The Competitive Advantage
of Industrial Districts

D1502548

Contributions to Economics

Christoph M. Schneider
Research and Development Management:
From the Soviet Union to Russia
1994. ISBN 3-7908-0757-5

Lars Olof Persson/Ulf Wiberg
Microregional Fragmentation
1995. ISBN 3-7908-0855-5

Ernesto Felli/Furio C. Rosati/
Giovanni Tria (Eds.)
The Service Sector:
Productivity and Growth
1995. ISBN 3-7908-0875-X

Giovanni Galizzi/
Luciano Venturini (Eds.)
Economics of Innovation:
The Case of Food Industry
1996. ISBN 3-7908-0911-X

David T. Johnson
Poverty, Inequality and Social
Welfare in Australia
1996. ISBN 3-7908-0942-X

Rongxing Guo
Border-Regional Economics
1996. ISBN 3-7908-0943-8

Oliver Fratzscher
The Political Economy of Trade
Integration
1996. ISBN 3-7908-0945-4

Ulrich Landwehr
Industrial Mobility and Public Policy
1996. ISBN 3-7908-0949-7

Arnold Picot/Ekkehard Schlicht (Eds.)
Firms, Markets, and Contracts
1996. Corr. 2nd printing 1997
ISBN 3-7908-0947-0

Thorsten Wichmann
Agricultural Technical Progress and
the Development of a Dual Economy
1997. ISBN 3-7908-0960-8

Ulrich Woitek
Business Cycles
1997. ISBN 3-7908-0997-7

Michael Carlberg
International Economic Growth
1997. ISBN 3-7908-0995-0

Massimo Filippini
Elements of the Swiss Market for
Electricity
1997. ISBN 3-7908-0996-9

Frank Hoster/Heinz Welsch/
Christoph Böhringer
CO_2 Abatement and Economic
Structural Change in the European
Internal Market
1997. ISBN 3-7908-1020-7

Christian M. Hafner
Nonlinear Time Series Analysis
with Applications to Foreign Exchange
Rate Volatility
1997. ISBN 3-7908-1041-X

Sardar M. N. Islam
Mathematical Economics of
Multi-Level Optimisation
1998. ISBN 3-7908-1050-9

Sven-Morten Mentzel
Real Exchange Rate Movements
1998. ISBN 3-7908-1081-9

Lei Delsen/Eelke de Jong (Eds.)
The German and Dutch Economies
1998. ISBN 3-7908-1064-9

Mark Weder
Business Cycle Models
with Indeterminacy
1998. ISBN 3-7908-1078-9

Tor Rødseth (Ed.)
Models for Multispecies Management
1998. ISBN 3-7908-1001-0

Michael Carlberg
Intertemporal Macroeconomics
1998. ISBN 3-7908-1096-7

continued on page 232

Michele Bagella · Leonardo Becchetti (Eds.)

The Competitive Advantage of Industrial Districts

Theoretical and Empirical Analysis

With 10 Figures
and 80 Tables

Physica-Verlag

A Springer-Verlag Company

Series Editors
Werner A. Müller
Marina Bihn

Editors
Prof. Michele Bagella
Dr. Leonardo Becchetti

University of Rome Tor Vergata
Faculty of Economics
Department of Economics and Institutions
Via di Tor Vergata snc
00133 Rome
Italy

ISBN 3-7908-1254-4 Physica-Verlag Heidelberg New York

Die Deutsche Bibliothek – CIP-Einheitsaufnahme
The competitive advantage of industrial districts: theoretical and empirical analysis / ed.: Michele Bagella; Leonardo Becchetti. – Heidelberg: Physica-Verl., 2000
   (Contributions to economics)
   ISBN 3-7908-1254-4

© Physica-Verlag Heidelberg 2000
Printed in Germany

Softcover-Design: Erich Kirchner, Heidelberg

SPIN 10746551   88/2202-5 4 3 2 1 0 – Printed on acid-free paper

Foreword

Almost all papers collected in this volume originated from a bilateral CNR research project (University of Rome, Tor Vergata – Stanford University) on the effects of open regionalism in Europe and in Latin America. This research focused on how different regional aggregations, based on internal and external liberalisation processes (UE, Mercosur, etc.), stimulated geographical agglomeration of productive units and how much geographical agglomeration could, in turn, account for accelerating economic growth and improved export performance. Papers collected in this book mainly respond to the second question.

We decided to concentrate our attention on Italian industrial districts as this particular organisational form is considered by domestic and foreign literature one of the main determinants of the most recent Italian industrial development. The opportunity for directing our empirical investigation on the issue was offered by the cooperation between the *Osservatorio sugli Intermediari e la Finanza Internazionale* of *CEIS-Tor Vergata* and the *Osservatorio sulla Piccola e Media Impresa* of *Mediocredito Centrale*. The *Mediocredito Centrale* supported the research with its rich database which collects information on a balanced sample of around 4000 firms. Thanks to this cooperation we could overcome the barrier of the insufficient availability of quantitative (balance sheet) and qualitative (interfirm agreements, export capacity, participation to subsidised credit programs, etc.) firm data which is typical of Italian databases. These data were combined with information from the Italian Census used for the definition of district and non-district areas in the country and resulted crucial to the analysis of the impact of geographical agglomeration on the behavior and on the performance of Italian firms.

The main paradigm on which most of the theoretical and empirical analysis of the book is based emphasises that geographical agglomeration has positive effects on effort in multiwinner games in which benefits from increased cooperation are higher than costs from increased competition (such as the provision of export services for small-medium firms). On the contrary, agglomeration has negative effects on effort in winner-takes-it-all games (such as the race for a breakthrough innovation) in which benefits from increased cooperation are lower than costs from increased competition.

To give an example, in R&D games, geographical proximity enhances positive spillovers and, consequently, payoffs from *free riding* on the quasi-public good of technological knowledge. As a consequence, the relative costs of individual R&D expenditures turn out to be higher than those of substitutes such as imitation, *learning on the job* and learning through job force relocation.

On the contrary, export games for small-medium firms, whose productive scale is relatively small with respect to demand, are much closer to multiwinner games. In this case geographical proximity enhances cooperation in the provision of services as individual effort has nonnegative effects on other agents payoffs. As a consequence, the development of common export services has positive impact on export performance.

Under the above described general perspective the book collects several interesting results on the economics of industrial districts.

The first part ("**Industrial districts: crucial competitive factors, research activity and productivity**") investigates over *internal* determinants of industrial district competitiveness looking at internal productivity, at patterns of innovation and at those factors which create a favorable industrial atmosphere. The first chapter empirically addresses the issue of the industrial districts' favorable *industrial atmosphere* and its link with the district economic performance. The central explanatory elements found are widespread human capital and the local availability of financial services, while family-based business does not appear to enjoy a crucial advantage anymore. The second chapter presents a theoretical model in which geographical proximity positively affects imitative capacity by increasing technological knowledge spillovers from firms with positive R&D expenditures to neighboring firms. The model shows that aggregate R&D effort is likely to be lower for firms agglomerated in «industrial districts» than for isolated firms. Empirical results presented in the chapter support this hypothesis. The third chapter provides an evaluation of the effects of industrial district external economies on firms' productivity and profitability. The 'district effect' on firms' profitability is shown to be quite strong: it depends on the measure of profitability and the period and varies between two and four percentage points. An econometric model confirms that ID firms tend to display higher technical efficiency than isolated firms do. All results are particularly strong for 'light' manufacturing industries, where districts play a major role. The fourth chapter shows that firms in industrial districts demonstrated to be relatively more efficient in the management of public subsidies. Subsidised district firms exhibit in fact a relatively better performance in terms of medium term profitability than subsidised non-district firms do

The second part of the book («**Industrial districts and foreign competitiveness: export and internationalisation performance**») investigates over foreign competitiveness of industrial districts focusing on the performance of export and of other forms of internationalisation. The first chapter of the second part presents a stylised model in which geographical proximity is assumed to increase private firm benefits from generating export services. On these premises the model shows that export intensity is higher for firms agglomerated in «industrial districts» than for isolated firms. The empirical part of the paper provides partial support to this theoretical hypothesis showing that benefits from geographical agglomeration in terms of higher export intensity and higher export participation are decreasing in firm size and generally higher in sectors characterised by forms of competition based on horizontal product differentiation The second chapter shows that the positive impact of geographical agglomeration on export performance is much stronger for firms whose specialisation matches that of the industrial district in which they are located. The third chapter presents results which are consistent with those illustrated in the previous two chapters by showing that the competitive advantage of industrial districts on export performance is stronger towards areas (such as non-EEC markets) where entry barriers for small-medium firms are presumably higher. The fourth chapter explores the impact of district organisation on more complex forms of internationalisation. It shows that a district small-medium firm, especially if the district has significant product specialisation, may have greater access to a wide range of information on foreign markets, alternative products, technologies and sources of finance. Conversely, when it comes to making productive investments abroad, whatever the form and nature, such an advantage decreases substantially. The district small firms need to invest in acquiring quantitative and qualitative information and "relational goods». This investment considerably increases not only internationalisation costs but also the variance of expected returns from the project. The realisation of the project within a district may help the small firm to mitigate the above mentioned negative effects due to the opportunity of sharing the project with an enterprise that belongs to a district and is considered a market leader. The fifth chapter analyses the hypothesis that inter-firm relationships in the form of a group of firms or of an "industrial district (ID)" may enhance the internationalisation of SMEs, especially in developing countries and studies the hypothesis of the internationalisation of the ID driven by a "leader firm". In the model, co-operation with the developing country enterprise is shown to ease the productive undertaking in the developing country. As a preliminary test of this hypothesis the paper analyses the social and economic context of Latin America, the experience of groups of SMEs and of "quasi-IDs" in some countries (Argentina, Brazil, Mexico), with the perspective of future co-operation with the Italian IDs, and further international expansion.

Acknowledgements

Theoretical and empirical papers collected in this book have been discussed in several seminars. We remember in particular the European Conference of the European Association of Regional Science (ERSA) (August 1997) and the International seminar organised by CEIS - Tor Vergata together with Fondazione Tagliacarne (Giugno 1997). In addition to the authors of book chapters we thank all those who contributed to this research and in particular G. Becattini, M. Bellandi. R. Cappellin, G. Dei Ottati, G. Esposito, M. Lo Cicero, G. Pellegrini, C. Pietrobelli, S. Rossi, G. Scanagatta, F. Sforzi, F. Trau. A special thanks goes to M. Fusco and R. Bruno for her precious assistance in the preparation of the book.

Table of Contents

The District Advantage in Small-Medium Firm Internationalisation 165

M. Bagella

From SMEs to Industrial Districts in the Process of Internationalisation: Theory and Evidence 175

M. Bagella and C. Pietrobelli

Appendix 195

Part I: Industrial Districts: Crucial Competitive Factors, Research Activity and Productivity

Competitiveness and its Socio-Economic Foundations: Empirical Evidence on the Italian Industrial Districts

Carlo Pietrobelli

University of Rome "Tor Vergata", Dipartimento di Economia e Istituzioni, via di Tor Vergata snc, 00133 Rome, Italy, Ph. +39.6.72595700-16, Fax: +39.6.2020500, E-Mail: carlo.pietrobelli@uniroma2.it .

Abstract: The superior international and overall performance of the Italian Industrial Districts (IDs) is by now acknowledged and has been shown by many different studies. Research at the theoretical level has focused on numerous socio-economic explanations, including the favourable industrial atmosphere within the ID and the ensuing lower transactions costs, its higher innovation record, its better human capital and widespread entrepreneurship in the area. In this paper we empirically address the issue of the IDs' industrial atmosphere and their economic performance. We use data from the Italian Population and Industry Censi and from other sources to test the prevailing theories of the socio-economic determinants of the IDs' industrial atmosphere and performance. We conclude that among the central explanatory elements are the local availability of good and widespread human capital, local financial services. Family-based business does not appear to enjoy a crucial advantage anymore. Smooth and frequent inter-firm linkages appear to play a role, but better statistical indices and data are still needed.

J.E.L. Classification: L1 (Market structure, firm strategy and market performance), D23.

Keywords: Industrial districts, Organisational behaviour, transaction costs

4   C. Pietrobelli

1 Introduction[*]

The theoretical and empirical literature has widely acknowledged the remarkable economic performance of the Italian Industrial Districts (IDs). The pioneering work of Becattini (Becattini, 1979, 1987, 1989) and his emphasis on the Marshallian external economies, opened the way to several studies. Thereafter, the IDs have been taken to represent a pattern of industrial development different from that pursued by large firms as well as by many isolated small and medium-sized enterprises (SMEs), constrained by their small size. Later, the concept of ID has been applied to the case of other industrial countries (Pyke et al., 1991, Garofoli, 1989, Onida et al., 1992) as well as developing countries (van Dijk and Rabellotti, 1997, Schmitz, 1995, UNCTAD and Deutsches Zentrum für Entwicklungstechnologien, 1994).

Within this context, the present study addresses the issue of the relationship between the IDs' economic and international performance and their geographical localisation, with the use of available data derived from the latest Industrial and Population Censi. Thus, this paper investigates the correlation between the IDs' performance and the structural characteristics of the areas where they are located.

Two features of this study are notably new in literature: first of all, a quantitative assessment of many of the theoretical hypotheses that are discussed in the literature, in spite of the limits imposed by the drawbacks of the dataset available is attempted; secondly, we try to move a step forward and away from the many reasonable idiosyncratic explanations of their superior performance, and find some general determinants on the basis of a representative sample of Italian IDs.

2 Background and Theoretical Hypotheses

The role and the importance of Industrial Districts (IDs) is by now a fact well acknowledged in the literature, and supported by substantial empirical evidence. Nonetheless, in order to clarify our focus, it is necessary to remind that, while each district has its own specific characteristics due to the historical and social events that contributed to its emergence and growth, a definition that serves a concrete methodological purpose is needed. Thus, an ID may be defined as a system of firms and local institutions (Bianchi, 1993, p.16). This theoretical paradigm of industrial district does not exist in its pure form, and each district has its own specific characteristics. However, four main common elements may be highlighted:

---

[*] This paper was presented at the 6th International Conference on the Economics of Innovation, "Networks of Firms and Information Networks", University of Piacenza, Cremona 5-7 June 1996. I wish to acknowledge Michele Bagella, Marco Bellandi, Monica Cracchi Bianchi and Luigi Speranza for the many useful discussions. However, I remain the only responsible for the opinions expressed in the paper.

- a district is <u>a system</u>; in other words the relationships among independent agents inside the district are ruled by a set of norms - generally informal - which characterise and shape the kind of social aggregation and the nature of the district itself.

- the agents inside the district are <u>independent firms</u> which maximise their profits through an external and interdependent specialisation of tasks. Each firm is specialised in one or few phases of the production cycle and has well-established relationships with other independent firms.

- the relationships inside the district are enforced and enhanced by <u>institutions</u> which encourage the growth of the whole district. Firms and institutions interact with one another within a system of informal relations, allowing the exploitation of flexible production achieved through an external division of labour.

- the district has a <u>local dimension</u>, geographically limited, in which a particular productive cycle is carried out by the multiplicity of actors belonging to the district itself.

The definition of such a theoretical paradigm is a first and necessary condition towards the comparative analysis of the performance of a sample of IDs. In order to better understand the nature of the theoretical hypotheses that we attempt to address here with some statistical information available, it is worthwhile briefly recalling the historical pattern of development of the IDs, and the role played by external factors inducing the change of their internal organisation.

Beginning in the early 1970s, small and medium-sized enterprises (SMEs) belonging to IDs, developed the capability to fill market *niches* that larger enterprises were not able to satisfy. These firms also indirectly benefited from the restructuring process of big Fordist enterprises "based on the decentralisation of productive phases already functioning within the large firm, towards small firms" (Bianchi 1993, p.17). Thus, overall the competitive advantage of IDs during this period may have been driven by external factors.

However, in that same period, the IDs succeeded in a rapid accumulation of skills and in deepening a productive specialisation through an efficient division of labour, and this has become the source of endogenous competitive advantage based on flexibility. The nature of flexibility in production depends on the particular kind of organisation which characterises the production cycle inside the district. More specifically, the flexibility depends on the specialisation of tasks among a set of firms, each of them being highly specialised in one or few phases of the production cycle. In other words, firms' specialisation enhances the ID's flexibility.

Specialisation is the key element governing flexibility in a context characterised by a multiplicity of independent and complementary enterprises, where there is no hierarchical decision-making structure. "A more fully entrepreneurial ID is one in which associations of firms along the production chain can collectively and simultaneously redesign products. This requires close consultation along the production chain. A fully developed ID would behave like a collective entrepreneur: it would possess the capacity to redesign process and organisation as well as product." (Best 1990, p. 206)

In fact, the way in which specialisation occurs is the result of a decentralised co-operative decision taken by individual agents active in the district, and it is part of a co-operation process reinforced by the culture and the know-how shared by all agents. In other words, the *industrial atmosphere*, following Marshall's definition, diminishes the costs of relations among agents, and operates as a sort of *social glue* stabilising relationships by allowing co-operation because it changes slower than market relations[1].

Specialisation is also the basis on which the endogenous determinants of development have matured, In particular, specialisation directed the pattern of accumulation of entrepreneurial capabilities and skilled labour, as well as the strengthening of social cohesion.

The *industrial atmosphere* is made of a set of intangible assets, which have both the nature of a public good, fostering the dynamic efficiency of all components of the district, and represents a collective sunk cost constraining rapid changes in the organisation of the district itself (Bianchi, 1993). External economies, agglomeration economies and the industrial atmosphere are the three elements characterising an industrial district in Marshall's terms.

Flexibility and efficiency through specialisation are the result of a collective process which has been successful between the mid-'70s and the mid-'80s. However, the collective nature of the organisation of production has also been the main source of rigidities and of delays in restructuring and change. Even if decentralised know-how and co-operation guide the innovation process among SMEs (Santarelli, 1990), it is necessary that the adjustment to changing market conditions occurs quickly. Otherwise, the same collective nature turns out to be a structural disadvantage, inducing inefficiencies and losses in competitive advantage due to low organisational and operational capacity of adaptation to a changing environment (Gandolfi, 1990).

Empirical evidence shows some directions that this process of adjustment has taken in the late '80s (Gandolfi, 1990). The causes of this process are both internal and external to the district. In particular, among the internal determinants, the division of labour among independent agents and the small dimension of each agent sometimes have been deemed responsible for the loss of competitiveness of the IDs. The external causes have been related to the general conditions of the

---

[1] The term *social glue* has been introduced by Becattini, 1990, writing on the relationships between the firm - not belonging to the district - and its suppliers.

economy. These may have strengthened the renewed competitive advantage of large firms achieving efficiency through the same elements previously developed by small firms (i.e. flexibility, specialisation, learning, decentralisation of some phases of production, relationships with customers and suppliers), as well as a more variable demand.

In other words, the same structural elements which had represented the key for their success in the mid-'70s and mid-'80s, may have been a cause of the slowness in their long-run restructuring process. As the social glue inside the district plays a crucial role in shaping the structure of the production system, the slow process of change of the extra-economic elements (beliefs, culture, knowledge, rules and institutions) may have affected the path of restructuring of the district. Therefore, whilst collective agents such as networks of enterprises, *milieu* and districts, reduce uncertainty and allow the adjustment to small and incremental changes, they are also the main obstacles to long run restructuring, because of the absence of a well defined strategic decision-making structure.[2] In this context, the restructuring may have been facilitated by the operations of institutions supporting the organisation of production, implementing the process of aggregation of firms, supplying semi-skilled workers through training programmes organised locally (Brusco, 1991).

In addition, the evidence on the performance of the IDs during the '90s suggests that the pattern of restructuring has been reinforced through more "formal" relations with subcontractors, together with an active capability of taking advantage of the favourable exchange rate and strengthening their competitive position on foreign markets (Istituto Tagliacarne, 1995).

Moving from such a rich variety of theoretical interpretations and detailed empirical analyses on specific cases to a careful measurement of the relevant variables is a hard task. This has often been attempted at a disaggregated level with case studies on specific experiences. Following a previous methodological paper[3], here we shall make a preliminary effort to use some available data in order to break the concept of *industrial atmosphere* into a number of social and economic components.

The measurement of the hypotheses that the theoretical literature considers to be central determinants of the IDs' international performance is riddled with difficulties. The ID is a socio-economic concept, that requires both economic and social data for its measurement. The difficulties are reinforced by the fact that most of the statistics available have not been constructed to serve the purpose of this study. The identification of the ID with the local community (at the level of the smallest geographical unit, the *comune*, on which data are available) is also

---

[2] For an optimistic view on the IDs' capability to face discontinuous radical technological changes, see Bellandi, 1996.

[3] Bagella and Pietrobelli, 1995.

risky. However, we still attempt to go beyond idiosyncratic and location-specific explanations, and make the best possible use of the available evidence. To this aim, we use some statistical evidence available from various sources, including the 1991 Italian Industry and Population Censi. We are aware, however, that in this way there is a risk of losing some systemic elements that go beyond individual firms and institutions, and are related to the quality and effectiveness of their interaction.

The explanation of the IDs' performance calls for many different and inter-related factors. Thus. for example, the main source of competitiveness is flexibility, that in turn reflects the quality of entrepreneurship, the skilfulness of the workers, and the availability of efficient markets of intermediate inputs, or institutions remedying for the possible failures. In fact, the innovation process inside the districts is a process concerning the way of organising production and of achieving flexibility among the workers, shifting from one task to another without losing their specific knowledge. It is not an easy task to measure all these components. However, in an effort to summarise some of the main theoretical hypotheses, and proxy them with statistical measures obtainable from the statistical database available, we have constructed a number of variables, that may be grouped to express six theoretical hypotheses (Table 1). We see them in sequence:

- Human capital and skills of a technical nature, acquired on the job or through formal education, have been acknowledged to be important conditions for the competitiveness of the ID. Various indicators of human capital in the area have been used to proxy the local availability of different skills, general or specialised, applied and technical (GENSK, GENSK2, HSK, TECSK, APPLSK). The simple correlations among these indicators are quite high (Table A1). However, among the pitfalls of such data, we cannot know whether these are the skills actually demanded by the manufacturing firms. Nowadays specialised workers are often trained inside the firm, and data on this phenomenon were lacking. Moreover, specialised workers might come from outside the *comune* to work in the ID.

- In the first phase of development of the IDs, that was spurred by the crisis of large firms, the role of family linkages and tradition was significant and played a role of buffer during periods of varying demand. It is interesting to look at the role of these linkages now that a radical process of restructuring has been completed. Data from the Census enable us to measure the importance of family components working inside the firms on the district's aggregate performance (FAM).

- The institutional framework has been deeply studied and it seems really important in shaping and fostering the competitive advantage of IDs, and supporting their internationalisation. Institutions act to support and strengthen the *industrial atmosphere*, but this may be done efficiently only insofar as they are able to understand the relevance of local externalities. For this reason, the local dimension of institutions plays a fundamental role. The coherence and efficiency of local institutions has been proxied by INST.

- The diffused entrepreneurial culture, grown out of a long-established tradition of production (and craftsmanship), has also been considered a crucial component of positive performance (ENTR).

- The local availability of real and financial services may help. They may be more effective locally, as they are provided by agents and institutions that know the users' needs better, as they belong to the same tradition and have a continuous acquaintance with the productive sector (RSERV, RESERV2, FSERV). The presence of an ID may also allow the reduction of uncertainty, and this is further reinforced by the provision of financial support to the ID firms, that increases the degree of trust among firms and between firms and the banking system (Dei Ottati, 1992, Lo Cicero, 1995).

- The entrenched tradition of co-operation and inter-firm collaboration has been highlighted as another determinant of economic success. This would reduce transaction costs, increase enterprises' "X-efficiency", and raise the convenience to carry out market (or quasi-market) transactions, rather than simply internalise transactions and missing markets as a large enterprise would do (Bagella and Pietrobelli, 1995). Thus, smooth and effective inter-firm linkages are crucial in all market conditions, and ID are deemed to favour them.[4] Unfortunately, there is no available statistics on the numerosity and the quality of inter-firm linkages, unless for very specific case studies. In the present exercise, we tried to proxy it with the number of firms in the district (NFIRMS), or with its reverse, the ID firm average size (AVGSIZE), under the assumption that, *coeteris paribus*, a larger number of firms active in the ID would raise the convenience to rely on externalised transactions.[5]

Table 1. List of variables employed in the study

Theoretical Hypotheses	Variable	Description	Source
Dep. Variable	XPROP	Export propensity (Exports/Sales)	2
	GENSK	Population with primary education /total population in the relevant *comune*	1
Human Capital	GENSK2	Secondary school/Total population	1
And Skills	HSK	Graduates/total population in the relevant *comune*	1
	TECSK	Technically educated (diploma)/total population	1
	APPLSK	self employed in manual activities in industry/active population	1

[4] In the presence of efficient competitive markets it would be optimal to carry out all market transactions through the market. However, this is rarely the case, and "institutions" are called to remedy and correct market imperfections.

[5] This indicator may be affected by the nature of the activity and the technology in use. A better indicator would be desirable, but it was not available and should be constructed on the basis of detailed microeconomic observation.

Theoretical Hypotheses	Variable	Description	Source
Family-business	FAM	family-employed workers/active population	1
Institutional Performance	INST	Index of "Institutional Performance"	3
Entrepreneurship	ENTR	entrepreneurs and professionals in industry (engaged only in management and organization)/ active population	1
Real and financial services	FSERV	Employed in monetary and financial intermediation/active population	1
	RSERV	Employed in "real" services (i.e.housing, renting, informatics, research, others) / active population	1
	RSERV2	entrepreneurs and professionals in service activities /active population	1
Inter-firm	AVGSIZE	Average firm-size in the ID	2
Linkages	NFIRMS	Number of firms in the ID	2

Table 1. Continuation

Sources: 1. 7° Censimento Generale della Popolazione, and 7° Censimento Generale dell'Industria e dei Servizi, 21.10.1991, ISTAT Roma, 2. Moussanet and Paolazzi, 1992, 3. Putnam, 1994.

The performance indicator chosen as the dependent variable is export propensity (i.e. the share of exports over total sales), as it is often done in other empirical analyses of competitiveness. This index may reflect a structural characteristic of the industry, as well as the sector's evolution at the national level. However, the identification of the ID with a single product following the industrial classification was often difficult, as in most cases the IDs are not specialised in only one product, but in some products along the *filiére*. Thus, it was hard to compare the ID's performance with the industry national average.[6] However, it has been acknowledged that IDs are more export oriented than other Italian firms in the same sectors (Istituto Tagliacarne, 1995). Thus, export propensity captures an element of differential performance that needs to be explained.

3 Some Econometric Evidence

In order to test some of the theoretical hypotheses often recalled in the literature, and briefly discussed in the section above, we selected a sample of Italian IDs on which some performance indicators were available[7], and measured the correlation of their performance with some structural socio-economic features of the areas where they are located. The latter was made possible by the availability of socio-

---

[6] Similarly, a comparative analysis with different counterfactuals would have been desirable, such as on non-exporting IDs, or on firms not belonging to an ID. However, such sample could not be easily constructed, and work in progress by the author is explicitly addressing this issue.

[7] Based on studies reported in Moussanet, Paolazzi, 1992.

economic data on the Italian *Comune,* the smallest geographical unit on which statistics are collected, that is sufficiently small to allow a good overlapping of the ID with its geographical localisation. In fact, socio-economic data coinciding exactly with the ID are not collected. The ID might extend across more than one Comune, as well as a Comune might host more than one ID. In order to reduce the risk of such errors, we excluded those IDs where geographical localisation was not sufficiently circumscribed, as well as those nearly mono-firm (i.e. where the expectation of a peculiar structure of the ID, dominated by a "leader-firm", was justified).

All data are for 1991. However, in the absence of longer time series, this does not seem to represent a major problem, as the components of the industrial atmosphere pointed out so far have a structural nature, and due to their "sunkness" they are not expected to change rapidly. This allows us to consider the results of the empirical analysis valid beyond the specific year of observation. The interest of this exercise lays in interpreting those social factors related to the human capital, the institutions' performance, the inter-firm relationships as determinants of the industrial atmosphere, and in trying to propose some proxies for their measurement. Interestingly, the Census data refer to 1991, when the ID restructuring process was almost completed, and the positive effects of the depreciation of the Lira and the ensuing increased competitiveness of the Italian firms on international markets had not shown up yet.

Econometric testing of the model consists of two stages, and follows the general to specific modelling technique (Hendry, 1979). First a general model is defined on the basis of the theoretical model, eliminating from the set of independent variables those very highly correlated with each other (Table A1) and then estimated using ordinary least squares (OLS) assuming zero lags on the independent variables. Secondly, in order to move from a general model to our "best" specific equation, we gradually drop independent variables one by one, on the basis of their explanatory power. At each stage in moving from our general equation to our "best" equation we need to test the acceptability of the restrictions we are imposing on the model. The principle of parsimony guides the exercise, to obtain a simple model that contains all the essential independent variables and excludes the rest. The most commonly used test is the F-test, and on the basis of it, candidates for exclusion are TECSK, ENTR, INST, RSERV, and NFIRMS (Table 2).[8]

---

[8] Table 2 contains the F statistics and the details of their calculation. Based on the null hypothesis that the restrictions are true (i.e., that the variable can be omitted from the equation), the test statistic has a Fisher's F-distribution with d and (n-k) degrees of freedom. The decision rule is: the null hypothesis will be accepted at the 5 % significance level if $F <$ Fd, n-k and rejected otherwise.

Following this procedure, as well as additional tests and economic assessment, the least significant variables are parsimoniously eliminated one by one to reach a specific model (Table 3).[9]

The specific model provides good results, with high significance of the whole regression and of the individual variables. The model explains a large proportion of the variation in industrial districts' economic performance: the R^2 is satisfactorily high for a cross-section.

First of all, the results reveal that the performance of the Italian IDs is a multidimensional phenomenon, that rejects simple and unidimensional explanations. In fact, the specific model obtained after a process of gradual and parsimonious simplification contains a number of variables that suggest various interpretations and point at areas for further research.

Table 2. Restriction test for general model

	RSSU	RSSR	RSSR-RSSU/d	RSSU/n-k	FStat
FAM	1.0906	1.3312	0.2405	0.0404	5.954
GENSK2	1.0906	1.1899	0.0992	0.0404	2.457
HSK	1.0906	1.3477	0.2570	0.0404	6.363
NFIRMS	1.0906	1.0984	0.0078	0.0404	0.193
TECSK	1.0906	1.0908	0.0002	0.0404	0.004
ENTR	1.0906	1.0926	0.0020	0.0404	0.049
INST	1.0906	1.1160	0.0253	0.0404	0.626
RSERV	1.0906	1.0917	0.0010	0.0404	0.025
FSERV	1.0906	1.2365	0.1459	0.0404	3.611

Notes: F statistics is defined as: $F= [(RSSR-USSR)/r]/[(USSR/(n-k-1)]=F_{(r,n-k-1)}$ where RSSR and USSR are respectively the sum of the squared residuals of the restricted and unrestricted models (the specific and the general model), r is the number of the restrictions imposed to the general model (i.e. no.of coefficients imposed to be =0), (n-k-1) is the number of degrees of freedom of the unrestricted model. This ratio follows a $F_{(r,n-k-1)}$ distribution. If the computed F-value is higher than the value reported in the F-tables, we reject the null hypothesis that coefficients = 0 (i.e. $H_0=\beta_1=\beta_2=...=\beta_n=0$). $F(1,27)=4,21$ (7,68 at 1%).

A first result is that secondary education appears to matter more than university-level education. The positive and significant coefficient of a measure of the availability of basic skills (provided by secondary education, GENSK2) and the negative coefficient of an indicator of higher skills (HSK), proxied by the employed with education at the graduate level, suggest this interpretation. Due to the correlation of the various indicators of technical skills and human capital, we were forced to test the model without all indicators simultaneously in the same

---

[9] Given the sectoral nature of the data for all the independent variables, high heteroskedasticity was expected and has been detected and corrected with the White method (White, 1980).

regression. Thus, the availability of good and widespread general skills in the area appears as a crucial pre-condition for a positive performance of an ID.[10] Secondary education, providing the basic preliminary technical skills, seems to matter more than primary education. Overall, technical skills importantly contribute to the growth of the IDs: in the first phase they were often provided by the personnel coming after an experience with large enterprises, that externalised part of their production. Afterwards, the existence of the ID itself enhanced the accumulation of technical skills, sparking an interesting cumulative process. It would have been interesting to include in the analysis also the professional and training courses financed by the European Union and by the Regions, but such information was not available.

Secondly, and perhaps surprisingly, our indicator of family-based business is significantly negatively correlated to economic performance. This may be interpreted in at least two possible ways: (i) our indicator does not capture the degree of family cohesion and collaboration that many authors consider a central determinant of the success of the IDs, reinforced by a long historical tradition; (ii) the evolution of the internal organisation of production and commercialisation of the firms in the ID has developed in a way whereby the employment of a large share of family-workers is not anymore a signal of internal solidity and dynamism. In fact, the firms of the ID that had initiated their activity with a family-run business, by now have evolved towards an organisation that does include members of the family only at the high levels of management and direction of production. This shows up in low values of the index FAM employed in the present analysis.

Table 3. Determinants of industrial districts' performance: Results of OLS estimations

	FAM	GENSK2	HSK	FSERV	CONST	R2	F	SE	DW
Specific Model	-7.53***	1.76*	-13.9***	14.0**	0.08	0.42	5.89	0.18	2.45
	(-5.51)	(1.93)	(-3.60)	(2.57)	(0.26)				

Note: Dependent Variable = XPROP, Year 1991, No.of observations = 37

Sources: See Table 1. NOTES: t-statistics in parentheses. These are all heteroskedastic-consistent estimates (White, 1980). *, **, ***, stand respectively for 90, 95, 99 percent of significance.

Interestingly, local financial services appear to matter for ID performance, with FSERV positively and significantly correlated to performance. The availability of financial services locally is expected to serve the purposes of the users better. They are provided by agents and institutions that know the users' needs better, as

---

[10] We need to remind, however, that the direction of causality may run both ways, with education coming after economic performance, as well as influencing it.

they belong to the same tradition and have a continuous acquaintance with the productive sector. Moreover, the presence of an ID may also allow the reduction of uncertainty, that increases the degree of trust among firms and between firms and the banking system (Dei Ottati, 1992, Esposito, 1995). A sort of collective insurance operates, through the working of mutual knowledge and interlinked control (Lo Cicero, 1995).

The other variables do not reach reasonable levels of statistical significance.

The measure of "institutional performance" computed by Putnam (1994) in his study on the Italian regions is not significant, but this is not surprising. This is an index only computed at the regional level, and not at the Comune as it would be required here. In fact, most of the sample districts belong to regions with very high indexes of institutional performance, thereby revealing, though indirectly, the relevance of Putnam's conclusions. This cannot show up in our analysis, as choosing IDs already predetermines and biases the analysis in favour of high values of the INST index. In order to test the hypothesis on the role of the institutional consistency and efficiency that much historical and sociological research puts at the core of the ID phenomenon, we should need a different indicator, computed at the level of a smaller localisation unit.

Similarly, all the measures of the availability of real services in the area are not statistically significant. This is probably due to the nature of the statistics available, that do not capture effectively the flow of services and linkages between firms and individuals that often take informal means, nor it does distinguish between services relevant to the enterprises' manufacturing and commercialisation activities, and other services not pertinent to enterprises' activities.

Finally, the indicator of inter-firm linkages (NFIRMS) is positively correlated with economic performance, but with too low significance to be included in the specific model. Neither the indicator of the opposite phenomenon of larger average firm-size within the ID (AVGSIZE) did turn out significant in alternative specifications of the econometric model. Both measures depend on the stringent assumption that a larger number of firms in the ID would itself facilitate fruitful linkages and collaboration. These indices appear too crude to capture effectively the extent and the richness of inter-firm linkages, flows of knowledge and collaboration, and test their effect on IDs' performance. Theoretical analyses have emphasised the relevance of effective inter-firm linkages to reduce transaction costs and raise X and collective efficiency (Bagella and Pietrobelli, 1995, Esposito, 1995).[11] New indicators are needed after more careful microeconomic scrutiny than it has been possible with the available data.

---

[11] For a recent paper on various forms of inter-firm partnerships having a central technological element, and involving firms from developed and developing countries, see Pietrobelli, 1996.

4 Summary and Conclusions

This paper, and the evidence presented using Italian Census data confirms the idea that the industrial district is intrinsically a multidimensional phenomenon, as many historical, economic and sociological analyses have well documented. However in spite of the many "idiosyncratic" elements of so many different experiences of IDs, the present study has been able to outline some regularities across a large sample of Italian IDs. Statistical evidence on the determinants of their economic performance is provided, to conclude that the availability of technical skills and financial services in the area appear essential. Family-run businesses were central in the initial stages of the evolution of the IDs, but today, after important restructuring processes, have lost their central role. Instead, excessive reliance on family-based activities appears a sign of weakness. Additional specific hypotheses such as the role of smooth and frequent inter-firm linkages and knowledge transfers, or the role of local institutions, could not be tested adequately. Additional detailed statistical information is needed to this purpose.

In sum, further statistical analyses to explain the evolution and the performance of the Ids are needed, and there is still ground to cover to obtain the indicators required to address the issues raised by theoretical research. However, this paper has pointed to promising areas of research and has provided original empirical evidence on the determinants of the competitiveness of the Italian industrial districts. Future analysis on the field and at the microeconomic level will have to proceed together with the search for good statistical indicators. Promising avenues appear the nature, dynamics and effects of inter-firm linkages, and their measurement, as well as the factors that determine the endogenous resilience of the industrial districts.

Table 4. Correlation matrix

	FAM	GENSK2	HSK	NFIRMS	TECSK	ENTR	INST	RSERV	FSERV	XPROP
FAM	1									
GENSK2	0.1315	1								
HSK	-0.2654	-0.5487	1							
NFIRMS	0.2820	-0.1146	0.0263	1						
TECSK	-0.2829	-0.4998	0.8401	0.0738	1					
ENTR	0.0595	0.2466	-0.4170	0.0056	-0.3585	1				
INST	0.2230	0.3466	-0.2052	0.2264	0.0745	0.0503	1			
RSERV	-0.1074	-0.2340	0.7103	0.2051	0.7859	-0.4087	0.2669	1		
FSERV	-0.0993	-0.3838	0.8067	0.1627	0.8385	-0.4212	0.1350	0.8097	1	
XPROP	-0.1829	0.4280	-0.4095	-0.0293	-0.2653	0.1157	0.1536	-0.1576	-0.1683	1

16   C. Pietrobelli

Table 5. Industrial districts in the sample. Basic indicators

	main product	sales bn.lire	exp. bn.lire	xprop	p.c.exp. mill.lire	nfirms	Empl	avgsize	Pop
S. Daniele del Friuli	Ham	450	81	0.18	10.6	26	700	26.92	7631
Montebelluna	sport shoes	1.237	866	0.70	34.6	701	8204	11.70	25055
Possagno	Bathware	60	2	0.03	1.1	10	250	25.00	1840
Castelgoffredo	women socks	654	362	0.55	42.5	422	7500	17.77	8511
Viadana	brooms brushes	79	12	0.15	0.8	120	1300	10.83	15950
Gardone Valtrompia	Weapons	500	350	0.70	32.1	100	4000	40.00	10887
Lumezzane	metal working	950	428	0.45	18.3	983	7000	7.12	23395
Arzignano	leather dying	3.087	2.315	0.75	109.7	600	7050	11.75	21108
Bassano	Furniture	1.000	175	0.18	4.5	500	2500	5.00	39112
Solofra	leather dying	900	585	0.65	52.7	150	3500	23.33	11105
Barletta	Shoes	600	294	0.49	3.3	308	3163	10.27	89054
Casarano	Shoes	560	180	0.32	9.1	67	3177	47.42	19861
Prato	textile garments	5.150	2.575	0.50	15.6	11850	48000	4.05	165449
Frosolone	Knives	11	1	0.09	0.3	9	130	14.44	3412
Cerea/Bovolone	Furniture	1.300	120	0.09	4.4	3000	15000	5.00	27512
Carrara	Marble	2.300	1.800	0.78	26.8	1200	9000	7.50	67049
Valduggia	Valves	350	240	0.69	101.0	110	1400	12.73	2377
Carpi	textile garments	1.740	470	0.27	7.8	2630	13120	4.99	60341
Mirandola	Biomedicals	360	180	0.50	8.4	80	2300	28.75	21508
Castelfidardo	musical instrum.	222	109	0.49	7.1	400	3150	7.88	15286
Gallarate	Embroidery	270	11	0.04	0.2	390	2000	5.13	45457
Manzano	Chairs	1.250	812	0.65	113.3	800	2500	3.13	7164
Matera	Furniture	400	80	0.20	1.5	80	2120	26.50	53877
Pesaro	Furniture	1.600	200	0.13	2.2	1000	10000	10.00	89780
Civita Castellana	Ceramics	200	100	0.50	6.5	43	2000	46.51	15473
Santa Croce	leather dying	2.500	500	0.20	40.6	880	10000	11.36	12318
Vigevano	shoe machinery	600	350	0.58	5.8	90	3000	33.33	60030
Vigevano	Shoes	400	300	0.75	5.0	50	800	16.00	60030
Valenza	Goldware	1.500	750	0.50	35.4	1300	7500	5.77	21166
Premana	knives scissors	80	28	0.35	13.1	140	1000	7.14	2134
Grumello del Monte	buttons knife mach	280	184	0.66	30.7	128	1740	13.59	5984
Palosco	Compasses	30	21	0.70	4.3	25	200	8.00	4828

	main product	sales bn.lire	exp. bn.lire	xprop	p.c.exp. mill.lire	nfirms	Empl	avgsize	Pop
Teramo	textile garments	650	108	0.17	2.1	1150	15700	13.65	52040
Settimo Torinese	Pens	500	350	0.70	7.7	200	4000	20.00	45187
Tolentino	leather goods	800	360	0.45	19.7	120	2000	16.67	18230
Cembra	Porphyry	115	50	0.43	29.5	154	1600	10.39	1693
Maniago	Knives	89	44	0.49	4.0	200	1180	5.90	11077

Table 5: Continuation

Sources: See Table 1 in the text

References

Bagella M. (ed.), 1996, *Internazionalizzazione della piccola e media impresa in America latina. Teorie ed evidenza empirica*, Bologna: Il Mulino

Bagella M. and Pietrobelli C., 1998, From SMEs to Industrial Districts in the Process of Internationalisation: Evidence, in this volume.

Bagella M. and Pietrobelli C., 1995, Internazionalizzazione dei distretti industriali. Elementi teorici ed evidenza dall'America Latina, *Economia e Politica Industriale*, 86.

Becattini G., 1990, Dall'impresa alla quasi-comunità: dubbi e domande, *Economia e Politica Industriale*, 68.

Becattini G., 1989, *Modelli locali di sviluppo*, Bologna: Il Mulino.

Becattini G. (ed.), 1987, *Mercato e forze locali: il distretto industriale*, Bologna: Il Mulino.

Becattini G., 1979, Dal settore industriale al distretto industriale. Alcune considerazioni sull'unità d'indagine dell'economia industriale, *Economia e Politica Industriale*, 1.

Becattini G. and Rullani E., 1993, Sistema locale e mercato globale, *Economia e politica industriale*, 80.

Bellandi M., 1996, Innovazione e cambiamento discontinuo nei distretti industriali, presented at the 6th International Conference on the Economics of Innovation, University of Piacenza, Cremona 5-7 June 1996.

Bellandi M., 1993, Structure and change in the industrial district, *Studi e discussioni*, Dipartimento di Scienze Economiche, Università di Firenze.

Best M., 1990, *The New Competition*, Cambridge Polity Press.

Bianchi P., 1993, Industrial Districts and Industrial Policy: The New European Perspective, *Journal of Industry Studies*, 1.

Brusco S., 1991, The Genesis of the Idea of Industrial District, in Pyke *et al.*.

Camagni R., 1989, Cambiamento tecnologico, milieu locale e reti di imprese: verso una teoria dinamica dello spazio economico, *Economia e politica industriale*, 64.

Dei Ottati G., 1992, Fiducia, transazioni intrecciate e credito nel distretto industriale, *Note Economiche*, XXII no.1-2.

van Dijk M.P. and Rabellotti R. (eds.), 1997, *Enterprise Clusters and Networks in Developing Countries*, London: Frank Cass.

van Dijk M.P., 1995, Flexible Specialization. The New Competition and Industrial Districts, *Small Business Economics*, 7.

Esposito G.F., 1995, I distretti industriali tra impresa e mercato: alcuni elementi analitici per una riconsiderazione, *Rassegna Economica*, 1.

Ferrucci L., and Varaldo R., 1993, La natura e la dinamica dell'impresa distrettuale, *Economia e politica industriale*, 80.

Franchi M., Rieser V. and Vignali L., 1990, Note sul modello organizzativo dell'impresa distrettuale, *Economia e politica industriale*, 66.

Gandolfi V., 1990, Relazionalità e cooperazione nelle aree-sistema, *Economia e politica industriale*, 65.

Garofoli G., 1989, Industrial Districts: Structure and Transformation, *Economic Notes*, 1.

Hendry D.F., 1979, Predictive Failure and Econometric Modelling in Macroeconomics: The Transactions Demand for Money, in P. Ormerod (ed.) *Economic Modelling*, London: Heinemann.

Istituto G. Tagliacarne, 1995, *Rapporto sull'impresa e sulle economie locali 1995*, Milan: Franco Angeli.

Lo Cicero M., 1995, Internazionalizzazione dei distretti industriali: un ruolo possibile per il merchant banking, *Economia e Diritto del Terziario*, 1.

Moussanet M . and Paolazzi L. (eds.), 1992, *Gioielli, Bambole Coltelli*, Milan: IL Sole 24 Ore Libri.

Onida F., Viesti G. and Falzoni A.M., 1992, *I distretti industriali: crisi o evoluzione?*, Milan: EGEA.

Pietrobelli C., 1998, *Industry, Competitiveness and Technological Capabilities in Chile: A New Tiger from Latin America?*, London-New York: Macmillan/St.Martin's Press.

Pietrobelli C., 1998, The Socio-Economic Foundations of Competitiveness: An Econometric Analysis of the Italian Industrial Districts, *Industry and Innovation*, Vol.5, No.2, December.

Pietrobelli C., 1997, On the Theory of Technological Capabilities and Developing Countries' Dynamic Comparative Advantage in Manufactures, *Rivista Internazionale di Scienze Economiche e Commerciali,* Vol.XLIV, No. 2, June.

Pietrobelli C., 1996, *Emerging Forms of Technological Cooperation: The Case for Technology Partnerships - Inner Logic, Examples and Enabling Environment,* Science and Technology Issues, Geneva: UNCTAD.

Pyke R., Becattini G. and Sengenberger W. (eds.), 1991, *Industrial Districts and Inter-firm Cooperation in Italy,* Geneva: ILO.

Putnam D., 1993, *Making democracy work: civic traditions in modern Italy,* Princeton: Princeton University Press.

Rabellotti R., 1997, *External Economies and Cooperation in Industrial Districts: A Comparison of Italy and Mexico,* London: Macmillan.

Sforzi F., 1989, The Geography of Industrial Districts in Italy, in Goodman E. and Bamford J. (eds.), 1989, *Small Firms and Industrial Districts in Italy,* London and New York: Routledge.

Sabel C., 1988, The reemergence of regional economies, Papers de seminari 29-30, Centre d'estudis de planificació.

Santarelli E., 1990, Organizzazione dell'attivitá innovativa e dimensione efficiente. C'é ancora spazio per le piccole imprese?, *Economia e politica industriale,* 66.

Schmitz H., 1995, Collective efficiency: rowth path for small-scale industry, *Journal of Development Studies,* Vol.31 No.4, April.

Traú F., 1991,La performance relativa delle piccole imprese industriali negli anni ottanta: una rassegna dell'evidenza empirica, *Economia e politica industriale,* 71.

UNCTAD and Deutsches Zentrum für Entwicklungstechnologien. 1994. *Technological Dynamism in Industrial Districts: An Alternative Approach to Industrialization in Developing Countries?* (UNCTAD/ITD/TEC/11). New York and Geneva: United Nations.

White H., 1980, A Heteroskedasticity-Consistent Covariance Matrix Estimator and a Direct Test for Heteroskedasticity, *Econometrica,* No.48.

Geographical Agglomeration in R&D Games: Theoretical Analysis and Empirical Evidence

Michele Bagella

University of Rome "Tor Vergata", Faculty of Economics, Department of Economics and Institutions, Via di Tor Vergata snc, 00133 Rome. E-mail: bagella@uniroma2.it

Leonardo Becchetti

University of Rome "Tor Vergata", Faculty of Economics, Department of Economics and Institutions, Via di Tor Vergata snc, 00133 Rome. E-mail: becchetti@uniroma2.it

Abstract: The chapter presents a theoretical model in which geographical proximity positively affects imitative capacity by increasing technological knowledge spillovers from firms with positive R&D expenditures to neighbouring firms. The model shows that aggregate R&D effort is likely to be lower for firms agglomerated in "industrial districts" than for isolated firms. This is because, without geographical proximity, the only feasible Weak Renegotiation Proof (WRP) equilibrium is one where both firms always invest in R&D, while, with geographical proximity, this equilibrium is not in the set of strictly individually rational payoffs. The validity of this conclusion is analysed under different frameworks such as infinitely repeated noncooperative and cooperative games with perfect and imperfect information and games with payoff relevant strategies. The empirical part of the paper provides partial support to this theoretical hypothesis showing that geographical agglomeration, - even though not always significantly for all macroareas, macrosectors and size classes - reduces private firm R&D expenditures and firm decision to invest in R&D (R&D participation).

JEL Classification: R3

Keywords: Localisation externalities, innovation.

1   Introduction*

A distinctive feature of Italian industrial development is the tendency to form the so called *industrial districts* ("distretti industriali") by agglomerating in geographically delimited areas which do not often coincide with urban agglomerations. An *industrial district* may then be defined by the following three features: i) large number of independent productive units; ii) geographical contiguity; iii) intense market and non market interchange of public and private goode and services among these productive units generating positive spillovers in the area (Marshall, 1920). Theoretical literature recently started to formalise the structure of districts (Dobkins, 1996) in theoretical models thereby generating an independent sub-branch from the traditional literature of externalities and urban agglomeration (Rivera-Batiz, 1988a,b; Abdel-Rahman and Fujita, 1990). In these studies spillovers are determined, according to various authors, by communication among firms, by sharing of factor advantages or by the presence of a monopolistically competitive service sector supplying differentiated goods to the tradable good sector. Recent theoretical and empirical work on the development of privately financed schemes for the implementation of services in industrial areas shows that the relatively higher propensity to cooperate and to share information in industrial districts is a crucial factor in fostering endogenous development mechanisms based on the development and the implementation of these schemes (Becchetti, 1997). These results help us to understand persistence in uneven geographical development in Italy between areas where firms are clustered in industrial district and the rest of the country.

Theoretical literature thoroughly investigated potential advantages in maintaining a decentralised organisation, such as that prevailing in industrial districts, vis-à-vis generating a giant firm. A comparative advantage of the former organisational form may occur when: i) transaction costs among small independent firms are relatively lower than coordination costs within a vertically integrated group; ii) dynamic learning economies of scale and economies of scale on the division of the production cycle prevail for certain activities over static economies of scale (Senegenberger-Pyke, 1992; Pike-Becattini-Senegenberger, 1991). An important advantage of *"industrial districts"* is in fact their higher capacity to adapt to external perturbations, given that reduced firm size, lower amount of sunk costs and higher input flexibility make it easier to reallocate labour and capital after a shock occurs.

* The paper is part of an empirical work on Italian industrial districts supported by Italian Center of National Research and has been presented at the 1997 Conference of the European Regional Studies Association (ERSA) and at the International Workshop on "Italian industrial districts: internationalisation and export performance", held at Istituto Tagliacarne in 1997. Even though the paper is fruit of common research L.Becchetti wrote sections 2 and 3.3, while M.Bagella wrote sections 3.1 and 3.2. Introduction and conclusions are in common. The authors thank M.Bellandi, R.Cappellin, L. Lambertini, C.Pietrobelli, F.Sforzi for helpful comments and suggestions.

While theoretical literature has analysed determinants and effects of the generation of industrial districts, the empirical literature is far behind in assessing the relative costs and benefits of geographical agglomeration at firm level

A widespread theoretical opinion identifies, for instance, the "decentralisation of the sources of new knowledge about production processes and about the activities of the use of products" (Bellandi, 1996) as a main feature of industrial districts (from now on also ID). According to this assumption, R&D expenditures of individual firms should be lower in ID where technological innovation also follows alternative paths of learning on the job, product imitation and learning through exports [1].

The aim of this paper is to shed some light on this issue with a simple theoretical framework and an empirical analysis on the effects of geographical agglomeration on private firm R&D expenditures at microlevel on a sample of around 4000 small-medium Italian firms. The paper is organised as follows. The first section presents the model using a game theoretical approach and the second section provides results on private R&D investment and R&D participation by macroareas, macrosectors and size classes for firms included in the Mediocredito sample.

2   The Partnership Stage Game

Consider a simple two players' game with the following payoff matrix:

Fig.1. The one stage R&D game.

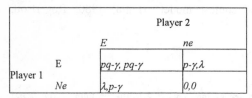

		Player 2	
		E	ne
Player 1	E	pq-γ, pq-γ	p-γ, λ
	Ne	λ, p-γ	0,0

In this stage game each player i (i=1,2) simultaneously chooses a (pure) action a_i or a mixed action α_i from a finite set A_i with m_i elements. The two pure actions *(e,ne)* in this game represent respectively the decision to exert or not R&D effort through positive R&D expenditures.

---

[1] Bagella-Becchetti-Sacchi (1998) and Becchetti-Rossi (1998) show that export intensity is higher for firms agglomerated in "industrial districts" than for isolated firms. Benefits from geographical agglomeration in terms of higher export intensity and higher export participation are decreasing in firm size and generally higher in sectors characterised by forms of competition based on horizontal product differentiation.

The game is based on four fundamental parameters: i) p which is the "stand-alone effort" output; ii) q which is the marginal effect of opponent's effort on an individual player (for simplicity we assume that players have homogeneous skills and that $q_i = q_j = q$); iii) γ which is the effort cost;[2] and iv) λ which is the imitative/free-riding output.

Players are small-medium firms, effort is equal to private firm R&D expenditure and output is the innovative product generated by research.

A first crucial assumption in the model is that the degree of geographical proximity among players *(gp)* increases player's capacity of producing imitative/free riding output so that $\lambda'(gp) > 0$.[3] The rationale for this assumption is that some of the R&D effort of firms located in an "*industrial district*" is public good. This rationale is strongly supported by the empirical literature on endogenous growth and Marshallian externalities (Romer, 1990; Lucas, 1988).

A second crucial assumption is that the joint effort (the situation in which both players incur in nonnegative R&D investments) is less than superadditive in the R&D game as the marginal effect of opponent's effort on an individual player q is less than 1. This is intuitively clear in case of breakthrough innovation if we set the prize of the R&D race to a fixed level and we consider that noncooperative joint effort reduces player's probability of winning the race. In case of incremental innovation the same assumption may be supported considering that, in models with vertical product differentiation (Shaked-Sutton, 1983), an improvement in the quality of product may significantly reduce the opponent's market share and even eliminate her from the market. More in general, the negative effect of one player's effort on opponent's utility is a common feature of almost all R&D models from deterministic "non tournament" models (Dasgupta-Stiglitz, 1980; Flaherty, 1980; Beath-Ulph, 1990) to probabilistic contest models (Futia, 1980; Rogertson, 1982).[4]

---

[2] Given that the imitative/free riding choice assigns payoff λ to the imitator in the *(e,ne)* solution of the game, γ may be alternatively interpreted as the differential between R&D expenditure and imitation costs in order to avoid a too restrictive assumption on costless imitation.

[3] We are implicitly assuming to live in an economy in which technological innovation in telecommunications has not eliminated positive effects of geographical agglomeration on capacity of absorbing technological spillovers. In other terms following Gaspar-Glaeser (1996), we assume that geographical proximity matters because electronic proximity is a complement and not a substitute of it.

[4] Given that our results crucially depend on this assumption, if it is considered too restrictive, we may alternatively argument that, only when the R&D game is not superadditive, a negative correlation between aggregate R&D expenditure and geographical agglomeration exists.

In the light of these assumptions, the aim of the model is to show how geographical agglomeration affects aggregate effort and aggregate output in the game. The effect of geographical agglomeration on R&D effort will be examined within two different frameworks: R&D games with low effort cost and R&D games with high effort costs.

2.1 R&D Game in the Low Effort Cost Scenario

The most important effect of effort cost is that of changing the relative payoff between imitative/free riding outcomes and outcomes in which the individual player exerts her effort. A convenient assumption to distinguish the low effort cost from the high effort cost game is then that $\lambda \in [0, p-\gamma]$ (and, respectively, $\lambda \in [p-\gamma, \infty])$ [5] in the low (high) effort cost version of the game described in this (the next) section.

By analysing equilibria in the one shot stage game it is clear that the low effort cost game described in Fig. 1 has a unique Nash equilibrium (e,e) when $\lambda \in [0, pq-\gamma)$.

When geographical agglomeration is higher, so that $\lambda \in (pq-\gamma, p-\gamma]$, the one shot stage game has two NE in pure strategies (e,ne) and (ne,e) - none of which Pareto dominates the other - and a third equilibrium in mixed strategies where each player plays e with probability π where $\pi = (\gamma-p)/(p(q-1)-\lambda)$.

The simple analysis of this stage game shows that, when $\lambda > pq-\gamma$, aggregate effort cannot be higher than when $\lambda < pq-\gamma$ and geographical agglomeration is lower.

Does this conclusion still hold in a framework of infinitely repeated games with observed actions? To evaluate which equilibria may be supported in this case, consider that Folk Theorem applies only for those payoff vectors v with $v_i > \underline{v}_i$ for all players i, where:

$$\underline{v}_i = \min_{\alpha_{-i}} \left[\max_{\alpha i} g_i(\alpha, \alpha_{-i}) \right] \tag{1}$$

is the minmax strategy of a player deviating from the equilibrium and also her reservation utility. In our game it is possible to show that $\underline{v}_i = \pi^* \lambda$ where $\pi^* = (\gamma-p)/(p(q-1)-\lambda)$. It is also clear from simple calculations that $\pi^* \lambda > pq-\gamma$ only when $\lambda > pq-\gamma$, while when $\lambda < pq-\gamma$ $\underline{v}_i = pq-\gamma$.

As a consequence:

---

[5] In this case effort cost is so high that imitation gives higher utility than positive R&D expenditure.

$$\underline{v}_i = \max\left[\pi *i, pq - \gamma\right] \tag{2}$$

and the minmax will be a pure strategy when $\lambda \in [0, pq-\gamma)$ and a mixed strategy when $\lambda \in (pq-\gamma, p-\gamma]$.

So, only with a low degree of geographical agglomeration it is possible to support an (e,e) equilibrium which generates the maximum aggregate R&D effort. One stage game conclusions on the effects of geographical agglomeration are then confirmed when the game is infinitely repeated and action is observed. With $\lambda \in [0, pq-\gamma)$ the set of feasible strictly individually rational payoffs $\{v \in V | v_i > \underline{v}_i \forall i\}$ is empty and the pure strategy equilibrium giving the minmax payoffs (e,e) is the only attainable. On the contrary, with $\lambda \in (pq-\gamma, p-\gamma]$, V is nonempty but $(e,e) \notin V$ (Fig. 2).

The result for the case with $\lambda \in [0, pq-\gamma)$ may change if side payments among players are allowed.

Individual players have no incentive to deviate from (e,e), but they may both gain from an (e,ne) outcome if the player exerting effort has enough extra gains to compensate the shirker for her loss. An alternative feasible equilibrium (e,ne) may be in fact devised when $(p-\gamma)-(pq-\gamma) > (pq-\gamma)-\lambda$ or $q < 1/2+(\gamma+\lambda)/2p$ and player 2 is compensated for her shirking by player 1 with a share of $((p-\gamma)-(pq-\gamma))-((pq-\gamma)-\lambda)$. We define this equilibrium as a $(e,ne|\varepsilon)$ equilibrium.

Two problems occur for the attainment of a $(e,ne|\varepsilon)$ equilibrium. How the two counterparts decide about who is going to shirk and how the extra profit share is bargained? Do Folk Theorem results apply to the $(e,ne|\varepsilon)$ equilibrium considering that player 1 may have an incentive to renegate side payments (see Folk Theorem below)? To the first point we may reasonably assume that players bargaining strength is a function of q and λ $(BS_i=f(q_i, \lambda_i))$. If, as it is assumed in the basic stage game, $q_i = q_{-i} = q$ and $\lambda_i = \lambda_{-i} = \lambda$, players have equal bargaining strength and a $(\frac{1}{2}-\frac{1}{2})$ division of extra profits is fixed. The two counterparts are then indifferent to whom is going to shirk. To the second point, we may apply Folk Theorem to see that there exists a $\underline{\delta} < 1$ such that:

$$(1-\underline{\delta}_i) \max_a g_i(a) + \underline{\delta}_i \underline{v}_i = v_i \tag{3}$$

where (3) corresponds in this case to

$$(1-\underline{\delta}_i)(p-\gamma) + \underline{\delta}_i(pq-\gamma) = p-\gamma-\varepsilon$$

with

$\varepsilon = 1/2((p-\gamma)-2(pq-\gamma)+\lambda)$ and $q<1/2+(\gamma+\lambda)/2p$.

Then, for all $\delta \in [\underline{\delta}_i, 1]$, the $(e, ne|\varepsilon)$ equilibrium can be supported in the infinitely repeated game described in Fig. 1.

The usual objection to this application of the Folk Theorem is that it is not subgame perfect as unrelenting punishment from player 2 when player 1 renegates side payments is a costly strategy for the first player. To overcome the objection we may check that Perfect Folk Theorem (Aumann-Shapley, 1976) may be applied to this type of game. In fact, if players evaluate sequences of stage-game utilities by the time-average criterion, the (e, ne) equilibrium, with side payment of $\varepsilon = 1/2((p-\gamma)-2(pq-\gamma)+\lambda)$ from the non shirker to the shirker when $q<1/2+(\gamma+\lambda)/2p$, is a subgame perfect equilibrium of the game. To obtain the result just check that an N exist such that:

$$\max_a g_i(a) + N\underline{v}_i < \min_a g_i(a) + Nv_i \tag{4}$$

if the deviator is minmaxed with mixed strategies or check that an N exist such that:

$$\max_a g_i(a) + N\underline{v}_i < Nv_i \tag{5}$$

when the deviator is minmaxed in pure strategies, where N is the number of periods for which player 1 is minmaxed if she deviates from the equilibrium. It is clear that, in our example, $N=(p-\gamma)/(p(1-q)-\varepsilon)$. The intuition for this result is that for "infinitely patient" agents costs of punishing the deviator are irrelevant. The assumption is quite unrealistic and it is interesting to see if subgame perfection of the Folk Theorem may be supported by relaxing it.

An alternative Perfect Folk Theorem moving in this direction allows us to say that the $(e, ne|\varepsilon)$ equilibrium may be shown to be subgame perfect by removing the extreme assumption of time-average criterion and assuming overtaking criterion with strategies in which punishment grows exponentially (Rubinstein, 1979).[6]

The main problem for the stability of the $(e, ne|\varepsilon)$ equilibrium, though, is that it is not possible to assume that, if it has been established through a negotiation, it

---

[6] The overtaking criterion represents a small departure from "infinite patience". It establishes that, given two payoff sequences $g=(g^0, g^1, ...)$ and $\hat{g} = (\hat{g}^0, \hat{g}^1, ..)$, the former is preferred to the latter if and only if there exists a time T' such that, for all T>T', the partial sum $\sum_{t=0}^{T} g^t$ strictly exceeds the partial sum $\sum_{t=0}^{T} \hat{g}^t$ (Fudenberg-Tirole, 1992).

cannot be subject to negotiation in case of deviation from the equilibrium. We then need to check if Weak Renegotiation Proofness (WRP) or Pareto-Perfection may be applied to the equilibrium. Given that punishment inflicted to player 1 does not reward player 2, the existence of a trade-off between rewarding player 2 and punishing player 1 prevents the $(e, ne|\varepsilon)$ equilibrium from being WRP.

The main problem here is that the bargaining power of the two counterparts remains completely balanced and that, even though we may devise strategies which may eliminate the trade-off, it is impossible to enforce them and therefore they remain not subgame perfect.

Consider for example the following strategy: *in stage one play an $(e, ne|\varepsilon)$ equilibrium with $\varepsilon = 1/2((p - \gamma) - 2(pq - \gamma) + \lambda)$ and $q < 1/2 + (\gamma + \lambda)/2p$; if player 1 does not renegate side payment ε, keep on playing the $(e, ne|\varepsilon)$ equilibrium in any of the following games, if player 1 does renegate side payment ε, play in the second stage an $(ne, e|\varepsilon_1)$ equilibrium where $\varepsilon_1 = \varepsilon + \xi(\xi > 0)$ is the side payment from player 2 to player 1 and then reverts to the $(e, ne|\varepsilon)$ equilibrium in all the following stages of the game.*

In this case the trade-off between rewarding player 2 and punishing player 1 is eliminated but the equilibrium is still not WRP as, if player 1 renegates side payment at the end of stage 1, there is no way to enforce her to accept the punishment.

Another serious limit to the feasibility of the $(e, ne|\varepsilon)$ equilibrium in infinitely repeated games arises if we pass from a perfect information to an imperfect information framework. Consider in fact a realistic situation in which player's level of effort is unobservable. Consider also two different R&D games: i) a breakthrough innovation game where $p \in [0,1]$ is the probability that an innovation will be obtained; ii) an incremental innovation game where $p \in [0, \infty]$ is the payoff for an innovative output which will be, in any case, obtained at the end of any stage. In the first case, the breakthrough innovation game, the Folk Theorem does not hold as the public outcome Π reveals too scarce information about players' actions. In fact, public outcome includes two uncertain states of nature (innovate and then $\Pi=1$, non innovate and then $\Pi=0$). Given that there is a nonzero probability that:

$$\Pi(a'_i, a_{-i}) = \Pi(a) \tag{6}$$

action a is in fact non enforceable. In the second R&D game with incremental innovation, the full-rank condition needed for application of Folk Theorems is respected given that there are as many publicly observed outcomes as actions for any player.

Dynamics may render the $(e, ne|\varepsilon)$ equilibrium even more unfeasible. Consider what happens when strategies are payoff-relevant and the game changes in each period.

Assume that our game is now a sequential game (Fudenberg-Tirole, 1992) with: i) a countable set of players, i=0,1...; ii) a state variable $k^t \in K \subseteq \Re$ with evolution equation $k^t = f_{t+1}(a^t)$; iii) a sequence of action spaces $A^t(k^t) \subseteq \Re$; iv) an objective function for each player of the form: $u_t = g_t(k^t, a^t) + w_t(k^{t+1}, a^{t+1}, a^{t+2}, ...)$; v) perfect information (player i knows $h^t = (a^0, ..., a^{t-1})$ before choosing action a^t.

The evolution equations which matter in this game are $q_{it}(a_{-it-1})$ and $\lambda_{it}(a_{it-1})$. In particular:

$$q_{it}(e_{-it-1}) = q_{it-1} \ and \ q_{it}(ne_{-it-1}) > q_{it-1} \ with \ q \in [0,1] \tag{7}$$

as the marginal effect of opponent on individual player payoff decreases if the former does not exert any effort in the one lag period. In addition:

$$\lambda_{it}(e_{it-1}) = \lambda_{it-1} \ and \ \lambda_{it}(ne_{it-1}) < \lambda_{it-1} \tag{8}$$

as the imitative capacity of a player decreases if no R&D effort (and expenditure) is exerted in the one lag period.

The rationale behind this specification is based on the dual role of R&D effort (pursuit of product and process innovation but also capacity to assimilate and to imitate external available information, (Cohen-Levinthal, 1989)). An extreme example justifying (6) is a deterministic patent race model (Dasgupta-Stiglitz, 1980). In fact, in a deterministic framework with no leapfrogging, the innovator, even though he is just one experiment behind, has no chances of winning the race, so that $q_{it}(ne_{-it-1})=1$. Given these two assumptions the payoff matrix of the dynamic stage game may be rewritten as (Fig. 2):

Fig. 2. The dynamic one stage game.

		Player 2	
		e	ne
Player 1	e	$p_{1t} \, q_{1t}(a_{2t-1}) - \gamma, \ p_{2t} \, q_{2t}(a_{1t-1}) - \gamma$	$p_{1t} - \gamma, \lambda_{2t}(a_{2t-1})$
	ne	$\lambda_{1t}(a_{1t-1}), \ p_{2t} - \gamma$	$0,0$

By using the structure of the game when geographical agglomeration is low and considering $\lambda \in [0, pq-\gamma]$, we have a unique Markov Perfect Equilibrium (e, e) with maximum aggregate effort.

On the contrary, the $(e, ne|\varepsilon)$ equilibrium cannot be Markov Perfect. In fact, imagine that players stick to it in the initial stage of the game. At the beginning of the second stage player 2, which does not invest in R&D effort in period 1 but invest in period 2, will find herself with lower imitative capacity and lower capacity of reducing the payoff of player 1. As a consequence $BS_2=f(q_2, \lambda_2)< BS_1=f(q_1, \lambda_1)$. Player 1 knows it and may renegate side payment to player 2. If this happens a new agreement may be renegotiated with worse terms for player 2 given the unbalance in bargaining strengths. Following this reasoning it will be impossible to enforce for more than one period any $(e, ne|\varepsilon)$ equilibrium given that the side which will accept to play the passive (ne) strategy will see her bargaining strength reduced and will obtain worse conditions in the next stage in case the agreement is renegotiated.

The dynamic game with high geographical agglomeration has a different outcome. When in fact $\lambda \in [pq-\gamma, p-\gamma]$ the analysis of the infinitely repeated static game shows that several equilibria with payoff v for each player i such that $\{v \in V | v_i > \underline{v}_i \forall i\}$ exist. For instance, the two equilibria in pure strategies, (e, ne) and (ne, e), are contained in the set V. These pure strategies, though, are not Markov Perfect Equilibria in the game in which strategies are payoff relevant. In fact the infinite repetition of the (e, ne) or of the (ne, e) equilibrium is not an equilibrium for the player i, who, without R&D effort, reduces her imitating and innovating capacity given that, after a certain number of stages, $\lambda_i < (pq_{-i}-\gamma)$. All equilibria in mixed strategies belonging to V are instead Markov Perfect Equilibria as far as the randomisation of strategies does not generate a sequence of games without R&D switch between players long enough that $\lambda_i < (pq_{-i}-\gamma)$ for some player i.

Theoretical predictions from the dynamic R&D game induce us to think that, in those sectors in which imitative capacity decreases when individual R&D effort is not exerted, the (e, ne) equilibrium is not Markov Perfect even with high geographical agglomeration. This conclusion creates then a discriminant between sectors with "highly depreciable imitating capacity" (such as High-Tech sectors and partially Specialised sectors) and sectors with "nondepreciable imitiating 1capacity" (such as Traditional sectors).

The conclusion of the R&D game in the low effort cost scenario is that geographical agglomeration is likely to reduce aggregate R&D effort. For $\lambda>pq-\gamma$ (high geographical agglomeration) the maximum aggregate R&D effort strategy is not a Nash Equilibrium of the stage game and is not contained in the set V of feasible strictly individually rational payoffs in the infinitely repeated game. For $\lambda<pq-\gamma$ (low geographical agglomeration) the only Nash Equilibrium of the one stage game is the (e, e) strategy which is also the strategy generating the maximum

aggregate R&D effort. An alternative $(e, ne|\varepsilon)$ equilibrium with lower aggregate effort may be supported by Perfect Folk Theorems under quite restrictive assumptions but this equilibrium is not WRP and cannot be supported with imperfect information and when the game is changed into a payoff-relevant strategy game under reasonable assumptions.

2.2 R&D Game in the High Effort Cost Scenario

The structure of the R&D game may change only when R&D effort cost is so high that it changes relative values of R&D effort toward imitation. It may then happen that, when geographical agglomeration is high, $\lambda \in [p-\gamma, \infty]$. The assumption that imitation gives higher payoffs than "stand-alone effort" research seems counterintuitive. It may become reasonable, though, if we assume that the probability of innovation is low and that R&D effort crowds out resources from production. In this case the imitator may find herself better off than the innovator. Let us consider the case where $pq-\gamma>0$. Here again in the stage game we have two NE in pure strategies - (e,ne) and (ne,e) -, none of which Pareto dominates the other. We also have an equilibrium in mixed strategies where each player plays e with probability π where $\pi=(\gamma-p)/(p(q-1)-\lambda)$. The important difference in the high effort cost scenario with respect to the previous scenario is that, with $\lambda \in [p-\gamma, \infty]$, the condition $q<1/2+(\gamma+\lambda)/2p$ for the feasibility of $(e,ne|\varepsilon)$ equilibria is always respected. This does not mean, though, that $(e,ne|\varepsilon)$ equilibria are more likely to occur considering that, as demonstrated in section 1.2, Folk Theorem and Perfect Folk Theorems may be applied to them. In fact, the $(e,ne|\varepsilon)$ equilibrium does not pass renegotiation proofness and cannot be reached in a dynamic game where strategies are payoff relevant and imitation and innovation capacity deteriorate if R&D effort is not exerted.

3   The Methodological Approach of the Empirical Analysis

The empirical analysis on the Mediocredito database[7] aims at testing theoretical predictions from the model presented in sections 1.2 and 1.3. Descriptive features of this sample illustrate some important characteristics of Italian economy: i) a

---

[7] The Mediocredito database is made of a sample of more than 5000 firms drawn from the universe of Italian manufacturing firms (64.463 firms at 1992 according to Cerved database). The sample is stratified and randomly selected (it reflects sector, geographical and dimensional distribution of Italian firms) for firms from 11 to 500 employees. It is by census for firms with more than 500 employees. For a subsample of 3852 firms both qualitative and quantitative data (balance sheets for the period 1989-1991) are available. Qualitative data provide, among other things, information on firm property, degree of internationalisation, entitlement to state subsidies and conclusion of agreements with partners and competitors.

relative specialisation in Traditional sectors and a despecialisation in High-Tech sectors; ii) a relevant weight of very small firms (with no more than 50 employees) in a system where small-medium firms represent the large majority; iii) the striking difference between firms in the North and firms in the South which are on average smaller, younger and have lower export capacity (Tab. 1).

To classify firms in the sample according to their degree of geographical proximity we use a criterion of pure geographical agglomeration. This criterion (Sforzi, 1995) calculates a coefficient of geographical concentration, using as indicator the share of local employment in the manufacturing sector and it considers as a threshold the national average (firms are "geographically agglomerated" if they are localised in an area where the above mentioned share is higher than average and not otherwise). In particular geographical agglomeration (GA) is calculated as:

$$GA = (E_{m,ls} / E_{t,ls}) / (A_{m,i} / A_{t,i}) \tag{7}$$

where $E_{m,ls}$ is the number of employees in firms with less than 250 employees for the manufacturing sector in the local system, $E_{t,ls}$ is the number of employees in the manufacturing sector in the local system, $A_{m,i}$ is the total number of employees in firms with less than 250 employees for the manufacturing sector in Italy and $A_{t,i}$ is the total number of employees in the manufacturing sector in Italy.

3.1 Empirical Descriptive Results

By applying the first criterion we may see that 47.7% of firms in the Mediocredito sample are geographically agglomerated. Descriptive statistics from Tab. 2 clearly show small firms' locational preference for geographical agglomeration in all

Table 1. Macroregional features of the Mediocredito sample (values in %)

	North West	North East	Centre	South	Italy
Firms with 0-50 employees	31.9	37.8	46.1	49.7	37.5
Firms with 50-500 employees	53.8	54.0	45.0	43.7	51.7
Firms with more than 500 employees	14.4	8.2	8.9	6.6	10.8
Firms with 0-10 billion liras net sales	35.1	38.7	47.7	55.7	40.0
Firms with 10-50 billion liras net sales	38.1	39.9	33.3	28.3	37.1
Firms with more than 50 billion liras net sales	26.7	21.4	18.9	16.0	22.9
	North West	North East	Centre	South	Italy
High-tech sectors	4.6	1.6	4.7	4.0	3.6
Specialised sectors	24.1	26.7	15.5	11.1	22.5
Scale sectors	28.8	27.7	27.1	28.6	28.2
Traditional sectors	40.1	42.0	49.4	53.4	43.3
Other non manufacturing	2.4	2.0	3.3	2.9	2.5
	North West	North East	Centre	South	Italy

Firm affiliated to groups	65.8	70.0	74.0	77.1	69.4
Firms participated for less than 50%	3.6	2.5	2.7	3.1	3.1
Firms participated for more than 50%	30.7	27.5	23.3	19.7	27.6
	North West	North East	Centre	South	Italy
Firms receiving subsidised credit	54.3	53.6	48.6	58.9	53.7
Firms non receiving subsidised credit	45.7	46.4	51.4	41.1	46.3
Exporting firms	77.3	73.1	61.4	40.9	70.3
Non exporting firms	22.7	26.9	38.6	59.1	29.7
Average size (n. of employees)	470	201	233	160	319
Average size (net sales in billion liras)	116	49	117	45	87
Share of exports sales on total sales	23%	26%	22%	11%	23%
Average foundation year	1964	1971	1971	1974	1968

Table 1. Continuation

areas with the exception of the South. Tab 3 shows a locational preference for geographical agglomeration of firms in Traditional and Specialised sectors, but not for firms in High-Tech sectors. This is consistent with the hypothesis that geographical agglomeration reduces the appropriability of nonpatented R&D knowledge, thereby generating benefits of agglomeration for R&D followers and costs of agglomeration for R&D leaders.

Table 2. Sample firms by area, size and geographical agglomeration (GA)

Size	North-East GA		North-East non GA		Total	
	N°	%	N°	%	N°	%
Small	277	37%	202	38%	479	38%
Medium	413	56%	278	52%	691	54.%
Large	50	7%	53	10%	103	8%
Total	740	100%	533	100%	1273	100%
	North-West GA		North-West non GA		Total	
	N°	%	N°	%		
Small	260	35%	232	27%	492	31%
Medium	421	57%	441	52%	862	55%
Large	52	7%	175	21%	227	14%
Total	733	100%	848	100%	1581	100%
	Centre GA		Centre non GA		Total	
	N°	%	N°	%	N°	%
Small	131	52%	124	42%	255	46%
Medium	120	47%	127	43%	247	45%

Large	3	1%	46	15%	49	9%
Total	254	100%	297	100%	551	100%

	South GA		South non GA		Total	
	N°	%	N°	%	N°	%
Small	32	64%	138	48%	170	51%
Medium	18	36%	127	45%	145	43%
Large	0	0	20	7%	20	7%
Total	50	100%	285	100%	335	100%

Table 2. Continuation

Small firms: firms with 0-50 employees; Medium firms: firms with 51-500 employees; Large firms: firms with more than 500 employees. GA firms: firms located in an area where the coefficient of geographical agglomeration is higher than 1; non GA firms: firms located in an area where the coefficient of geographical agglomeration is lower than 1.

Table 3. Geographical agglomeration (GA) and manufacturing macrosector

Sector by Pavitt classification	GA firms	Non GA firms	Total
Scale sectors	24%	33.2%	28.8%
Specialised sectors	24.3%	21.8%	23%
Traditional sectors	50.2%	39.4%	44.6%
High-tech sectors	1.5%	5.5%	3.5%

Table 4. Locational choice of manufacturing firm by sector and macroarea

Sector	NE GA	NE non GA	NW GA	NW non GA	C GA	C Non GA	S GA	S non GA
Specialised	26.3%	30.6%	23.8%	34.4%	20.2%	35.0%	14.0%	33.1%
Scale	27.7%	27%	25.7%	23.0%	14.3%	17.9%	4.0%	12.7%
Traditional	44.9%	40.3%	48.8%	35.5%	64.0%	39.3%	78.0%	49.8%
High-tech	1.109%	2.11%	1.7%	7.1%	1.6%	7.9%	4.0%	4.4%
Non-metallic mineral products	8.8%	8.6%	1.9%	2.9%	5.9%	5.7%	2.0%	9.1%
Chemicals	2.0%	3.2%	3.1%	6.0%	1.6%	5.4%	2.0%	4.9%
Pharmaceuticals	0.5%	0.8%	0.3%	2.7%	0	4.4%	0	0
Artificial fibres	0.1%	0	0.3%	0.5%	0	0.3%	0	0
Metal products	13.5%	12.9%	15.8%	15.0%	8.7%	7.4%	14%	13.7%
Mechanical Equipment	19.2%	15.2%	16.0%	12.3%	5.5%	6.4%	0	6.0%
Office equipment and computers	0.1%	0.6%	0	0.9%	0	0.7%	2.0%	0.4%
Electronics and electrical equipment	7.0%	9.2%	7.0%	11.3%	4.7%	10.1%	4%	6.3%

Sector	NE GA	NE non GA	NW GA	NW non GA	C GA	C Non GA	S GA	S non GA
Vehicles and vehicle components	1.6%	2.1%	1.5%	2.1%	0.8%	0.7%	2%	2.8%
Other means of transport	0.1%	1.1%	0.3%	0.7%	0	1.3%	0	0.7%
Precision instruments and apparels	1.1%	3.0%	0.5%	2.0%	0	1.3%	0%	1.1%
Food	3.2%	3.9%	2.6%	2.0%	2.8%	7.1%	2%	6%
Sugar, tobacco, etc...	1.8%	1.9%	1.0%	1.9%	1.2%	1%	0	4.6%
Textile	6.9%	4.7%	18.4%	8.8%	12.6%	3.4%	12%	2.5%
Leather	2.2%	0.8%	1.2%	0.5%	3.5%			
Shoes and clothing	10.5%	6.8%	5.3%	4.0%	26.0%			
Wood and wooden furniture	4.7%	6.8%	3.4%	1.5%	8.7%			
Paper and printing	6.6%	8.8%	6.4%	9.7%	7.1%			
Rubber and plastics	5.3%	3.8%	7.2%	5.0%	3.5%			
Other manufacturing	3.0%	3.2%	5.9%	4.8%	5.9%			

Table 4. Continuation

3.2 Descriptive Statistics on the Relationship between R&D and Geographical Agglomeration

Descriptive evidence shows that geographically agglomerated (from now on GA) firms generally spend less in R&D, have less R&D employees and participate less to R&D than their non geographically agglomerated counterparts (Tab. 5). This result is quite clear cut at a national level but it is not homogeneous across macroareas, size classes and macrosectors. The negative difference in R&D participation between GA and non GA firms seems in fact more pronounced in the North-West and in the Centre and for Specialised and High-tech firms (Tab. 6).

Table 5. Geographical agglomeration (GA), R&D expenditures and R&D employees

Firms	Number	Average	Standard deviation	Confidence Interval
		R&D expenditures on total assets		
No GA firms	1963	0.14%	0.159	0.08% - 0.22%
GA firms	1777	0.06%	0.006	0.03% - 0.09%
All firms	3740	0.10%	0.124	0.06% - 0.15%
		R&D employees		
No GA firms	1963	2.20	5.42	1.96 - 2.44
GA firms	1777	1.83	4.84	1.61 - 2.06
All firms	3740	2.03	5.16	1.86 - 2.19

Table 6. R&D participation by macroarea, macrosector and size

	R&D		No R&D	
	GA firms	No GA firms	GA firms	No GA firms
Macroarea				
North-East	40%	43.9%	60%	56.1%
North-West	37.5%	46.2%	62.5%	53.8%
Centre	29.9%	35.7%	70.1%	64.3%
Size				
Small firms	19.4%	20.7%	80.6%	79.3%
Medium firms	46%	45.1%	54%	54.9%
Large firms	67%	67.6%	33%	32.4%
Macrosector				
Scale	42.4%	40.2%	57.6%	59.8%
Specialised	45.1%	53.2%	54.9%	46.8%
Traditional	30.4%	30.9%	69.6%	69.1%
High-Tech	38.5%	60.2%	61.5%	39.8%

3.3 Results from Econometric Analysis

Longitudinal regressions try to provide a breakdown by size, macroarea and macrosector for the net effect of geographical agglomeration on private firm R&D expenditure and R&D participation. A synthetic description of the results is presented in Tab. 7-8 while full results are presented in the Appendix. Tab. 7 present coefficients and T-statistics on the net impact of geographical agglomeration (GA) on private firm R&D intensity from the following Tobit specification:

$$Rsotat = \alpha_0 + \sum_{i=1}^{22} \alpha_i Dset_i + \sum_{i=1}^{3} \gamma_k Darea_k + \beta_1 Size + \beta_2 Group + \beta_3 GA + \varepsilon \quad (8)$$

where *Rstotat* is the three year (1989-91) average of the share of R&D expenditure on total assets, *Dset* are 22 sector dummies, *Darea* are three macroarea dummies, *GA* is a dummy which takes value of 1 if the firm is located in an industrial district (is geographically agglomerated) and zero otherwise, *Size* is three year (1989-91) average of firm's employees, *Group* is a dummy which takes value of one for firms affiliated to groups (subsidiaries or parent companies) and zero otherwise.

The presence of sector controls is crucial as it helps to detect the right causality link between locational choice and R&D effort. In fact a significantly negative β_3 coefficient without sector controls might be explained by the fact that firms in R&D intensive sectors avoid to locate themselves into industrial districts. It is still possible, though, after sector controls, that differences in R&D intensity within sectors affect locational choice. Even if this interpretation which reverts the causality link between locational choice and R&D intensity, is accepted, it does not contradict the theoretical hypothesis on the relative disadvantage of private R&D effort in geographically agglomerated areas.

Results from Tobit estimates clearly show that GA has a negative and significant effect on R&D intensity, while other significant factors affecting the dependent variable are, as expected, firm size in the sample of small-medium firms and dummies of sectors in which Italy has a relative specialisation (Mechanical Equipment, Office equipment and computers, Electronics and Electrical Equipment).

Tab. 8 presents results on the impact of GA on "R&D participation" (decision to afford private R&D expenditure) from multivariate logit regressions performed by macrosectors, macroareas and size classes. To this purpose we use the following specification:

$$Rspart = \alpha_0 + \sum_{i=1}^{3} \alpha_i Dma_i + \sum_{k=1}^{22} \delta_k Dset_k + \beta GA + \gamma Size + \varepsilon \qquad (9)$$

where *Rspart* is a dummy which takes value of one if the firm has nonzero average R&D expenditures in the period 1989-91 and zero otherwise, *Dset* are 22 sector dummies, *Dma* are three macroareas dummies and *Size* is three year (1989-91) average of firm's employees. In all the performed regressions geographical agglomeration presents the expected negative sign even though the coefficient is not always significant. Geographical agglomeration and participation to an industrial district seem to be more effective in reducing R&D participation in the full sample regression in the North-East, in the Centre, and in Traditional and Scale sectors. This is consistent with the idea that in High-Tech sectors an imitative strategy with no R&D expenditure is not efficient, even with geographical agglomeration, because nonparticipation to R&D reduces the "absorptive capacity" necessary both for active research and imitation (Cohen-Levinthal, 1989). The same should occur in Specialised sectors where the main direction of technological accumulation is in process innovation. On the contrary, in Scale and Traditional sectors technological accumulation occurs through product development and product design, so that an imitative strategy with no R&D participation may be successful when the level of geographical agglomeration is high.

Table 7. Tobit estimates on the determinants of R&D intensity in Italy (Dependent variable: R&D/Total Assets)

	All firms		Firms with less than 250 employees		Firms with less than 100 employees	
	Coeff.	T stat	Coeff.	T stat	Coeff.	T stat
Size	1.6E-07	0.463	5.5E-05	2.40	0.0002	3.248
North-West	0.008	1.731	0.010	1.792	0.006	0.971
North-Easth	0.005	1.152	0.008	1.358	0.003	0.470
Centre	0.007	1.270	0.008	1.260	0.004	0.498
Group	0.002	1.007	0.003	0.887	0.002	0.477
Non-metallic mineral products	-0.040	-2.620	-0.008	-0.926	-0.004	-0.328
Chemicals	-0.022	-1.497	0.012	1.465	0.022	2.127
Pharmaceuticals	-0.014	-0.844	0.034	2.725	0.019	0.755
Artificial fibres	-0.002	-0.076				
Metal products	-0.032	-2.248	0.002	0.316	0.002	0.222
Mechanical Equipment	-0.015	-1.050	0.021	3.434	0.025	3.018
Office equipment and computers	-0.008	-0.445	0.042	2.621	0.061	3.201
Electronics and electrical equipment	-0.022	-1.494	0.017	2.514	0.021	2.332
Vehicles and vehicle components	-0.022	-1.349	0.021	1.803	0.033	2.048
Other means of transport	-0.019	-1.024	0.018	0.971	0.020	0.782
Precision instruments and apparels	-0.033	-1.919	0.006	0.442	-0.006	-0.300
Food	-0.024	-1.580	0.016	1.943	0.021	1.888
Sugar, tobacco, etc	-0.022	-1.375	0.018	1.675	0.030	2.316
Textile	-0.038	-2.561	0.000	-0.041	0.004	0.465
Leather	-0.036	-2.029	-0.008	-0.547	0.002	0.140
Shoes and clothing	-0.045	-2.986	-0.014	-1.621	-0.020	-1.631
Wood and wooden furniture	-0.034	-2.234	0.002	0.277	0.004	0.318
Paper and printing	-0.046	-3.016	-0.009	-1.184	-0.009	-0.893
Rubber and plastics	-0.021	-1.418	0.019	2.594	0.021	2.328
Other manufacturing	-0.029	-1.916				
Other non manufacturing	-0.023	-1.507				
Electrical measure, equipment and telecommunications	-0.030	-1.609	0.031	2.26	0.012	1.98
GA location	-0.008	-3.129	-0.010	-3.371	-0.008	-2.129
Constant	-0.028	-1.958	-0.073	-8.921	-0.082	-7.495
Left censored observations	3479		2816		2000	
Uncensored observations	343		259		167	
χ^2	112.91		115.5		96.64	
Log Likelihood	-41.34		-53.49		-45.84	

The table reports magnitude and T-statistics (in parenthesis) of the following Tobit estimate:

$$Rsotat = \alpha_0 + \sum_{i=1}^{22} \alpha_i Dset_i + \sum_{i=1}^{3} \gamma_k Darea_k + \beta_1 Size + \beta_2 Group + \beta_3 GA + \varepsilon$$

where *Rstotat* is the three year (1989-91) average of the share of R&D expenditure on total assets, $Dset_i$ are 22 sector dummies, $Darea_k$ are 3 macroarea dummies (NEST, NOVEST, CENTRE), *GA* is a dummy which takes value of 1 if the firm is located in an area in which the coefficient of geographical agglomeration is higher than 1 and zero otherwise, *Group* is a dummy which takes value of one for firms affiliated to groups (subsidiaries or parent companies) and zero otherwise.

Vertical headers for any of table cells indicate the subsample on which the regression is performed. Estimate disturbances are controlled for normality and heteroskedasticity.

Table 8. The marginal impact of geographical agglomeration on R&D participation - Synthesis of empirical results

Sample	All firms	Firms with less than 500 employees	Firms with less than 300 employees	Firms with less than 100 employees
All firms	**-0.40 (9.83)**	**-0.44 (10.56)**	**-0.46 (10.77)**	**-0.31 (3.07)**
North-East	**-0.66 (8.77)**	**-0.59 (6.44)**	**-0.54 (5.14)**	-0.34 (1.22)
North-West	-0.003 (0.0003)	-0.06 (0.07)	-0.09 (0.17)	0.03 (0.009)
Centre	**-2.69 (6.73)**	**-2.64 (6.44)**	**-2.59 (6.17)**	**-2.42 (5.17)**
Traditional sectors	**-0.41 (3.27)**	**-0.55 (5.2)**	**-0.61 (5.88)**	**-0.8 (5.4)**
Specialised sectors	004 (0.02)	0.1 (0.16)	0.17 (0.42)	0.45 (1.77)
Scale sectors	**-1.36 (15.72)**	**-1.37 (14.22)**	**-1.33 (13.18)**	**-1.14 (6.12)**
High-tech sectors	-0.66 (0.34)	-0.76 (0.44)	-1.16 (0.83)	

The table reports coefficient and Wald-statistics for the geographical agglomeration dummy coefficient β in a logit which controls for macrosector, size and other variables.

$$Rspart = \alpha_0 + \sum_{i=1}^{3} \alpha_i Dma_i + \beta GA + \gamma Size + \varepsilon$$

where *Rspart* is a dummy which takes value of one if the firm has nonzero R&D expenditures as a three year (1989-91), *Dset* are 22 sector dummies, *GA* is a dummy which takes value of 1 if the firm is located in an area where firms are geographically agglomerated (higher than average share of local employment in the manufacturing sector) and zero otherwise, *Size* is the three year (1989-91) average of firm's employees.

Vertical and horizontal headers for any of table cells indicate the subsample on which the regression is performed. Full econometric results are provided in the Appendix.

4 Conclusions

Industrial districts are generally intended as geographical agglomerations of small-medium firms which decide to locate themselves next to each other. A decentralised small-medium firm network is preferred to vertical integration when Marshallian externalities generated by proximity of potential competitors are higher than costs from increased competition.

A potential effect of geographical agglomeration, though, is that of reducing the appropriability of nonproprietary knowledge which is the typical intermediate output of interim stages of research. Thus, geographical agglomeration may increase the relative advantage of imitation on independent R&D effort, thereby reducing firm's private R&D expenditures.

This paper provides a theoretical rationale for this hypothesis and tests theoretical predictions at microlevel on a sample of around 4000 firms for which information on locational choice and R&D expenditures is available.

The theoretical section shows, in a simple two players' game, that, with no geographical proximity, the only feasible Weak Renegotiation Proof equilibrium is one where both firms always invest in R&D, while, with geographical proximity, this equilibrium is not in the set of strictly individually rational payoffs. The robustness of this conclusion is analysed under different frameworks such as infinitely repeated noncooperative and cooperative games with perfect and imperfect information and games with payoff relevant strategies.

The empirical section tests this theoretical prediction using size classes, macroareas and industrial sectors as sample discriminants or control variables. Findings from this section show that R&D expenditure and R&D participation is significantly reduced, even though not in all specifications, by geographical proximity. This effect is stronger in sectors in which imitation is an efficient alternative to private R&D and zero private R&D expenditure does not reduce too much absorptive capacity needed for successful imitation (Traditional and Scale sectors).

Even though the geographical agglomeration-reduction in R&D expenditure effect seems to occur, this result must not induce to the conclusion that aggregate level of technological innovation in industrial districts is insufficiently low. Other forms of innovation (product/process imitation, learning by doing, learning through export) may be developed alternatively and seem to have a relative advantage over private R&D expenditures when firms are geographically agglomerated.

Fig. 3. The feasibility of R&D game equilibria in the infinitely repeated game

Case 1 Low geographical proximity

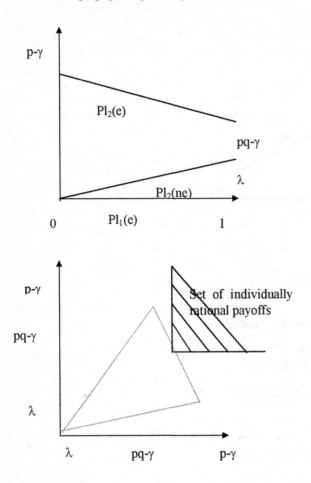

Minmax is pq-γ for both players. Consequently (e,e) is the only outcome which is in the set of individually rational payoff (V) and the aggregate effort is maximum

Case 2 High geographical proximity

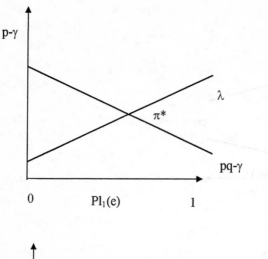

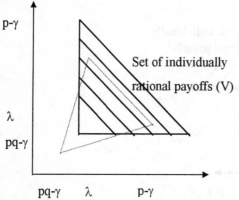

Minmax is p*λ for both players. Consequently (e,ne) and (ne,e) are in the set of individually rational payoffs, while (e,e) is out of it. The aggregate R&D effort must be lower than in case 1.

Fig. 3. Continuation

References

Abdel-Rahman, H. and Fujita M., 1990, Product Variety, Marshallian Externalities, and City Sizes, *Journal of Regional Science*, 30.

Aumann R. and Shapley L., 1976, Long Term Competition - a Game Theoretic Analysis, mimeo.

Bagella M. and Becchetti L., 1999, Business Cycle and Growth in an Economy with Financial Market Imperfections, in E.Phelps, M.Baldassarri, L.Paganetto (eds.) *Finance, Research, Education and Growth,* Mc Millan (forth.).

Bagella M., Becchetti L. and Sacchi S., 1998, The positive impact of geographical agglomeration on export intensity, *Economic Notes*.

Bagella M., Becchetti L. and Caggese A., 1996, Finanza, Investimenti ed Innovazione in Italia: il divario Nord-South in B.Quintieri (ed.) *Finanza, Istituzioni e sviluppo regionale: il problema del Mezzogiorno,* Il Mulino.

Beath J. and Ulph D., 1990, The Trade-Off between Static and Dynamic Efficiency in a Non-Tournament Model of Innovation, *University of Bristol, Discussion Paper 90/286*.

Becattini G.,1987, *Mercato e Forze Locali: Il Distretto Industriale*, Bologna, Il Mulino.

Becchetti L. and Rossi S., 1999, The positive effect of Industrial District on the export performance of Italian firms, *The Review of Industrial Organisation*, (forth.).

Bianchi P., 1989, *Concorrenza Dinamica, Distretti Industriali e Interventi Locali*, In F. Gobbo Distretti Industriali e sistemi produttivi alla soglia degli anni 90, Milano, F. Angeli.

Cohen W. and Levinthal D., 1989, Innovation and Learning: the two Faces of R&D, *Economic Journal*, 99.

Dasgupta P. and Stiglitz J., 1980, Industrial Structure and the Nature of Innovative Activity, *Economic Journal*, 90.

Dobkins L.H., 1996, Location, Innovation and Trade; The Role of Localization and Nation-Based Externalities, *Regional Science and Urban Economics*, 26.

Flaherty M., 1980, Industry Structure and Cost Reducing Investment, *Econometrica*.

Fudenberg D. and Tirole J.J., 1992, Game Theory, MIT Press, Cambridge Massachussets

Futia C., 1980, Schumpeterian Competition, *Quarterly Journal of Economics*, 93.

Gaspar J. and Glaeser E.L., 1996, Information technology and the future of cities, *NBER Working Paper, n.5562*.

Goffman E., 1988, *L'interazione Strategica*, Bologna, Il Mulino.

Marshall A., 1920, Principles of Economics, 8th edition. (Procupine Press, Philadelphia, 1982).

Mistri M., 1993, *Distretti Industriali e Mercato Unico Europeo,* Istituto G. Tagliacarne, Milano, F. Angeli.

Momigliano F. and Dosi G., 1983, *Tecnologia e organizzazione Industriale Internazionale,* Bologna, Il Mulino.

Nuti F., 1992, I Distretti Industriali Manifatturieri, Vol.1, CNR.

Onida F., Viesti G. and Falzoni A.M., 1992, *Distretti Industriali: Crisi o Evoluzione?,* CESPRI, Egea,1992.

Porter M., 1991, *Il vantaggio Competitivo delle Nazioni,* Milano, Mondadori.

Pyke F. and Sengenberger W., 1992, *Industrial District and local Economic Regeneration,* Geneva, International Institute for labour Studies.

Rivera-Batiz F.L., 1988a, Increasing Returns, Monopolistic Competition and Agglomeration Economies in Consumption and Production, *Regional Science and Urban Economics,* 18.

Rivera-Batiz F.L., 1988b, Modeling urban Agglomeration : Producer Services, Linkage Externalities and Specialisation Economies, in : M.H. Mickel and V.Vogt, eds., *Modeling and Simulation* (Instrument Society of America, Research Triangle Park, NC).

Rogertson W., 1982, The Social Cost of Monopoly and Regulation: A Game- Theoretic Analysis, *Bell Journal of Economics,* 13.

Rubinstein A., 1979, Equilibrium in Supergames with the Overtaking Criterion, *Journal of Economic Theory,* 21.

Sforzi F., 1991, Sistemi Locali di Piccola e Media Impresa, IRPET.

Sforzi F., 1995, *Sistemi Locali di Impresa e Cambiamento Industriale in Italia,* AGEI-Geotema n°2.

Shaked A and Sutton J., 1983, Natural oligopolies, *Econometrica,* Vol. 51.

Efficiency and Localisation: the Case of Italian Districts

S. Fabiani

Banca d'Italia, Servizio Studi, via Nazionale 91, 00184 Roma

G. Pellegrini

Università di Bologna, Dipartimento di Scienze Statistiche, via Belle Arti 41, 40126 Bologna

E. Romagnano

Banca d'Italia, Servizio Studi, via Nazionale 91, 00184 Roma

L.F. Signorini

Banca d'Italia, Servizio Studi, via Nazionale 91, 00184 Roma

Abstract: Despite the large interest devoted by the literature to the role of industrial districts (IDs) in the Italian economy, the factors underlying the successful performance of firms which are part of IDs are scarcely analysed from an empirical point of view. This paper presents a quantitative comparison between the performance, in terms of profitability and technical efficiency, of ID and isolated firms. The measurement of technical efficiency, based on statistical parametric methods, allows to assess whether the "success" of ID firms is due to factors related to a more efficient use of inputs and technologies or to causes that are external to the structure of the organisation. The analysis, based on the balance sheets of a panel of small and medium sized manufacturing firms drawn from the Centrale dei Bilanci *database, covers the whole manufacturing sector and, as far as the availability of data allows, all Italian IDs. The identification of IDs utilises the procedure developed by Sforzi (1990) and Istat (1996), based on the sub-provincial aggregation of areas in the so-called "local labour systems".*

JEL Classification: R3.

Keywork: Technical efficency, Industrial Districts.

1 Introduction*

Italy is peculiar among large industrialised countries because of the overwhelming dominance of small firms and traditional sectors in the manufacturing industry. According to one comparison, for example, the textile and clothing industry employs almost a quarter of the manufacturing labour force in Italy, as against 10 per cent in the US, 6 per cent in Japan and 5 per cent in Germany (Signorini and Visco, 1997); also, in 1991 71 per cent of the Italian manufacturing labour force was employed by firms with fewer than 250 employees, as against, say, 38 per cent in Germany, 47 in France, 45 in the UK, 37 in the US (Brusco and Paba, 1997)

This kind of industry and size specialisation makes Italy much more similar to many emerging economies than to the average G-7 country. This has long been considered both a puzzle and (to many) a source of concern. First of all, why is Italy so different, i.e. what makes such a specialisation efficient, in some sense, for Italy? And, secondly, how can its manufacturing industry ultimately face the double competition of low-cost NICs and hi-tech, large-scale productions in other advanced countries?

The concern has so far proved unfounded. In the long run, Italy has grown more than most other G-7 countries (though, of course, less than many NICs); and small firms have remained, by and large, the most dynamic part of the Italian manufacturing industry. Despite occasional setbacks in some regions and/or industries, their share of the manufacturing labour force has continued to grow, at least until the latest industrial census. Many 'light' industries, where the predominance of small firms is even more marked than in manufacturing as a whole, have consistently generated trade surpluses, and have made a decisive contribution to the substantial surplus of the current-account balance that Italy has enjoyed since 1993. The day of reckoning may yet come; but, so far, the peculiar industry and size structure of Italy's manufacturing sector has not seriously hindered its development.

Which leaves us with the puzzle about the efficiency of such a structure. To solve it, one strand of the literature has long claimed that looking at firms in isolation and using simple industry classifications may be misleading (see, for instance, Becattini, 1990 and Brusco, 1986). In certain industries, *internal* economies of scale may be more or less irrelevant beyond a (small) minimum efficient scale; much more important are the *external* economies produced by the special 'industrial climate' which is said to predominate in certain local agglomerations of small firms, all specialised in one industry and sharing idiosyncratic, community-

---

* The views expressed in this work do not necessarily reflect those of the Bank of Italy, and any error is the authors' responsibility. Although the paper is the result of the authors' joint effort, sections 1 and 5 were written by L.F. Signorini, section 2 by G. Pellegrini, section 3 by E. Romagnano and section 4 by S. Fabiani.

dependent externalities. Following early descriptions by Marshall, these agglomerations are called industrial districts (ID). In this view, generic statements about 'small firms' or 'traditional sectors' are largely meaningless; it is the interplay between size, industry and location that determines the competitiveness and development potential of industry.

While the early literature on IDs was almost exclusively qualitative and case-based, the more recent literature has also a quantitative dimension. One aspect of this is an attempt to measure the share of ID production in the Italian manufacturing industry. This implies the difficult task of specifying which areas qualify as districts in the strict Marshall-Becattini sense. The Sforzi (1990) - Istat (1996) classification is based on local labour systems (LLSs), defined as areas which are more or less closed with respect to daily commuting trips. An LLS is then classified as an industrial district if it meets some criteria (manufacturing vocation, industry specialisation, small firm size), judgmentally specified in advance by the authors in a way that is compatible, in some general sense, with the qualitative descriptions of IDs found in the relevant literature. Sforzi and Istat find that over 40 per cent of Italian manufacturing (measured in terms of labour) is concentrated in industrial districts as they define them.

On the other hand, there are very few attempts to measure the size of the supposed competitive advantage of IDs with respect to other forms of productive organisation. This is surprising, given the large body of qualitative literature on Italian industrial districts that has amassed over the last two decades, where such an advantage was always assumed but never empirically demonstrated. One of us (Signorini, 1994) has tried to measure an 'industrial district effect' in one specific instance (the Italian wool textile industry), by comparing several measures of performance between district and non-district firms in this industry. We are aware of no comprehensive quantitative study of the existence and size of 'district effects' in Italy.

This paper (which is part of a wider Bank of Italy research project on regional and local development) makes a first attempt at such a comprehensive study. Basically, using the Centrale dei Bilanci database, we take balance-sheet data on over 10,000 small and medium-sized firms belonging to all branches of the manufacturing industry and all regions of Italy. We classify each firm as ID or non-ID ('isolated'), on the basis of the Sforzi-Istat map. We then compare a number of key firm-level characteristics in ID and isolated firms. The methodology adopted for the identification of ID firms and the construction of the database is presented in section 2.

The main object of the analysis is the economic efficiency of production in industrial districts. If ID external economies exist, they should be detectable in some measures of productivity and/or profitability. As a first step, in section 3 we present some descriptive evidence based on balance-sheet data on profitability as well as on some key variables which can be influenced by the characteristics of the organisation of the productive process in IDs (labour cost, capital intensity, cost of credit). The data mainly refer to 1995, although for some variables we present evidence for the period 1982-1995. Results are presented separately for each of 13 manufacturing industries. In almost every industry, productivity and profitability appear to be considerably higher for ID firms.

Section 4 contains an econometric analysis of efficiency. We estimate industry-level stochastic frontier production functions, with random inefficiency terms which are assumed to depend, among other things, on whether a firm belongs to an ID or not. The estimation is based on balanced panels covering the period 1991-1995. Being in a district generally improves the technical efficiency (closeness to the frontier) of a firm in a strongly significant way. Only in a few industries (such as paper and printing, chemicals and transport vehicles) where districts are known to be largely irrelevant this result does not hold.

2   The Identification of Districts and District Firms

The operational identification of districts and their boundaries is somewhat arbitrary. Sforzi (1990) and Istat (1996) proposed a multi-step procedure, which is widely used.[1] In the first step, the Sforzi-Istat procedure identifies travel-to-work areas, called 'sistemi locali del lavoro' (local labour systems or LLS). Italy is partitioned into 784 LLSs, i.e. groups of neighbouring municipalities (comuni) that are largely self-contained with respect to daily commuting (the data are drawn from the 1991 Population Census). An LLS is defined as an ID if (1) the share of manufacturing workers in the LLS labour force is larger than the national average; (2) the LLS is specialised in one particular manufacturing industry; (3) LLS employment is concentrated in productive plants with no more than 250 employees. For 1991, the Sforzi-Istat criteria identify 199 industrial districts, which account for 42.5 per cent of total Italian manufacturing employment.

Clearly, this procedure is less than ideal from a purely theoretical point of view. Thresholds are somewhat arbitrary (e.g., why 250 employees and not, say, 100?). 'Social' variables (attitudes, information flows, etc.), so central to ID theory, are not considered for lack of reliable data. Urban agglomerations, which sometimes display district-like characteristics, are usually excluded from the list of IDs because of a high share of employment in services (Brusco and Paba, 1997). Furthermore, the specialisation of districts may not be well captured by considering industries rather than 'filières' (which would include complementary activities, e.g. the production of shoe-production machinery if the ID is specialised in shoes). On the other hand, given the limitations of the available data, the Sforzi-Istat criteria may be considered a reasonable approximation of the ID concept.

---

[1] For a detailed description of the procedure see also Brusco and Paba (1997) and Appendix 1 in Baffigi, Pagnini and Quintiliani (1997).

Therefore, their list of districts is widely adopted in the recent literature; it will be used in this paper.[2]

The analysis of this paper is based on firm-level data.[3] Data on ID firms may be collected in several ways. Some recent studies (for example, Brusco and Bigarelli, 1997) were based on field investigations. With this approach the list of firms to be interviewed, and of questions to be asked, can be precisely focused. However, there are practical limits to the size of the sample and the amount of quantitative information that can be gathered in this way. Another approach, adopted in Signorini (1994), is to use a large enterprise database, like Centrale dei Bilanci, and select the firms that belong to districts. In Signorini (1994) the boundaries of IDs were approximated by those of the administrative provinces that contained them. In that paper only a single micro-industry (the wool textile industry) was considered, and it was safe to assume that most wool-textile firms in the (two) provinces considered were actually located in the ID areas within each province. But, in general, provinces cannot be used for this purpose. There are about 100 provinces and almost 800 LLSs in Italy; thus LLSs (and hence IDs, which are a subset of them) are usually much smaller than provinces. Moreover, LLSs often straddle province boundaries. Therefore, we used postal-code data to identify the LLS to which a firm belongs.[4]

To focus on the size classes that are relevant for ID theory, we considered only firms with no more than 250 employees.

Within that limit, our definition of ID firms is based only on location: all firms located in an LLS that the Sforzi-Istat procedure identifies as a district are considered ID firms. Obviously, many firms located in an ID produce goods that are not related to the district specialisation; call them non-specialised ID firms. It is not entirely clear, in principle, whether non-specialised ID firms should be grouped with specialised ID firms or with isolated firms. While some of the competitive advantages of districts (e.g. knowledge of technologies and markets) are industry-specific, others (e.g. social attitudes, enterprise-friendly local governments, etc.) affect all local firms in much the same way. If industry-specific effects prevail, then a 'wide' definition of ID firms (i.e., one based only on location) may distort the results for those industries where IDs are relatively unimportant (such as chemicals, transport vehicles, paper, electrical equipment),

---

[2] See Brusco and Paba (1997), Baffigi, Pagnini and Quintiliani (1997).

[3] Given the existence of multi-plant firms, it might be argued that plant-level data would, in principle, be preferable. However, no such data exist at the required level of geographical disaggregation.

[4] It is impractical to use the denomination of municipalities for classification, because of small differences in the way they can be written (abbreviations, blanks, and so on). The postal code is a 5-digit numeric code. Some ambiguous cases were solved by a a double check between postal code and denomination of the municipality.

because ID firms in those sectors will turn out to be, to a large extent, non-specialised. On the other hand, if district-wide effects prevail, then an alternative, 'narrow' definition (i.e., one based on location+specialisation) would be unduly restrictive. Also, many ostensibly non-specialised ID firms may in fact belong to complementary ('*filière*') industries, related to the main specialisation of the district: e.g. packaging, machinery, and so on. For all these reasons, while we maintain the wide definition as our basic definition of an ID firm, in the next section we also present some descriptive evidence based on a narrow definition to check for the robustness of the main results.

The data on firms are drawn from the Centrale dei Bilanci company account database (CB).[5] CB covers about 30,000 firms in all sectors of the Italian economy. We considered only manufacturing firms. CB is not a statistical sample, because the selection criteria are not rigorously defined (Cannari, Pellegrini and Sestito, 1996). The coverage increases with size: with respect to the Census of 1991, CB covers 16 per cent of the firms with 10 employees or more (and 45 per cent of their workers), but only 6 per cent of the firms in the smallest size class (10-19 employees). The coverage rises to 28 per cent of firms (29 per cent of workers) in the class 20-99, to which most of the firms analysed in this paper belong.

To account for any distortion linked to the size bias of the CB sample, we present separate results for each size class. Apart from the size distribution, CB is likely to be reasonably representative of small and medium sized firms. Because of the original purpose of the CB database[6], one peculiarity is that it includes only companies that entertain (or used to entertain at some point in the past) multiple bank relationships. It is unclear whether, and how, this fact might bias the selection of firms from the point of view of the analysis of efficiency; besides, any such bias is unlikely to affect ID firms in a different way from non-ID firms. However, this point being particularly important for very small firms, data on them should be regarded with some caution.

Company accounts are sometimes suspect as a source of data for economic analysis, because the accounting values of some items (e.g., fixed assets) is dictated, to a certain extent, by legal convention. The accounting data may also be affected by exceptional events, mistakes in reporting and other noise. Although some distortions may be significant in general, we find no reason for any ID-specific effect; since we are only interested in the difference between ID and non-ID firms, we are confident that accounting distortions will add noise, but not bias, to our results. To avoid some obvious trouble, we selected only firms that presented a complete balance sheet, that were not affected by mergers or

---

[5] For more information on Centrale dei Bilanci see Centrale dei Bilanci (1991), Signorini (1994), Cannari, Pellegrini and Sestito (1996).

[6] CB is jointly owned by the Bank of Italy and a number of commercial banks, who wanted to share information on company accounts.

acquisitions, and whose accounting values for sales, capital stock and other basic items was greater than one.[7] We also excluded firms with less than 10 employees, of which only a tiny (and possibly distorted) fraction is sampled by CB. To further increase the robustness of results with respect to outliers, in the descriptive evidence we present medians rather than arithmetic means.

3   Some Preliminary Evidence

This section presents some descriptive evidence on the differences between ID and isolated firms. We consider three main aspects: profitability, cost and productivity of labour, financial costs.

The year 1995 is the latest date for which complete information is available in the CB database. Thus we mostly used company balance sheets for that year, for which we had data on 10,939 firms. Of those, 70 per cent are in the 20-99 size class, 21 per cent in the 100-250 class and the rest in the 10-19 class. We present separate data for 13 manufacturing sectors. The largest sectors, by number of firms, are the machinery industry (15 per cent of the sample), the textiles industry (14), the electric and electronic industry (13), the food and beverages industry (11); the smallest is the wood industry (2 per cent). Further details on the size and industry distribution of the 1995 sample are contained in table A1 in the Annex.

Out of 10,939 firms, 6,389 (58 per cent) are located in a district (table A2 in the Annex). They account for 57 per cent of the 747,000 employees in the sampled firms. ID firms are concentrated in the 20-99 size class (71 per cent of district firms, 42 of the whole sample); their average size (67 employees) is slightly smaller than that of isolated firms (70). The share of ID firms is higher than 60 per cent in the textile, leather, wood, mechanical and 'other manufacturing' sectors.[8] The share of ID firms is lower than 50 per cent in the food, paper and printing, chemicals, electrical equipment, and transport vehicles sectors.

The positive externalities which are assumed to exist in a district should increase the profitability of ID firms with respect to isolated ones. This is clearly the case in our sample.

Profitability is measured by return on investment (ROI) and return on equity (ROE). Both present higher values in districts, for every size class and industry[9] and for almost every size/industry cell (tab. 1 and tab. 2). On average, in 1995

---

[7] A conventional value of 1 lira is sometimes attributed to items that are worthless in accounting terms.

[8] Also in the Istat data for 1991, the share of employment in district firms is particularly high in these sectors (see Baffigi, Pagnini and Quintiliani, 1997).

[9] A lone exception is ROE for the 'other manufacturing' industry, a heterogenous grouping where a mix effect is likely to prevail.

ROI is higher in district firms by two points, ROE by more than four points. These results for 1995 are not exceptional: figure 1 shows that, from 1982 to 1995, profitability was always higher in ID firms. The data seem to suggest that the size of the gap is pro-cyclical.

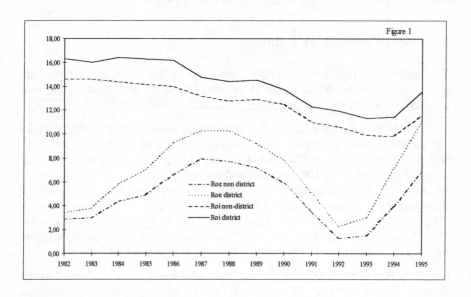

Table 1. Return on investment – 1995 (percentage values)

| | Non-district | | | | District | | | |
	10-19	20-99	100-25	Total	10-19	20-99	100-25	Total
Food, beverages, tobacco	9.38	8.31	7.88	8.43	11.17	9.73	8.62	9.65
Textile	13.08	11.53	9.79	11.36	16.71	13.69	10.93	13.29
Leather industries	13.86	13.70	12.52	13.78	14.20	15.29	13.87	14.59
Wood and wood products	13.76	11.72	13.14	12.10	10.25	12.47	10.42	12.24
Paper, paper products, printing, publ.	14.70	11.98	9.42	11.74	18.74	13.88	13.34	13.88
Chemicals	14.85	11.96	8.55	8.27	14.12	13.53	8.94	8.82
Rubber, plastic products	16.30	13.66	13.48	13.78	21.18	16.01	15.38	16.07
Non-metallic mineral products	10.25	8.85	8.45	8.88	14.05	11.79	10.69	11.78
Metal and metal products	16.83	14.90	11.96	14.52	19.82	15.59	14.87	15.55
Mechanical equipment	21.97	13.77	12.81	13.67	18.59	15.40	13.95	15.19
Electrical equipment	16.80	12.18	9.92	11.98	19.08	14.38	13.08	14.44
Transport (vehicles)	9.92	14.83	14.78	14.48	13.93	14.88	14.56	14.56
Other manufacturing	10.62	10.70	13.21	10.91	10.62	11.36	11.24	11.28
Total	12.77	11.71	10.56	11.55	15.25	13.66	12.39	13.54

Larger profits may be due to greater efficiency, lower factor costs, or both.

An econometric analysis of technical efficiency is presented in the next section. As preliminary evidence, we present here data on just one aspect of efficiency, labour productivity (measured by per capita value added; tab. 3). This is slightly greater in ID firms in most sectors (exceptions are wood, electrical equipment and transport vehicles). Thus efficiency appears to be part of the explanation of the ID/non-ID profitability gap. We do not pursue this point further at this stage; we turn to a brief analysis of factor costs.

Table 2. Return on equity – 1995 (percentage values)

	Non-district				District			
	10-19	20-99	100-25	Total	10-19	20-99	100-25	Total
Food, beverages, tobacco	2.01	2.54	1.89	2.40	7.33	4.23	3.69	4.37
Textile	4.90	6.39	6.23	6.23	10.69	10.26	7.15	9.46
Leather industries	16.17	10.37	6.43	10.12	13.33	12.25	9.79	11.48
Wood and wood products	15.11	7.56	5.64	6.92	2.67	8.62	5.05	7.78
Paper, paper products, printing, publ.	9.55	5.83	4.55	5.82	13.46	13.08	14.07	13.52
Chemicals	11.38	5.99	6.22	6.36	7.88	12.59	3.08	10.91
Rubber, plastic products	7.24	9.43	15.40	11.02	16.51	16.89	18.08	16.91
Non-metallic mineral products	3.37	2.22	3.74	2.34	15.57	6.86	9.01	7.89
Metal and metal products	13.84	12.77	9.10	11.70	19.72	15.07	17.44	15.98
Mechanical equipment	10.59	11.26	9.18	10.11	16.50	12.70	12.38	12.73
Electrical equipment	9.53	8.93	7.12	8.29	24.65	11.84	14.45	12.94
Transport (vehicles)	6.34	12.53	14.49	12.56	4.64	16.17	13.70	14.44
Other manufacturing	5.12	6.27	9.77	6.73	3.58	4.14	9.60	4.58
Total	6.36	6.89	7.04	6.90	11.15	11.12	10.41	11.01

Consider first labour costs. One would expect wages to be higher in district firms, where the endowment of human capital should be higher and more sector-specific. The evidence is mixed. In the whole manufacturing sector, per capita labour costs are lower in district firms (tab. 4). This is true in each year from 1982 to 1995 (figure 2). There is an industry mix effect in this result, however. Some industries (food, textiles, leather, plastic, non metallic mineral product) where IDs are significant show a higher labour cost for ID firms, as expected.

Next, consider the cost of external finance. Although financial aspects are not the main focus of this work, it is useful to briefly examine the level and the cost of debt as elements that contribute to bottom-line profits. Theoretical predictions are ambiguous on this aspect. On the one hand, within industrial districts the existence of particularly efficient information channels and of long-run relationships among agents should reduce the information asymmetries that typically affect credit and financial markets. That may reduce the cost of credit and also, in the spirit of the Stiglitz-Weiss literature, credit rationing in IDs. On the other hand, the same

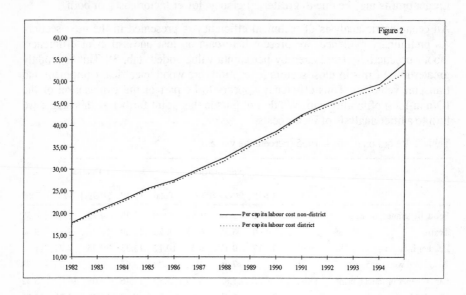

Figure 2

factors may be favourable to the development of inter-firm credit within the manufacturing sector (in the form of commercial credit or direct finance). This would reduce the banks' ability to control the destination of credit and increase asymmetries of information in the credit market (Baffigi, Pagnini and Quintiliani, 1997). In 1995, on average, ID firms are slightly more leveraged than isolated firms (tab. 5); this result holds for most sectors. It is not due to the smaller average firm size in districts, because even within the two smaller size classes the leverage of ID firms is lower (it is actually higher in the class 100-250). Also, the cost of debt (tab. 6) is slightly lower for ID firms; the weight of interest payments on operating revenues (tab. 7) is lower for ID firms in almost all sectors. Thus, also the financial side of the balance sheet appears to contribute to the larger profits of ID firms.

Table 3. Per capita value added – 1995 (millions of lire)

	Non-district				District			
	10-19	20-99	100-25	Total	10-19	20-99	100-25	Total
Food, beverages, tobacco	102.50	91.41	90.38	93.73	137.82	106.35	96.94	109.46
Textile	154.21	80.58	72.69	80.84	132.00	90.03	74.47	89.72
Leather industries	114.44	78.27	47.11	78.21	113.11	78.01	68.51	81.75
Wood and wood products	150.09	83.40	91.50	92.49	136.16	80.86	86.43	83.52
Paper, paper products, printing, publ.	137.21	91.53	104.28	98.98	133.00	99.64	111.34	101.38
Chemicals	171.46	113.92	105.96	116.52	153.27	121.55	104.24	121.59
Rubber and plastic products	101.63	86.00	91.47	87.02	167.98	99.38	93.58	99.80

Non-metallic mineral products	115.72	91.93	98.73	93.15	152.52	101.54	92.11	100.32
Metal and metal products	133.09	95.67	88.41	96.47	140.78	98.46	99.10	100.53
Mechanical equipment	119.64	94.18	89.26	93.51	124.04	93.74	90.35	93.97
Electrical equipment	137.00	93.05	81.41	93.48	170.47	87.96	90.01	90.06
Transport (vehicles)	125.34	81.94	88.24	86.61	71.41	89.12	82.01	85.18
Other manufacturing	89.30	76.40	77.54	77.54	101.73	72.45	77.96	73.63
Total	124.86	91.29	89.80	93.10	131.64	93.38	87.75	94.31

Table 3. Continuation.

The basic results (tables 1-7) are obtained using the 'wide' definition of ID firms (location only; see section 2). To check for robustness, in tables 8, 9 and 10 we present results based on the 'narrow' definition (location+specialisation). They confirm that, for all size classes and almost all industries, profitability indicators are higher in district firms than elsewhere, although the gap is - rather surprisingly - somewhat smaller than with the original definition (one point for ROI, two points for ROE). Labour productivity also appears to be higher in districts, as before. Another aspect that deserves investigation is capital intensity. Table 11 indicates that per capita fixed capital formation is generally lower in ID firms. This evidence, despite being very preliminary, since accounting data provide a raw evaluation of the stock of capital, suggests that the capital/labour ratio is not significantly different between ID and isolated firms.

Table 4. Per capita labour costs – 1995 (millions of lire)

	Non-district				District			
	10-19	20-99	100-25	Total	10-19	20-99	100-25	Total
Food, beverages, tobacco	50.43	51.41	57.35	51.63	56.14	54.48	60.35	55.26
Textile	48.07	46.02	46.00	46.06	51.46	47.25	47.42	47.63
Leather industries	47.68	42.56	43.60	43.22	44.79	43.82	42.86	43.83
Wood and wood products	44.93	45.37	46.84	45.61	43.80	44.86	50.60	45.10
Paper, paper products, printing, publ.	60.62	56.75	62.91	57.82	49.00	53.34	57.82	53.77
Chemicals	61.22	64.62	72.39	66.81	64.35	59.03	69.52	61.34
Rubber and plastic products	45.30	50.43	55.87	51.24	53.34	51.14	54.42	51.64
Non-metallic mineral products	57.00	51.94	61.39	54.53	55.95	56.74	57.57	56.81
Metal and metal products	51.79	54.11	58.30	54.83	53.05	53.98	58.18	54.58
Mechanical equipment	56.16	59.43	60.69	59.94	52.88	57.08	59.32	57.41
Electrical equipment	58.18	57.06	59.79	57.53	61.13	51.23	54.53	52.09
Transport (vehicles)	55.90	48.88	55.30	51.64	47.67	50.34	51.15	50.48
Other manufacturing	48.68	46.21	47.96	46.86	45.93	42.80	46.89	43.80
Total	52.66	53.28	58.04	54.25	51.58	51.62	54.37	52.17

Table 5. Leverage[*] - 1995

| | Non-district | | | | District | | | |
	10-19	20-99	100-25	Total	10-19	20-99	100-25	Total
Food, beverages, tobacco	4.86	3.97	4.43	4.27	5.09	4.76	4.64	4.82
Textile	4.64	4.93	4.27	4.79	5.67	4.68	4.28	4.72
Leather industries	7.09	5.33	5.08	5.58	7.12	5.96	4.74	5.76
Wood and wood products	4.79	4.33	4.63	4.52	3.78	4.61	4.37	4.47
Paper, paper products, printing ,publ.	6.63	4.82	4.71	4.87	5.68	4.97	4.01	4.81
Chemicals	4.20	4.33	4.25	4.29	4.36	4.68	4.41	4.60
Rubber and plastic products	5.50	4.17	4.29	4.23	4.40	4.56	4.36	4.53
Non-metallic mineral products	4.30	3.31	3.00	3.28	4.06	3.95	4.11	4.05
Metal and metal products	6.23	4.66	5.31	4.84	6.00	4.98	4.37	4.89
Mechanical equipment	6.98	4.91	5.19	5.13	6.32	5.21	5.10	5.28
Electrical equipment	4.97	4.96	4.42	4.84	6.34	5.25	4.29	4.94
Transport (vehicles)	7.12	4.63	4.33	4.55	6.66	4.74	4.65	4.89
Other manufacturing	6.13	5.66	5.14	5.28	7.19	4.75	4.76	4.84
Total	5.22	4.57	4.55	4.62	5.67	4.84	4.49	4.85

[*] Total assets/own capital

Table 6. Cost of debt[*] - 1995

| | Non-district | | | | District | | | |
	10-19	20-99	100-25	Total	10-19	20-99	100-25	Total
Food, beverages, tobacco	8.58	8.68	9.21	8.76	8.49	9.08	9.64	9.06
Textile	6.28	7.62	8.77	7.78	5.36	7.69	8.28	7.62
Leather industries	6.38	7.55	8.08	7.53	7.23	6.66	7.26	6.75
Wood and wood products	7.23	7.78	7.12	7.55	7.47	7.86	7.95	7.91
Paper, paper products, printing, publ.	6.61	8.01	9.39	8.20	6.83	8.26	8.34	8.08
Chemicals	5.75	7.72	8.84	8.03	6.75	8.02	8.44	7.92
Rubber and plastic products	7.27	7.21	8.33	7.49	6.13	7.52	8.62	7.68
Non-metallic mineral products	6.91	8.10	8.54	8.07	6.85	8.30	9.38	8.49
Metal and metal products	8.41	7.71	9.10	8.21	6.34	7.52	8.72	7.87
Mechanical equipment	7.24	7.32	8.37	7.70	5.72	7.07	8.54	7.25
Electrical equipment	5.29	7.81	8.92	7.86	8.39	8.07	9.41	8.25
Transport (vehicles)	8.26	7.73	7.86	7.79	8.50	7.86	7.84	7.88
Other manufacturing	8.06	7.78	8.11	7.89	7.68	7.34	8.79	7.51
Total	7.46	7.85	8.83	8.03	6.96	7.71	8.64	7.84

[*] Consolidated debt + financial debt within the subsequent year

Table 7. Gross interest payments/Gross operating profits - 1995

	Non-district				District			
	10-19	20-99	100-25	Total	10-19	20-99	100-25	Total
Food, beverages, tobacco	46.59	37.52	40.92	38.60	37.98	35.47	43.15	36.73
Textile	48.15	40.19	33.42	39.95	39.59	32.45	31.81	33.11
Leather industries	39.49	29.91	41.69	32.98	48.36	37.27	26.66	37.27
Wood and wood products	43.26	39.60	53.96	40.63	58.89	37.61	28.58	37.61
Paper, paper products, printing, publ.	28.32	28.28	33.74	29.98	27.83	25.13	19.71	23.48
Chemicals	24.98	29.53	27.56	28.69	23.39	22.50	30.16	24.79
Rubber and plastic products	49.83	26.95	18.08	26.14	19.77	25.64	21.58	25.16
Non – metallic mineral products	55.96	30.80	29.51	30.96	20.76	26.33	24.58	25.68
Metal and metal products	27.31	27.70	33.64	29.04	28.36	25.04	21.87	24.69
Mechanical equipment	31.84	27.02	30.29	27.94	37.00	27.93	26.89	28.03
Electrical equipment	32.92	30.79	29.72	30.73	13.91	27.73	19.50	26.03
Transport (vehicles)	37.09	25.33	21.85	26.12	67.63	23.43	22.65	23.43
Other manufacturing	47.57	37.46	40.14	39.55	51.48	35.40	30.93	35.27
Total	35.27	31.33	31.84	31.78	36.64	29.55	26.91	29.52

The evaluation of the statistical significance and the economic interpretation of these preliminary results require a more formal analysis. The next section focuses on productive efficiency and conducts an econometric test of the existence of a 'district effect', as distinct from more conventional effects like size, relative factor endowment and so on.

One particular point is worth highlighting. Since most Italian IDs are located in the North and Centre of the country, it is difficult to disentangle a true 'district effect' (ID firms versus non-ID firms) from a broadly geographical one (developed North versus struggling South). This point will be taken up in the next section, where the analysis will also take into account regional effects.

Table 8. Return on investment – 1995 (percentage values - narrow definition of ID firms)

	Non-district				District			
	10-19	20-99	100-25	Total	10-19	20-99	100-25	Total
Food, beverages, tobacco	10.14	9.10	8.10	9.05	10.27	10.05	8.62	9.79
Textile	14.17	12.75	9.91	12.18	17.44	13.60	11.37	13.43
Leather industries	13.86	14.11	14.38	14.11	14.55	15.57	12.50	14.84
Wood and wood products	11.87	12.19	11.69	12.15	22.99	12.83	9.68	12.46
Paper, paper products, printing, publ.	15.16	13.07	11.39	12.65	15.96	17.42	9.81	12.57
Chemicals	14.48	12.57	8.73	12.10	11.49	20.13	5.66	14.37
Rubber and plastic products	18.07	14.71	13.79	14.81	11.65	17.59	17.84	17.59
Non – metallic mineral products	11.60	10.16	9.57	10.01	14.05	12.79	11.54	12.45

58   S. Fabiani, G. Pellegrini, E. Romagnano and L.F. Signorini

Metal and metal products	17.71	15.40	13.51	15.04	-	12.39	21.74	17.07
Mechanical equipment	18.73	14.38	13.18	14.28	20.37	15.61	13.89	15.47
Electrical equipment	17.21	13.19	10.70	12.80	17.16	12.82	15.56	13.91
Transport (vehicles)	10.36	14.83	14.64	14.51	20.02	15.51	15.65	16.79
Other manufacturing	10.68	11.22	12.61	11.26	9.74	11.28	8.70	10.64
Total	13.63	12.76	11.36	12.57	15.69	13.82	12.29	13.59

Table 8. Continuation.

Table 9: Return on equity – 1995: (percentage values - narrow definition of ID firms)

	Non-district				District			
	10-19	20-99	100-25	Total	10-19	20-99	100-25	Total
Food, beverages, tobacco	4.04	3.22	2.84	3.29	7.90	6.26	2.26	4.45
Textile	5.77	7.67	5.80	6.88	12.22	10.50	8.22	9.91
Leather industries	16.17	11.34	9.14	10.92	13.33	12.41	9.94	11.48
Wood and wood products	7.74	8.23	5.79	7.63	5.63	9.74	0.96	7.81
Paper, paper products, printing, publ.	11.60	10.25	9.11	10.18	17.62	10.95	6.37	6.37
Chemicals	10.40	7.45	5.92	7.15	8.69	20.62	1.71	11.71
Rubber and plastic products	15.86	13.96	16.53	14.74	9.71	17.80	23.92	17.80
Non-metallic mineral products	3.58	4.25	4.26	4.23	49.81	5.68	11.62	9.42
Metal and metal products	17.44	14.38	13.55	14.28	-	12.50	23.40	17.95
Mechanical equipment	11.47	11.27	10.11	11.02	18.31	14.21	13.12	14.18
Electrical equipment	11.93	10.10	8.55	10.03	26.39	10.91	18.33	11.93
Transport (vehicles)	5.46	13.94	14.33	13.47	25.39	17.50	16.53	17.97
Other manufacturing	4.54	4.94	9.77	5.70	3.42	3.65	6.14	3.65
Total	7.94	9.00	8.60	8.82	11.62	11.32	9.80	11.11

Table 10. Per capita value added – 1995: (millions of lire - narrow definition of ID firms)

	Non-district				District			
	10-19	20-99	100-25	Total	10-19	20-99	100-25	Total
Food, beverages, tobacco	111.36	97.11	95.44	99.23	214.28	113.88	96.94	118.17
Textile	135.57	80.47	72.42	80.54	139.16	97.32	76.15	97.29
Leather industries	124.10	74.72	62.05	73.03	111.96	84.81	71.14	89.28
Wood and wood products	141.24	82.90	86.43	86.66	104.28	79.25	114.89	84.08
Paper, paper products, printing, publ.	135.77	95.78	108.09	100.40	137.17	108.55	86.34	94.98
Chemicals	161.74	115.56	105.47	116.71	164.88	141.26	121.48	141.26
Rubber and plastic products	144.97	95.11	92.04	95.58	82.43	100.25	117.52	101.50
Non-metallic mineral products	121.27	97.72	94.89	98.37	216.82	102.12	90.98	100.55
Metal and metal products	139.88	97.60	94.73	99.13	-	130.81	74.38	102.60
Mechanical equipment	127.53	93.41	90.08	93.43	120.45	96.70	91.38	95.63
Electrical equipment	137.00	92.76	86.91	93.04	183.60	82.51	85.72	86.37

	Non-district				District			
	10-19	20-99	100-25	Total	10-19	20-99	100-25	Total
Transport (vehicles)	95.76	86.43	88.16	86.67	70.71	85.18	79.58	84.00
Other manufacturing	100.41	73.95	77.54	75.65	69.26	66.00	77.96	67.95
Total	128.93	92.46	90.37	93.83	128.91	93.41	82.34	94.30

Table 10. Continuation.

Table 11. Per capita gross capital – 1995: (millions of lire - narrow definition of ID firms)

	Non-district				District			
	10-19	20-99	100-25	Total	10-19	20-99	100-25	Total
Food, beverages, tobacco	243.86	207.30	199.09	209.65	443.36	209.65	210.46	224.20
Textile	85.85	92.54	98.80	93.29	62.09	113.67	119.67	106.23
Leather industries	72.72	64.65	59.35	64.40	62.74	56.10	52.84	57.54
Wood and wood products	115.79	115.04	100.16	112.25	212.42	117.32	310.13	124.71
Paper, paper products, printing, publ.	129.88	148.36	162.90	149.60	219.41	188.77	222.08	222.08
Chemicals	177.28	160.57	162.69	162.60	215.91	161.19	157.09	157.09
Rubber and plastic products	166.48	143.76	167.45	146.41	209.37	136.60	154.02	136.60
Non-metallic mineral products	190.19	188.93	177.97	183.89	113.49	161.35	124.66	153.67
Metal and metal products	181.44	140.11	140.93	141.53	-	319.79	71.22	195.51
Mechanical equipment	87.72	81.99	100.53	86.70	89.21	89.04	97.20	90.98
Electrical equipment	69.08	78.96	102.81	83.53	137.91	75.74	85.27	79.43
Transport (vehicles)	86.05	91.21	98.28	91.37	63.57	116.45	138.33	115.28
Other manufacturing	106.00	86.35	111.23	91.74	80.57	86.20	75.91	80.57
Total	157.80	122.61	125.54	125.11	76.69	100.12	112.68	98.72

4 Technical Efficiency and Industrial Districts

4.1 Modelling and Measuring Firms' Efficiency

Productivity and, more generally, efficiency can differ across firms, locations and industries for various reasons. For example, firms may use different technologies or operate at different scales. Even allowing for such differences, however, there may still be considerable gaps in the quantity of output firms can produce from the same level of inputs. The failure to produce the maximum possible output for any chosen combination of inputs is called technical inefficiency. This concept includes, among other things, the inefficiency arising from the managerial and organisational structure and the socio-economic environment in which firms operate.

This section aims at capturing the influence of a 'district effect' on the productive performance of firms, due to externalities arising from such factors as the organisation of the labour market, the diffusion of knowledge, the social environment favouring integration among small and medium sized firms in industrial districts. To evaluate this effect one has to isolate it from a variety of other factors that can influence firms' efficiency.

Signorini (1994) provides a first attempt at quantitatively testing the existence of a district productivity effect, for the Italian wool textile industry. Using, basically, an OLS cross-section estimation of a production function that includes district dummies (both in level and interacted with factors' coefficients) among the variables explaining output, he finds that in that sector the total factor productivity of firms located in districts is significantly higher than elsewhere. Such a simple cross-section regression cannot identify firm-specific fixed effects, nor time effects in the structure of production, which could be investigated by panel data techniques. Moreover, since the variables that may affect technical (in)efficiency are directly included in the production function, the approach cannot model efficiency itself in an explicit way.

In order to overcome these drawbacks, in this paper we draw from some recent developments in the theoretical and empirical literature on technical inefficiency. More specifically, we employ the concept of a formally defined production frontier.[10]

The production frontier can be defined either as a production function (parametric approach), or on the basis of the best input-output combinations actually observed within a sector or an industry (non-parametric approach). In the former case, the form of the frontier production function is specified *a priori* and its parameters are empirically estimated. The residual is assumed to be composed of two independent elements: one is a symmetrical random error; the other, representing individual inefficiency, is a deterministic or stochastic asymmetrical term with negative mean, because each firm has to lie on or below the frontier, after allowing for purely random disturbances.

The non-parametric approach does not require the choice of a particular functional form for the production function. The frontier is computed on the basis of the performance of the most efficient units (the ones with the highest level of production for a given combination of inputs or with the lowest use of inputs for a given level of output), using linear programming techniques or simple comparisons of data. Efficiency is then measured as the distance from the

---

[10] See, among others, Jondrow, Lovell, Materov and Schmidt (1982), Battese and Coelli (1988, 1995).

frontier.[11] This method is statistically robust to the choice of the model, but very sensitive to outliers.

Conversely, parametric methods, by allowing for (potentially large) random variation across firms, avoid the risk of defining as 'best' some unusually large outlier. They have also the advantage of providing an economic interpretation for the coefficients of the frontier production function, and hence a theoretical framework for the analysis of efficiency. On the other hand, they depend on basically arbitrary assumptions concerning the functional form of the frontier and the distribution of the inefficiency residual.

Here we use a parametric technique. The basic model, applied on panel data, is specified as follows:

$$y_{it} = \beta'x_{it} + v_{it} - u_{it} \qquad (1)$$

where: y_{it} denotes the production of the ith firm at time t (i=1,...,N; t=1,...,T); x_{it} is a vector of inputs and other explanatory variables associated with the ith firm at the tth observation; β is a vector of unknown parameters, v_{it} and u_{it} are two residual independent components. The former is a symmetrical random term; the latter is a non-negative term which reflects inefficiency with respect to the frontier. In order to obtain consistent and efficient estimates the model requires precise assumptions on the distribution of the two residual components. We assume that v_{it} is iid N(0, σ^2_v). The distribution of the one-sided component u_{it} is specified below.[12]

Equation (1) can be extended to explicitly investigate the factors underlying technical inefficiency: Battese and Coelli (1995) propose a model in which u_{it} is assumed to be independently distributed as a truncated normal, with variance σ^2_u and mean $m_{it} = z_{it}\delta > 0$, where z_{it} is a vector of variables that influence individual inefficiencies, and δ a vector of unknown parameters. The whole model can be estimated simultaneously by maximum likelihood to provide efficient estimates.[13]

The likelihood function to be maximised is expressed in terms of the variance parameters $\sigma^2=\sigma^2_v+\sigma^2_u$ and $\gamma=\sigma^2_u/\sigma^2$, and the predicted measure of firm's inefficiency, which takes a value between zero and one, is derived as:

---

[11] The most widely used non-parametric methods are FDH (Free Disposable Hull) and DEA (Data Envelopment Analysis), where the latter requires the assumption of a convex set of attainable input-output combinations. See Farrell (1957), Deprins, Simar and Tulkens (1984), Deprins and Simar (1989), Tulkens (1993).

[12] In the literature, the truncated normal, the normal, the exponential and the gamma are the most commonly adopted distributions.

[13] Until recent developments of the literature (Battese and Coelli, 1995), applied works on stochastic frontier production functions have dealt with this issue mainly by adopting a two-stage approach in which the inefficiency effects predicted in the first step are regressed, in the second step, against some explanatory variables.

$$EFF_i = \frac{E(y_i|u_i, x_i)}{E(y_i|u_i = 0, x_i)} \quad (2)$$

which depends on the conditional probability function $f(u_i|v_i - u_i)$ and hence on the joint distribution assumed for (u_i, v_i-u_i).[14] The estimated value and the significance of the parameter γ allows the researcher to assess whether a stochastic frontier production function is required at all. The acceptance of the null hypothesis that the true value of the parameter equals zero implies that σ^2_u is zero and hence that the inefficiency term should be removed from the model.

4.2 Efficiency in Italian Manufacturing Firms and Localisation Effects

The econometric analysis focuses on 13 manufacturing industries (the ones considered in the previous section), for which balanced panels of firms have been selected, drawn from the CB database, for the period 1991-1995 (tab. 12).

Table 12. The panel selected for each sector (1991-1995)

	total	District	non-district
Food, beverages, tobacco	724	350	374
Textile	1025	772	253
Leather industries	339	274	65
Wood and wood products	150	107	43
Paper, paper products, printing, publ.	413	193	220
Chemicals	394	168	226
Rubber and plastic products	407	255	152
Non-metallic mineral products	449	238	211
Metal and metal products	949	585	364
Mechanical equipment	878	541	337
Electrical equipment	440	231	209
Transport (vehicles)	134	58	76
Other manufacturing	385	284	101

For each industry, the following Cobb-Douglas stochastic frontier production function is estimated:

$$\ln(y_{it}) = \beta_0 + \beta_1 trend + \beta_2 \ln(labour_{it}) + \beta_3 \ln(capital_{it}) + v_{it} - u_{it} \quad (3)$$

---

[14] The expressions for the conditional expectations, given the assumptions of the model, are presented in Battese and Coelli (1993).

where y indicates value added, *labour* the number of employees, *capital* the value of fixed assets net of depreciation, v_{it} is iid $N(0, \sigma^2_v)$ and the technical inefficiency effect u is specified as:

$$u_{it} = \delta_0 + \delta_1(district_i) + \delta_2 Y_1 + \delta_3 Y_2 + \delta_4 Y_3 + \delta_5 Y_4 + \omega_{it} \quad (4)$$

with the dummy variable *district_i* taking the value one if the firm i belongs to a district (wide definition) and zero otherwise and the dummy variables Y_j (j=1,2,3,4) taking the value one in period j and zero otherwise. These two factors allow inefficiency to vary with respect to time (to capture, possibly, cyclical effects) and to depend on the firm being located in a district or not. Finally, ω is a stochastic variable with a half-normal distribution. The expected sign of the coefficient δ_1 is negative, meaning that ID firms are expected to be less inefficient than isolated ones.

The maximum likelihood estimates, the asymptotic t-statistics and the variance parameters, obtained using an updated version of the program FRONTIER developed by Coelli (1992), are presented in table 13. The variance ratio γ is always significant and close to unity, meaning that individual inefficiency effects are a relevant factor. For 8 out of the 13 industries considered, the fact of being located in an ID significantly improves a firm's efficiency; this phenomenon seems to be particularly prominent in 'light' industries such as textiles, leather, wood, where IDs predominate; it is also important in the food, plastic and non-metallic minerals sectors.

Table 13. MLE efficiency estimation results

Model:

$$\ln(Y_{it}) = \beta_0 + \beta_1 trend + \beta_2 \ln(L_{it}) + \beta_3 \ln(K_{it}) + (v_{it} - u_{it})$$

$$v_{it} \text{ iid } N(0, \sigma_v^2)$$

$$u_{it} = \delta_0 + \delta_1(district_i) + \delta_2 Y_1 + \delta_3 Y_2 + \delta_4 Y_3 + \delta_5 Y_4 + \omega_{it}$$

$$\gamma = \sigma_u^2 / (\sigma_u^2 + \sigma_v^2)$$

	β_0	β_1	β_2	β_3	δ_0	δ_1	δ_2	δ_3	δ_4	δ_5	γ
Food, beverages, tobacco	3.990	0.053	0.678	0.227	-3.569	-4.629	-1.196	-2.237	-1.161	-1.204	0.930
	(73.3)	(7.88)	(61.5)	(31.9)	(7.12)	(8.26)	(6.59)	(8.75)	(7.87)	(9.14)	(112.3)
Textile	4.832	0.072	0.671	0.098	-1.746	-1.497	0.779	0.687	-0.022	-0.483	0.701
	(113.7)	(10.8)	(65.2)	(16.9)	(6.29)	(6.12)	(5.33)	(5.05)	(0.14)	(1.39)	(17.3)
Leather industries	4.341	0.076	0.626	0.179	-1.678	-3.630	-0.894	0.097	-1.009	-1.027	0.865
	(89.6)	(14.1)	(49.4)	(23.4)	(1.74)	(2.33)	(2.54)	(1.08)	(2.24)	(1.98)	(16.5)
Wood and	4.288	0.085	0.704	0.134	-1.469	-2.564	0.477	0.077	-0.494	0.247	0.763

	β_0	β_1	β_2	β_3	δ_0	δ_1	δ_2	δ_3	δ_4	δ_5	γ
wood products	(44.9)	(8.69)	(33.3)	(10.4)	(2.61)	(2.47)	(2.82)	(0.48)	(1.396)	(1.88)	(13.0)
Rubber, plastic products	3.840	0.079	0.690	0.213	-5.026	-3.209	-0.584	-0.532	0.284	0.496	0.939
	(68.4)	(13.2)	(51.1)	(23.0)	(4.14)	(5.34)	(4.34)	(3.57)	(2.48)	(3.67)	(69.8)
Non-metallic mineral products	3.963	0.040	0.736	0.208	-5.953	-4.593	0.230	1.308	-1.223	0.323	0.956
	(57.8)	(7.01)	(48.3)	(21.4)	(9.08)	(8.98)	(1.59)	(6.63)	(6.57)	(2.49)	(346.7)
Metal and metal products	3.961	0.099	0.756	0.162	-3.289	-0.301	-2.105	-0.502	0.751	0.675	0.839
	(100.0)	(26.2)	(88.5)	(29.6)	(6.26)	(5.22)	(5.91)	(3.90)	(9.06)	(9.36)	(40.5)
Mechanical equipment	4.411	0.088	0.830	0.073	-3.017	-0.370	-2.608	0.063	-0.307	-0.159	0.869
	(126.7)	(31.7)	(87.5)	(13.5)	(5.32)	(4.24)	(5.15)	(1.08)	(3.51)	(2.56)	(42.9)
Electrical equipment	4.494	0.066	0.752	0.115	-5.938	0.917	-1.848	0.479	-0.981	-0.695	0.886
	(75.4)	(12.4)	(51.1)	(13.1)	(8.50)	(7.21)	(5.54)	(4.62)	(5.08)	(4.52)	(67.8)
Transport (vehicles)	4.095	0.130	0.872	0.748	-3.087	0.975	-5.258	-3.242	-1.161	-0.596	0.893
	(33.2)	(9.98)	(29.3)	(4.18)	(3.51)	(3.89)	(3.64)	(3.75)	(3.76)	(2.643)	(40.4)

Table 13. Continuation.

Absolute values of t-statistics in parenthesis

The five cases where this does not occur can be divided into two groups. The first includes the chemical industry, the paper, printing and publishing industry and the 'other manufacturing' industry, for which technical inefficiency is not influenced by any of the factors explicitly considered here. (Results for these industries are not presented in the tables). The second includes the transport vehicles industry and the electrical equipment industry, for which the parameter of interest is significantly different from zero but has the wrong sign. These exceptions are all related to industries where districts are known to play a relatively minor role.

As already stated in the previous section, the district dummy may capture also positive externalities originating from geographical factors, i.e. the fact that IDs are generally located in the more developed parts of the country. To test for this possibility, we estimated model (3)-(4) on sub-panels including only firms located in the Centre and in the North, which represent, in all sectors, more than 80 per cent of the total number of firms.

The results, presented in table 14, show that the geographical effect is in fact the dominant source of higher efficiency of production in ID firms only as concerns the metal products industry. The district effect, on the other hand, remains statistically significant and with the expected sign in seven sectors, thus confirming that in the 'light' manufacturing industries (such as textile, leather, wood, rubber and plastic products) ID firms, irrespective of their geographical location, are more efficient than isolated ones.

Table 14. MLE efficiency estimation results: (Centre-North)

Model:

$$\ln(Y_{it}) = \beta_0 + \beta_1 trend + \beta_2 \ln(L_{it}) + \beta_3 \ln(K_{it}) + (v_{it} - u_{it})$$

$$v_{it} \text{ iid } N(0, \sigma_v^2)$$

$$u_{it} = \delta_0 + \delta_1(district_i) + \delta_2 Y_1 + \delta_3 Y_2 + \delta_4 Y_3 + \delta_5 Y_4 + \omega_{it}$$

$$\gamma = \sigma_u^2 / (\sigma_u^2 + \sigma_v^2)$$

	β_0	β_1	β_2	β_3	δ_0	δ_1	δ_2	δ_3	δ_4	δ_5	γ
Food, beverages, tobacco	3.96	0.06	0.72	0.21	-3.21	-2.19	-1.99	-3.37	-1.77	-1.23	0.90
	(70.1)	(10.6)	(62.6)	(25.3)	(5.80)	(7.81)	(7.14)	(7.31)	(7.81)	(8.01)	(67.8)
Textile	4.84	0.08	0.67	0.09	-2.97	-0.55	0.87	0.45	0.54	-1.56	0.73
	(138.4)	(14.7)	(74.7)	(17.2)	(11.8)	(10.4)	(7.69)	(4.80)	(5.91)	(4.93)	(46.5)
Leather industries	4.33	0.74	0.62	0.18	-3.89	-2.99	-	-	-	-	0.88
	(83.2)	(13.5)	(50.9)	(24.8)	(1.88)	(2.19)					(18.9)
Wood and wood products	4.14	0.08	0.68	0.16	-0.005	-0.14	0.11	0.06	0.08	0.99	0.003
	(26.9)	(6.63)	(30.1)	(9.58)	(0.06)	(1.71)	(1.03)	(0.61)	(0.96)	(0.93)	(0.47)
Rubber, plastic products	3.91	0.08	0.68	0.21	-5.13	-2.63	-0.51	-0.58	-0.10	0.63	0.93
	(67.6)	(15.0)	(48.3)	(24.2)	(3.01)	(4.18)	(4.36)	(2.76)	(1.03)	(3.51)	(46.3)
Non-metallic mineral products	3.99	0.04	0.70	0.22	-8.66	-1.34	-0.22	1.70	-0.99	0.83	0.95
	(61.5)	(7.79)	(52.3)	(23.2)	(5.43)	(5.49)	(1.76)	(4.57)	(4.48)	(4.38)	(100.5)
Metal and metal products	3.96	0.08	0.75	0.16	-0.08	0.05	0.08	0.14	0.15	0.13	0.001
	(99.7)	(15.9)	(79.9)	(29.5)	(2.20)	(3.06)	(1.59)	(2.53)	(3.92)	(4.34)	(1.09)
Mechanical equipment	4.38	0.09	0.83	0.07	-3.26	-0.16	-2.61	0.20	-0.25	-0.16	0.87
	(117.3)	(21.6)	(87.3)	(14.0)	(11.4)	(3.82)	(9.66)	(2.85)	(3.12)	(2.55)	(85.9)
Electrical equipment	4.45	0.06	0.77	0.10	-6.82	1.29	-1.44	0.45	-0.69	-0.36	0.91
	(83.8)	(13.8)	(56.1)	(12.3)	(3.98)	(3.88)	(3.46)	(2.41)	(2.86)	(2.48)	(48.5)
Transport (vehicles)	4.09	0.13	0.85	0.09	-2.50	1.27	-4.80	-3.10	-1.24	-0.52	0.87
	(35.1)	(8.50)	(29.1)	(5.28)	(4.05)	(4.14)	(3.40)	(3.50)	(3.50)	(2.14)	(33.9)

Absolute values of t-statistics in parenthesis

5 Conclusions

This paper provides an evaluation of the effect of industrial district external economies on firms' productivity ad profitability. The 'district effect' on firms' profitability is shown to be quite strong: depending on the measure of profitability and the period, it varies between two and four percentage points. An econometric model confirms that ID firms tend to display higher technical efficiency than isolated firms. All results are particularly strong for 'light' manufacturing industries, where districts play a major role.

These results are robust to different model specifications and in particular to explicit consideration of the North-South dimension. This is one of the crucial points of the analysis. Since most Italian IDs belong to the more developed regions of the Centre and North of Italy, it is necessary to separate a pure district effect, due to agglomeration externalities, from a broad geographical effect, due to area-wide elements such as the endowment of physical, human and social capital and the proximity of relevant markets. In this work, the fact that technical efficiency depends on whether a firm is located in an ID or not, after controlling for the geographical location of the firm itself, is interpreted as evidence in favour of a pure 'district effect'.

Clearly, as in most empirical analyses, the results obtained here depend on the assumptions we have made in order to translate the theoretical definition of ID into an empirical concept. The use of alternative criteria provides scope for further research. However, the main conclusions presented here are sufficiently clear-cut and robust to provide a first significant and broad-based empirical corroboration to the vast qualitative literature on industrial districts: which, in our opinion, much needed it.

ANNEX

Table A1. Distribution of firms in 1995 by sector and size class

	Dimensional class			Total	%
	10-19	20-99	100-250		
Food, beverages, tobacco	232	748	192	1172	10.7
Textile	198	1053	326	1577	14.4
Leather industries	73	383	88	544	5.0
Wood and wood products	20	172	35	227	2.1
Paper, paper products, printing, publ.	67	452	139	658	6.0
Chemicals	76	436	135	647	5.9
Rubber and plastic products	42	516	133	691	6.3
Non-metallic mineral products	39	500	134	673	6.2
Metal and metal products	116	1162	357	1635	14.9
Mechanical equipment	62	1032	351	1445	13.2
Electrical equipment	54	535	193	782	7.1
Transport (vehicles)	12	158	74	244	2.2
Other manufacturing	44	494	106	644	5.9
Total	1035	7641	2263	10939	100

Table A2. Distribution of firms by sector and size class in 1995: districts vs non-districts (percentages)

	District				Non-district				Total
	10-19	20-10	100-25	Total	10-19	20-10	100-25	Total	
Food, beverages, tobacco	8.70	30.38	7.25	46.33	11.09	33.4	9.13	53.67	100
Textile	10.21	49.21	15.03	74.45	2.35	17.5	5.64	25.55	100
Leather industries	11.76	52.57	12.50	76.84	1.65	17.8	3.68	23.16	100
Wood and wood products	3.08	53.74	10.13	66.96	5.73	22.0	5.29	33.04	100
Paper. paper products. printing, publ.	3.95	31.00	8.51	43.47	6.23	37.6	12.61	56.53	100
Chemicals	5.56	27.51	8.04	41.11	6.18	39.8	12.83	58.89	100
Rubber and plastic products	3.76	44.14	10.27	58.18	2.32	30.5	8.97	41.82	100
Non-metallic mineral products	2.67	39.08	10.10	51.86	3.12	35.2	9.81	48.14	100
Metal and metal products	3.67	44.10	12.05	59.82	3.43	26.9	9.79	40.18	100
Mechanical equipment	2.21	44.50	14.05	60.76	2.08	26.9	10.24	39.24	100
Electrical equipment	2.30	33.63	12.02	47.95	4.60	34.7	12.66	52.05	100
Transport (vehicles)	1.64	31.15	9.84	42.62	3.28	33.6	20.49	57.38	100
Other manufacturing	4.35	56.52	10.71	71.58	2.48	20.1	5.75	28.42	100
Total	5.32	41.66	11.40	58.38	4.14	28.1	9.29	41.62	100

References

Baffigi A., Pagnini M. and Quintiliani F., 1997, Industrial Districts and Local Bank: Do the Twins ever Meet?, Paper presented at the XXXVII ERSA Congress, Siracusa, October 1997.

Battese G.E. and Coelli T.J., 1988, Prediction of firm-level technical efficiencies: with a generalised frontier production function and panel data, *Journal of Econometrics*, Vol.38.

Battese G.E. and Coelli T.J., 1993, A stochastic frontier production function incorporating a model for technical inefficiency effects, *Working Papers in Econometrics and Applied Statistics*, N.69, University of New England, Armidale.

Battese G.E. and Coelli T.J., 1995, A model for technical inefficiency effects in a stochastic frontier production function for panel data, *Empirical Economics*, vol. 202.

Becattini G., 1990, The Marshallian districts as a socio-economic notion in Pyke, Becattini and Sengenberger (eds.), *Industrial districts and inter-firm co-operation in Italy*, Geneva.

Brusco S., 1986, Small firms and industrial districts: The experience of Italy, *Economia internazionale*, No. 2.

Brusco S. and Bigarelli D., 1997, Regional productive systems in the knitwear and clothing sector in Italy: Industrial structure and training needs, ESRC Centre for Business Research Working Paper No. 51, March 1997.

Brusco S. and Paba S., 1997, Per una storia dei distretti industriali italiani dal secondo dopoguerra agli anni novanta in F. Barca ed. *Storia del capitalismo italiano dal dopoguerra a oggi*, Donzelli.

Cannari L., Pellegrini G. and Sestito P., 1996, L'utilizzo di microdati d'impresa per l'analisi economica: alcune indicazioni metodologiche alla luce delle esperienze in Banca d'Italia, Temi di discussione, Banca d'Italia, No. 286.

Cannari L. and Signorini L.F., 1997, La geografia economica italiana: nuovi strumenti per la classificazione dei sistemi locali, mimeo.

Centrale dei Bilanci 1991, *Economia e finanza delle imprese italiane*, Milano, Il Sole-24 Ore.

Coelli T.J., 1992, A computer program for frontier production estimation: FRONTIER Version 2.0, *Economic Letters*, Vol. 39.

Deprins D., Simar L. and Tulkens H., 1984, Measuring labor inefficiency in post offices, in Marchand, Pestieau and Tulkens (eds.), *The Performance of Public Enterprises: Concepts and measurement*, Amsterdam, North-Holland, pp.

Deprins D. and Simar L., 1989, Estimating technical inefficiencies with correction for environmental conditions with an application to railways companies, *Annals of Public and Cooperative Economics*, Vol. 60.

Farrell M.J., The measurement of productive efficiency, *The Journal of the Royal Statistical Society*, A120.

Jondrow J., Lovell C.A.K., Materov I.S. and Schmidt P., 1982, On the estimation of technical inefficiency in stochastic frontier production models, *Journal of Econometrics*, Vol. 19.

Istat, 1996, *Rapporto annuale. La situazione del Paese nel 1995.* Istituto Poligrafico dello Stato.

Sforzi F., 1990, The quantitative importance of Marshallian industrial districts in the Italian Economy, in Pyke, Becattini and Sengenberger (eds.), *Industrial districts and inter-firm co-operation in Italy,* Geneva.

Signorini L.F. 1994, The price of Prato, or measuring the industrial district effect, *Papers in Regional Science,* No. 73.

Signorini L.F. and Visco I., 1997, *L'economia italiana,* Bologna, Il Mulino.

Tulkens H., 1993, On FDH efficiency analysis: some methodological issues and application to retail banking, courts, and urban transit, *Journal of Productivity Analysis,* Vol. 4.

Do State Subsidies Have a Stronger Impact when Provided to District Firms? An Empirical Analysis on Italian Data

Leonardo Becchetti

University of Rome Tor Vergata, Faculty of Economics, Department of Economics and Institutions, Via di Tor Vergata snc, 00133 Rome. E-mail: Becchetti@uniroma2.it

Stefania P.S. Rossi

Istituto Universitario Navale, Facoltà di Economia, Istituto di Studi Economici, Via Medina 40, 80133, Napoli. E-mail: Rossiste@unina.it

Abstract: The growing constraints on public expenditure imposed by the process of European Monetary Union are increasingly shifting the attention of policymakers to the quality of industrial policy. A recent address of Italian political economy emphasises the role of the so called "patto d'area" (a package of tax allowances, soft loans and services provided only to firms located in Marshallian Industrial Districts or aimed at "reproducing" them in new underdeveloped areas). The implicit assumption is that industrial policy is more effective on "fertile grounds" in which infrastructures and cooperation among firms are of good quality. Does past experience support this assumption and tell us that subsidies are more effective when provided in district than in non district areas? The present paper explores this hypothesis on a dataset of around 2000 firms showing that district subsidised firms seem to obtain better borrowing terms and, in the medium run, a relative improvement of their return on investment with respect to the control sample.

JEL Classification: R3

Keywords: Localisation externalities, innovation.

1   Introduction[*]

A large share of total credit in the Western countries has been constituted by subsidised credit programs in the last two decades (Gale, 1991). To face the growing public expenditure constraints policymakers were compelled to focus on the impact of state interventions on firms' financial and economic performance. As a consequence, the trade-off between supporting industrial activity and increasing the tax burden implied by government credit programs became much more binding.

Moreover, new important changes in the political and economic scenario reduced even more the room for independent macroeconomic policies of domestic governments in these last years. The process of European Monetary Union, by preventing the use of traditional policy instruments (exchange rate, monetary and "quantitative" fiscal policies) is increasingly shifting the attention of policymakers to the quality of industrial policy. Common currency and the removal of residual barriers to productive factor circulation is now pushing national and regional authorities in the EU to create the most favourable regulatory and fiscal environment which may foster self-employment and positively affect foreign investment decisions. In this framework, a recent address of the Italian industrial political economy emphasises the role of the so called "*patto d'area*" (a package of tax allowances, soft loans and services provided only to firms located in Marshallian Industrial Districts or aimed at transferring these districts in new underdeveloped areas). The implicit assumption is that industrial policy is more effective on "fertile grounds" in which infrastructures and cooperation among firms are of good quality.

This assumption, and generally all those related to the expected effect of credit subsidies, have never been supported by empirical evidence. In the last years in fact a growing demand for monitoring and evaluation of government credit programs has been seldom met by empirical literature due to the scarcity of dataset combining balance sheet data with qualitative and quantitative information on subsidies.

The aim of this paper is to evaluate the effect of state subsidies on financial and economic performance of firms belonging to industrial district versus non district firms. An *industrial district* (from now on also ID) may be defined as a network of small-medium firms located in a delimited area in which geographical proximity among different units generates positive spillovers. These spillovers are

---

[*] The authors thank M.Bagella, M. Bellandi, G.Dei Ottati, G.Esposito, K.Kaiser, G. Pellegrini, S. Sacchi, G. Scanagatta, for useful comments and suggestions. The usual disclaimer applies. Although this paper is a common research work section 2, 4 and 6 have been written by L. Becchetti and sections 1, 3 and 5 by S.P.S. Rossi.

determined, according to various authors, by communication among firms (Marshall, 1920), by sharing of factor advantages or by the presence of a monopolistically competitive service sector supplying differentiated goods to the traded good sector (Rivera-Batiz, 1988a,b ; Abdel-Rahman and Fujita, 1990; Dobkins, 1996). The hypothesis we explore is that an economic environment (such as an industrial district) characterised by more competitive features and a more balanced bargaining power between banks and firms might lead to a reduction in the cost of debt and to an increase in the return of investment for firms located in those areas.

Under the standard Stiglitz-Weiss (1981) approach, the subsidy rent is earned by the bank which has all the bargaining power (Bagella-Becchetti, 1998). As a consequence, subsidised firms do not result to have better borrowing terms than non subsidised. However, borrowing terms for subsidised firms may improve, if lender's market power is reduced.

In order to test this hypothesis we perform our empirical analysis on a sample of around 2000 (subsidised and non subsidised) district and non district firms for which we dispose of six years of balance sheet data and qualitative information about the provision of state subsidies.

The paper is divided into five sections. In section 1 we first discuss some stylised facts on Italian subsidised credit programs and we then present the theoretical predictions about subsidised credit effects on firm's financial and economic performance from credit rationing literature.

In the second section the two alternative approaches (Sforzi, 1995; Del Colle, 1997) adopted for identifying industrial district firms are discussed. In section 3 we present our data set and some descriptive evidence on financial and economic performance of subsidised district and subsidised non district firms versus a control sample of firms never subsidised in the sample period. The econometric analysis is presented in section 4, in which we test whether district location significantly affects borrowing terms and performance of subsidised firms. Our results show that, in the 1989-94 experience, district subsidised firms seem to experience a relatively lower cost of debt and a relative improvement of their return on investment with respect to the control sample. Conclusions on these results are drawn in section 5.

2   Subsidised Credit Programs and Theoretical Framework

Scope and justification for the intervention of a *benevolent planner* is the existence of several forms of market failures in real and financial markets. Relevant cases of market failures are those generated by insufficient private investment in public or semi-public goods, such as monitoring (Stiglitz, 1993) and technological knowledge (Grossman-Helpmann, 1991) and by informational asymmetries leading to financial constraints and credit rationing (Fazzari-Hubbard-Petersen 1988, Hoshi-Kashyap-Sharfstein 1992, Devereux-Schiantarelli 1989, Becchetti 1995, Schiantarelli-Georgoutsos, 1990; Bond-Meghir, 1994).

An important role in avoiding some of these market failures can be played by the governance of domestic financial systems. With its features of "bank-centred" and industrially "downsized" system, Italy can be viewed as a good example of a "credit view economy" in which the three Kashyap-Lamont-Stein (1993) conditions are met and where financial governance may generate those distortions that public intervention costly tries to correct.

Two are the main financial constraints of Italian firms in our sample period (1989-94). First, small-medium firms (most of them family owned) do not have access to foreign capital markets and therefore credit is the almost only source of external finance for them. Fiscal, transparency and equity dilution costs prevent small-medium firms from being listed, so that stock market capitalisation in Italy remains abnormally low with respect to other industrial countries. Moreover, financial markets do not represent a viable alternative to internal finance because corporate bonds are crowded out by Treasury bonds, not only in terms of risk-adjusted returns, but also in terms of market liquidity.

Second, the banking system, largely publicly owned, cannot issue reserve-free liabilities (the issue of reserve-free long term deposit certificates is penalised by unfavourable taxation) so that aggregate lending volumes are strongly dependent from the policy rate (*tasso di sconto*) fixed by the Bank of Italy.

Innovative firms, concentrated mainly in the Mechanical Equipment sector, are those who suffer more from credit constraints and financial distortions in Italy. These firms which are generally downsized have relatively lower availability of external finance with respect to innovating firms in the rest of Europe (Hoshi-Kashyap-Sharfstein 1992, Devereux-Schiantarelli 1989)[1].

---

[1] The anomaly may be easily explained in a Bernanke-Gertler (1987) framework. In an economy, which is neither downsized, nor "bank-centered", higher asymmetric information between external financiers and firms, when the investment is high-tech, is an incentive for financiers to transform themselves from external (credit) financiers into internal (equity) financiers. The market for venture capital participations in innovating activities develops due to financiers' migration and the innovating sector is not more financially constrained than other industrial sectors in equilibrium. In a "bank-centered" and industrially "downsized" system (such as Italy) in which debt favourable tax shield and the "equity dilution syndrome" of small-medium firm owners are two barriers to the development of a market for equity financiers, financiers' migration does not occur and innovating firms remain more financially constrained than traditional firms in equilibrium.

In the last decade state intervention mainly focused on alleviating the effects of these distortions through subsidy programs, instead of concentrating on governance reforms (fiscal reforms reducing cost differential between debt and equity financing, privatisation of the banking system) to correct these institutional distortions. The most relevant government credit programs are illustrated in Table 1. As shown in this table subsidies are given to the firms with an almost automatic procedure, given that geographical location and firm size are the only criteria for the identification of subsidy recipients.

Table 1. Summary features of state support to small-medium firm investment in Italy

Law	Interest Payment Provisions	Principal Provisions	Geographical Area	Limits to Potential Recipients
46/82 (R&D program)	Soft loans which cover from 35% to 70% of total investment costs. The rate is 40-50% lower (small-medium firms), 75% lower (firms from the South) than the market rate.	Grants up to 70% of investment costs	Italy	
64/86 (South and underdeveloped areas program)	Soft loans with interest rates at 36% of market rate up to 30 billion liras and at 60% of market rate above 30 billion liras:	Grants for 40% of total investment costs lower than 7 billion liras, for 30% for the part of them exceeding 30 billion liras up to 30 billions for the part of them exceeding 30 billion liras	South and underdeveloped areas	
657/77 (Guarantee program)	"Guarantee fund" for medium-long term bank credit up to 50% of investment financing		Italy	Small medium firms
1142/66 (BEI-EEC program)	Soft loans for investment projects of small-medium firms in domestic or foreign currency up to 50% of total investment costs. Currency specific rates are decided by BEI and may be either fixed or variable		Italy	Small medium firms
240/81 (Consortia program)	Soft loans for a maximum of 10 years for material and immaterial investments up to 70% of total investment costs. The rate is 60% of market rate for firms in the South.		Italy (firms belonging to consortia)	Firms
44/86 (Young entrepreneurs' program)			South, underdeveloped areas, mountain areas	Firms and individuals

Law	Interest Payment Provisions	Principal Provisions	Geographical Area	Limits to Potential Recipients
1329/65 (Sabatini program)	Soft loans for leasing or purchase of tangible investment goods by small-medium firms up to a maximum of 3 billion liras with a variable rate under the market rate according to firm size and location		Italy	Small medium firms
949/52 (SME program)	Soft loans for leasing or purchase of tangible investment goods by small-medium firms up to a maximum of 4 billion liras with a variable rate under the market rate according to firm size and location		Italy	Small medium firms
227/77 (Export program)	Soft loans for medium long term export commercial credit (up to 85% of total commercial credit). The incentive consists of the positive difference between the market rate and that applied by the Italian firm to the foreign importer		Italy	
394/81 (FDE program)	Soft loans for foreign direct investments of firms which are already exporting up to 85% of total investment costs with a ceiling of 3 billion liras. The rate is 40% of the market rate		Italy	Exporting firms
49/87 (LDC-FDE program)	Soft loans for investments in LDC countries at a rate of 1% for a maximum of 30 years		Italy	

Table 1. Continuation

Credit rationing models are the framework in which to analyse the effects of soft loans concession on bank-firm relationship and on changes in the cost of debt. According to this literature increases in the cost of debt can have two effects: a "cleansing effect" in which "only the fittest survive"(De Meza-Webb, 1987); or, alternatively, an adverse selection effect in which the pool of financed projects gets riskier (Stiglitz-Weiss,1981).

A De Meza-Webb (1987) banker will believe that the subsidy, by lowering the interest rate paid by the borrower, reduces instead the "cleansing effect" of the cost of debt therefore making the pool of selected firms riskier. As a consequence, the reduction in the supply of credit, coupled by an increase in demand, should increase the subsidy-gross cost of credit with no impact on volumes. If this positive effect is taken into account it may counteract the negative selection effect and dampen the movement of the supply curve.

A Stiglitz-Weiss (1981) banker will believe that, by lowering the cost of debt and therefore dampening the adverse selection effect, the subsidy reduces both risk and expected return of the pool of financed projects so the new point at which price and adverse selection effects exactly offset each other and profit is maximum will imply higher interest rates and higher lending volumes. As a consequence, he will offer in equilibrium more credit and at a higher cost, gross of subsidies.

The consequence is that, in equilibrium, a subsidy will tend to have two effects which are observationally equivalent to those of the De Meza-Webb (1987) model: an increase in the volume of credit and an increase in the subsidy-gross cost of credit. As a consequence, also in this model, subsidised firms are not likely to have significantly lower subsidy-net cost of debt than non subsidised firms.[2]

This conclusion, though, is correct if a fundamental and implicit hypothesis of the Stiglitz-Weiss (1981) model holds. The solution of this model through the maximisation of the bank profit function, in fact, implies that banks are monopolistic and have 100% bargaining power in their relationship with borrowing firms. If this assumption is relaxed, competition among banks or an increase in the bargaining power of borrowers may lead to non monopolistic solutions where the subsidy rent is shared more equally among counterparts and subsidised firms obtain significant discounts on the cost of their debt with respect to the Stiglitz-Weiss (1981) monopoly equilibrium.

The empirical section of this paper verifies whether competition among banks or an increase in bargaining power of borrowers may lead to these non monopolistic solutions. In order to ascertain this hypothesis we try to test whether credit subsidies were more effective for district than for non district firms by comparing bank debt conditions and return on investment for district against the non district subsidised firms.

3   Industrial District Indicators

Industrial districts have been widely analysed in the economic literature (Abdel-Rahman and Fujita, 1990; Becattini, 1991; Bellandi, 1996; Dobkins, 1996; Rivera-

---

[2] The only difference between the two models is that subsidised firms will tend to have, versus non subsidised, lower returns and lower risk in a Stiglitz-Weiss (1981) framework and lower return and higher risk in a De Meza-Webb (1987) framework. These two models obviously do not fully represent credit rationing literature. Other models: i) consider that collateral may eliminate (Bester, 1987) or not (Besanko-Thakor, 1993) the informational asymmetry; ii) depart from the assumption of indivisible projects and consider that firms may signal with the proportion of debt (Milde-Riley, 1988; Innes, 1992). The first type of models may be considered less important for our analysis given that asymmetric information is seldom single dimensional and, as such, it can not be eliminated by a single signal. The introduction of subsidies in the second type of models leads to results which are almost observationally equivalent to those from Stiglitz-Weiss (1981) and De Meza-Webb (1987). Subsidised firms, when recognised as such by banks, must in fact reinforce their signal by choosing a debt contract with higher cost and volume of debt (Innes, 1992).

Batiz, 1988a,b). We recall here only the main features of this form of industrial organisation: *i)* existence of a large number of small independent firms with or without the presence of a large firms having relationship with them; *ii)* concentration of these firms in a geographically delimited area; *iii)* network relationship between these firms consisting of large exchange flows of labour force and informal cooperation in the provision of public good and services such as information on process/product technological improvement.

The existing statistical indicators used for defining industrial districts may only partially capture these features. In order to check the robustness of the effects of geographical agglomeration on subsidies we use two indicators (Sforzi, 1995, and Del Colle, 1997) which are the most widely used in the statistical classification of industrial districts in Italy. The first (Sforzi, 1995) is a criterion of pure geographical agglomeration and is based on the share of local employment in the manufacturing sector considering the national average as a threshold[3]. According to this method firms are "geographically agglomerated" if they are localised in an area where the share of local employment is higher than average and not otherwise. This index has been recently adopted as a benchmark also by the Italian government to identify targets of industrial policy programs, following a new approach which aims at directing subsidised loans plus provision of services to district areas (L.142/90)

This indicator presents, however, several limits. First, it deliberately abstracts from product considerations. In fact any attempt at defining a "Marshallian district" on the product side is much more difficult and ambiguous as in all these areas we find a relative specialisation in at least two or three sectors with a mix of "horizontal" (multiple industrial units producing the same type of product) and "vertical" features (multiple units which are upstream and downstream integrated in the product chain). Moreover, the Sforzi method does not explicitly take into account the problem of physical distance among firms and it uses a level and not a flow variable.

The second method (Del Colle, 1997) used for defining ID or *locale* partially overcomes these pitfalls (Becchetti-Rossi, 1999b). First, this method is based on

---

[3] In particular geographical agglomeration (GA) is calculated as:

$$GA = (E_{m,ls} / E_{t,ls})/(A_{m,i} / A_{t,i})$$

where $E_{m,ls}$ is the number of employees in manufacturing firms with less than 250 employees in a town council, $E_{t,ls}$ is the number of workers in the manufacturing sector in a town council, $A_{m,i}$ is the total number of workers in manufacturing firms with less than 250 employees in Italy and $A_{t,i}$ is the total number of employees in the manufacturing sector in Italy. The same indicator is used to measure geographical agglomeration in the second chapter of the book (*Geographical Agglomeration in R&D Games: Theoretical Analysis and Empirical Evidence*).

two indices of spatial autocorrelation (Moran, 1950 and Getis-Ord, 1992) and takes into account the problem of spatial distance among firms. Moreover, it uses a flow indicator by considering the change of residence that occurred between the 1981 and the 1991 census years[4]. Since the flow variable (change of residence) is only indirectly related to economic activity, we associate to any *locale*, measured with Del Colle method, other two indicators providing additional information on industrial structure of the district: *i) Ulpop* (number of productive units per 1000 inhabitants); *ii) Addpop* (number of workers per 1000 inhabitants). By considering these indicators in the econometric analysis we also have the advantage of replacing a dichotomous variable, such as the (0-1) indicator from Sforzi (1995) with a continuous variable.

4   Empirical Evidence from the Sample

Data used in the analysis come from the Mediocredito dataset[5]. For a subset of around 2000 firms we dispose of balance sheet data integrated by qualitative information from two questionnaires which cover respectively the 1989-91 and the 1992-94 periods.

To analyse the effects of credit subsidies on firms located in an industrial district we divide them into four groups: *i)* firms which declared they obtained credit subsidies in the first period (1989-1991) but not in the second (1992-1994); *ii)* firms which declared they obtained credit subsidies in the second period (1992-1994) but not in the first (1989-1991); *iii)* firms which declared they obtained credit subsidies in both periods; *iv)* firms which declared they never obtained credit subsidies between 1989 and 1994. We define these four groups respectively as *sub8991, sub9294, sub8994* and *nevsub*. We then split the first and third group discriminating between firms located (*Sub8991d* and *sub8994d*) or not (*Sub8991n*

---

[4] The variable is computed as:

$$x_{ij} = \frac{E_{ij}}{\sqrt{P_i P_j}} 1000$$

where x_{ij} is the number of those changing residence from council i to council j during the considered period, while P_i and P_j are the average populations in the two councils between the 1981 and the 1991 census. The distance is computed by minimizing an objective function which weights two arguments: geographical distance and time needed to reach that distance by available means of transportation. This variable is, in turn, a function of road quality and of the type of transportation.

[5] Characteristics of this dataset are illustrated in Becchetti and Rossi (1999a) included in this volume.

and *sub8994n*) into industrial districts. We present descriptive evidence for five of these groups (*sub8991d, sub8991n, sub9294d, sub9294n* and *nevsub*) in tables 2-5. In tables 2-3 we compare the *sub8991d, sub8991n* and *nevsub* groups, while in tables 4-5 we compare the *sub9294d, sub9294n* and *nevsub* groups.

When we look at balance sheet indicators for district and non district firms subsidised in the first period (*sub8991d, sub8991n*) compared to firms never subsidised in the six years (*nevsub*), several findings from descriptive evidence seem to show that geographical agglomeration has some impact on bank-firm relationship and generates some advantages for subsidised firms located in industrial districts *vis a vis* subsidised firms which are not (Tab. 2-5)[6].

A first relevant result is that all groups of subsidised firms are more leveraged than non subsidised and, within subsidised, those located into districts have a higher bank debt/total asset ratio (0.10 against 0.089).

Table 2. Average (1989-91) balance sheet indicators for subgroups of firms

	Firms subsidised in 89-91, but not in 92-94 and not located in an ID			Firms subsidised in 89-91, but not in 92-94 and located in an ID			Firms never subsidised between 89 and 94		
	Mean	95%Conf. Int		Mean	95%Conf. Int		Mean	95%Conf. Int	
Number of employees (89-91 average)	247.818	186.144	309.491	191.798	147.884	235.712	123.970	103.347	144.592
Interest payments /total debts (89-91)	0.299	0.130	0.468	0.176	0.106	0.245	0.440	0.242	0.637
Operating income+depreciation (cash-flow)/total assets	0.049	0.043	0.055	0.053	0.049	0.057	0.054	0.051	0.057
Total debts towards banks /total assets	0.089	0.079	0.099	0.104	0.094	0.114	0.080	0.075	0.085
Short term debts towards banks /total assets	0.063	0.054	0.071	0.074	0.065	0.083	0.062	0.057	0.067
Total debt versus banks/total assets	0.276	0.259	0.294	0.299	0.281	0.317	0.265	0.255	0.275
Total debts towards banks/ total debts	0.284	0.260	0.309	0.312	0.291	0.332	0.256	0.243	0.269
Short term debts towards banks /total debts	0.218	0.197	0.240	0.246	0.228	0.265	0.204	0.192	0.215

[6] For any balance sheet indicator Tables 2-5 indicate average subgroup means and their 95% confidence intervals. Non overlapping intervals for means of two different subgroups are an indication that these means are significantly different from each other, indication that must be confirmed, though, by econometric results presented after in the paper.

	Firms subsidised in 89-91, but not in 92-94 and not located in an ID			Firms subsidised in 89-91, but not in 92-94 and located in an ID			Firms never subsidised between 89 and 94		
	Mean	95%Conf. Int.		Mean	95%Conf. Int.		Mean	95%Conf. Int.	
Short term debts towards banks / total sales	0.164	0.138	0.190	0.172	0.147	0.197	0.152	0.134	0.170
Short term debts towards banks /inventories	1.436	0.903	1.969	1.419	0.980	1.859	2.693	0.598	4.787
Gross profits/net total sales	0.029	0.014	0.043	0.033	0.023	0.044	0.025	-0.001	0.051
EBIT/total sales	0.027	0.011	0.044	0.032	0.018	0.047	0.025	-0.001	0.052
Cash flow/ Short term debts towards banks	17.972	-2.377	38.320	30.787	-2.054	63.627	27.218	4.595	49.841
Cash flow/ total sales	0.103	0.092	0.114	0.112	0.101	0.122	0.095	0.077	0.113
ROE	0.097	0.034	0.160	0.098	0.026	0.171	0.063	-0.147	0.272
Investments payments /total sales	0.045	0.039	0.050	0.045	0.040	0.050	0.040	0.036	0.044
ROI	0.074	0.060	0.088	0.079	0.070	0.088	0.090	0.082	0.098
Inventories/total sales	0.200	0.173	0.228	0.336	0.045	0.627	0.418	0.039	0.797
Total debts towards banks Short term debts towards banks	0.377	0.338	0.416	0.411	0.370	0.452	0.352	0.310	0.394
Short term debts towards banks /total sales	0.582	0.513	0.651	0.831	0.301	1.362	0.753	0.306	1.2
Short term debts /inventories	6.391	4.102	8.679	5.207	3.800	6.613	8.619	3.689	13.548

Table 2. Continuation.

Table 3. Average (1992-94) balance sheet indicators for subgroups of firms

	Firms subsidised in 89-91, but not in 92-94 and not located in an ID			Firms subsidised in 89-91, but not in 92-94 and located in an ID			Firms never subsidised between 89 and 94		
	Mean	95%Conf int		Mean	95%Conf int		Mean	95%Conf int	
Number of employees ('89-'91 average)	228.83	170.89	286.77	173.03	137.023	209.05	125.47	101.83	149.11
Interest payments /total debts (89-91)	0.193	0.148	0.239	0.194	0.103	0.285	1.264	-0.036	2.5642
Operating income + depreciation (cash-flow)/total asset	0.042	0.036	0.048	0.045	0.040	0.050	0.045	0.042	0.0487
Total debts towards banks /total asset	0.094	0.081	0.106	0.097	0.087	0.107	0.075	0.070	0.0811
Short term debts towards banks /total asset	0.073	0.063	0.083	0.073	0.065	0.081	0.062	0.057	0.0674

	Firms subsidised in 89-91, but not in 92-94 and not located in an ID			Firms subsidised in 89-91, but not in 92-94 and located in an ID			Firms never subsidised between 89 and 94		
	Mean	95%Confint		Mean	95%Confint		Mean	95%Confint	
Total debts towards banks/ total debts	0.289	0.260	0.318	0.293	0.271	0.316	0.253	0.239	0.2679
Short term debts towards banks /total debts	0.245	0.221	0.269	0.246	0.227	0.265	0.218	0.206	0.2304
Short term debts towards banks / total sales	0.211	0.174	0.248	0.175	0.152	0.199	0.151	0.135	0.1675
Short term debts towards banks /inventories	1.248	1.022	1.473	1.289	1.015	1.564	2.098	1.061	3.1361
Gross profits/net total sales	0.009	-0.004	0.022	0.013	-0.001	0.026	0.004	-0.029	0.0362
EBIT/total sales	0.005	-0.011	0.021	0.006	-0.012	0.025	-0.002	-0.038	0.033
Cash flow/ Short term debts towards banks	14.237	-1.494	29.968	52.820	-25.292	130.932	15.138	4.976	25.300
Cash flow/ total sales	0.096	0.085	0.108	0.093	0.083	0.103	0.064	0.011	0.1157
ROE	-0.017	-0.082	0.048	0.100	-0.322	0.521	-0.068	-0.289	0.1536
Interest payments /total sales	0.058	0.051	0.065	0.051	0.046	0.057	0.045	0.042	0.049
ROI	0.056	0.044	0.067	0.064	0.053	0.075	0.073	0.066	0.0812
Inventories/total sales	0.232	0.185	0.280	0.214	0.174	0.253	0.231	0.193	0.2699
Total debts towards banks / Short term debts towards banks	0.334	0.299	0.370	0.363	0.328	0.398	0.306	0.279	0.3334
Short term debts towards banks /total sales	0.675	0.594	0.756	0.597	0.538	0.656	0.539	0.498	0.5795
Short term debts /inventories	4.661	3.821	5.500	4.443	3.771	5.115	7.584	4.267	10.901
Change in the short term/long term bank debt ratio	-0.810	-16.025	14.405	2.583	-1.334	6.501	-2.560	-10.989	5.8698
Skilled workers hired	13.005	9.076	16.935	13.260	8.647	17.873	7.651	5.723	9.5795
Total workers hired	1.579	0.471	2.687	0.914	-0.170	1.997	0.913	0.247	1.5784

Table 3. Continuation

Table 4. Average (1989-91) balance sheet indicators for subgroups of firms

	Firms subsidised in 89-91, and in 92-94 not located in an ID			Firms subsidised in 89-91, and in 92-94 located in an ID			Firms never subsidised between 89 and 94		
	Mean	95%Conf.int.		Mean	95%Conf.int.		Mean	95%Conf.int.	
Number of employees (1989-91 average)	671.63	417.86	925.40	183.14	131.09	235.19	123.97	103.34	144.59
Interest payments /total debts (89-91)	0.180	0.111	0.250	0.251	0.116	0.386	0.440	0.242	0.638
Operating income + depreciation (cash-flow)/total asset	0.050	0.047	0.053	0.056	0.052	0.060	0.054	0.051	0.058
Total debts towards banks /total asset	0.097	0.090	0.103	0.099	0.093	0.106	0.080	0.075	0.086
Short term debts towards banks /total asset	0.062	0.057	0.068	0.068	0.063	0.074	0.062	0.057	0.067
Total debts towards banks/ total debts	0.321	0.306	0.335	0.308	0.293	0.323	0.256	0.243	0.270

	Firms subsidised in 89-91, and in 92-94 not located in an ID			Firms subsidised in 89-91, and in 92-94 located in an ID			Firms never subsidised between 89 and 94		
	Mean	95% Conf. int.		Mean	95% Conf. int.		Mean	95% Conf. int.	
Short term debts towards banks /total debts	0.220	0.206	0.234	0.236	0.223	0.250	0.204	0.192	0.216
Short term debts towards banks / total sales	0.163	0.146	0.180	0.179	0.152	0.205	0.152	0.134	0.170
Short term debts towards banks /inventories	1.319	0.999	1.639	1.429	1.100	1.758	2.693	0.598	4.788
Gross profits/net total sales	0.039	0.028	0.049	0.034	0.027	0.041	0.025	-0.001	0.051
EBIT/total sales	0.035	0.025	0.046	0.030	0.021	0.039	0.025	-0.001	0.052
Cash flow/ Short term debts towards banks	140.44	-94.423	375.30	14.320	-0.399	29.038	27.218	4.595	49.841
Cash flow/ total sales	0.117	0.108	0.126	0.118	0.110	0.125	0.095	0.077	0.113
ROE	0.067	0.021	0.113	0.102	0.072	0.133	0.063	-0.147	0.273
Interest payments /total sales	0.046	0.041	0.051	0.046	0.042	0.050	0.040	0.036	0.044
ROI	0.070	0.062	0.077	0.080	0.072	0.088	0.090	0.082	0.098
Inventories/total sales	0.227	0.198	0.256	0.198	0.175	0.221	0.418	0.039	0.797
Total debts towards banks / Short term debts towards banks	0.461	0.406	0.517	0.423	0.384	0.463	0.352	0.310	0.394
Short term debts towards banks /total sales	0.612	0.548	0.676	0.606	0.545	0.667	0.753	0.306	1.200
Short term debts /inventories	5.424	4.309	6.539	6.137	4.489	7.785	8.619	3.689	13.548

Table 4. Continuation

Table 5. Average (1992-94) balance sheet indicators for subgroups of firms

	Firms subsidised in 89-91, and in 92-94 and not located in an ID			Firms subsidised in 89-91, and in 92-94 and located in an ID			Firms never subsidised between 89 and 94		
	Mean	95% Conf. int.		Mean	95% Conf. int.		Mean	95% Conf. int.	
Number of employees (1989-91 average)	555.47	390.24	720.70	165.17	134.95	195.38	125.47	101.83	149.11
Interest payments /total debts (89-91)	0.170	0.133	0.207	0.171	0.134	0.209	1.264	-0.036	2.564
Operating income + depreciation (cash-flow)/total asset	0.045	0.042	0.048	0.048	0.044	0.051	0.045	0.042	0.049
Total debts towards banks /total asset	0.090	0.083	0.097	0.100	0.093	0.107	0.075	0.070	0.081
Short term debts towards banks /total asset	0.065	0.059	0.070	0.075	0.069	0.080	0.062	0.057	0.067
Total debts towards banks/ total debts	0.294	0.279	0.309	0.300	0.284	0.316	0.253	0.239	0.268
Short term debts towards banks /total debts	0.232	0.218	0.245	0.252	0.238	0.265	0.218	0.206	0.230
Short term debts towards banks / total sales	0.193	0.165	0.220	0.192	0.174	0.210	0.151	0.135	0.168

	Firms subsidised in 89-91, and in 92-94 and not located in an ID		Firms subsidised in 89-91, and in 92-94 and located in an ID		Firms never subsidised between 89 and 94	
	Mean	95%Conf.int.		Mean	95%Conf.int.		Mean	95%Conf.int.
Short term debts towards banks /inventories	5.552	-3.005	14.109	1.559	0.888	2.229	2.098	1.061	3.136
Gross profits/net total sales	0.016	0.001	0.032	0.015	0.007	0.023	0.004	-0.029	0.036
EBIT/total sales	0.013	-0.005	0.031	0.009	-0.001	0.020	-0.002	-0.038	0.033
Cash flow/ Short term debts towards banks	20.675	0.651	40.700	16.199	-2.477	34.875	15.138	4.976	25.300
Cash flow/ total sales	0.110	0.102	0.119	0.106	0.098	0.114	0.064	0.011	0.116
ROE	0.221	-0.169	0.611	-0.101	-0.267	0.064	-0.068	-0.289	0.154
Investments payments /total sales	0.063	0.049	0.077	0.055	0.051	0.059	0.045	0.042	0.049
ROI	0.058	0.051	0.065	0.062	0.055	0.070	0.073	0.066	0.081
Inventories/total sales	0.308	0.211	0.405	0.197	0.182	0.212	0.231	0.193	0.270
Total debts towards banks / Short term debts towards banks	0.378	0.351	0.405	0.376	0.346	0.405	0.306	0.279	0.333
Short term debts towards banks /total sales	0.704	0.589	0.819	0.646	0.606	0.686	0.539	0.498	0.580
Short term debts /inventories	17.389	-6.320	41.098	6.490	3.712	9.267	7.584	4.267	10.902
Change in the short term/long term bank debt ratio	0.093	0.062	0.124	0.073	0.039	0.108	0.062	0.034	0.091
Skilled workers hired	2.608	1.815	3.401	0.596	0.437	0.756	7.651	5.723	9.580
Total workers hired	26.976	18.365	35.586	11.329	9.412	13.245	0.913	0.247	1.578

Table 5. Continuation

In the medium term, though, subsidised district firms improve their indebtedness ratio which is no more significantly different from that of non district subsidised firms (0.097 against 0.094). Another crucial finding is that district subsidised firms have a lower cost of bank debt (0.176 against 0.299) besides being more leveraged than never subsidised firms, while non district subsidised firms cannot be distinguished in terms of cost of bank debt and leverage from never subsidised firms in the short run. In the medium run, though, non district subsidised result to be more indebted than district and never subsidised. Again, this seems consistent with the hypothesis that geographical agglomeration, probably via an increase in borrowers bargaining power, might reduce the subsidy rent share that the banking system obtains on soft loans. We will verify this hypothesis in the econometric analysis.

Geographical agglomeration seems also to have positive effects on firms performance. All (district and non district) subsidised firms seem to have at the beginning a lower return on investment (respectively 0.079 and 0.074) than firms never subsidised in the six years (0.090). After three years, though, only district subsidised firms partially catch up (0.064 against 0.056 of district non subsidised and 0.073 of never subsidised). The change in ROI does not seem dramatic but is much more relevant when we consider respective confidence intervals and econometric estimates presented below in the paper.

The comparison of balance sheet indicators for district and non district firms subsidised in the first period (*sub8991d, sub8991n*) compared to firms never subsidised in the six years (*nevsub*) does not allow to insulate medium term effects of subsidies (we do not have a testing period after the provision of subsidies where both groups did not receive soft loans anymore) but seems to confirm evidence of tables 2-3 both in terms of profitability and bank-firm relationship. District subsidised firms are more leveraged and then obtain more credit than non district subsidised firms, although profitability/indebtedness ratios are not significantly different across the two groups. This result is confirmed also when we analyse the period 1989-94. The evidence supports the implicit hypothesis of Stiglitz-Weiss (1981) model which predicts that in a more competitive economic environment and with lower informational asymmetries the subsidy rent is more equally shared among the counterparts and subsidised firms obtain better borrowing terms. Moreover, descriptive results from balance sheet indicators for district and non district firms subsidised in both periods (1989-91 and 1992-94) indicate that non district subsidised firms have a ROI significantly lower than non subsidised firms. This pattern does not occur in the case of district subsidised firms.

5   Econometric Results

Descriptive evidence on variables discriminating performance and borrowing terms of subsidised district *vis-a-vis* non district firms may be strongly biased by composition effects generated by the influence of other variables such as sector, geographical area, age and size. To evaluate the net effect of geographical agglomeration we propose econometric estimates in which the net effect of the district on the relevant dependent variables is evidenced.

In a first estimate we evaluate the impact of a set of regressors on changes in firm's average performance:

$$Droi = \alpha_0 + \sum_{i=1}^{3} \alpha_i Darea_i + \sum_{k=1}^{22} \vartheta_k Dset_k + \beta Size + \gamma Birth +$$
$$\delta Distr + \varepsilon \tag{1}$$

where *Droi* is the ratio between the 1992-94 and the 1989-1991 average return on investment for the i-*th* firm; *Darea$_i$* are three macroarea dummies, *Dset$_k$* are 3 Pavit macrosector dummies, *Size* is the three year (1989-91) average of firm's employees, *Birth* is the firm's foundation year, and *District* is a variable which assumes different specifications according to the selected district indicator. To evaluate the net impact of (1989-91) credit subsidies in the following three years we must select a group of firms which received them in the first but not in the second period (*sub8991*) and a control sample which never received them from 1989 to 1994 (*nevsub*). We restrict our sample only to these two groups of firms and we split the first group by separately considering firms located or not located into an industrial district. We distinguish among these two subgroups using alternatively Sforzi and Del Colle indicators: *i)* with *sub8991d* we consider firms subsidised in the 1989-91 period (but not in the 1992-94 period) which are located into industrial districts according to Sforzi classification; *ii)* with *sub8991ul* we consider firms subsidised in the 1989-91 period (but not in the 1992-94) using Del Colle indicator which measures industrial unit concentration within a district (number of industrial units per 1000 inhabitants); *iii)* with *sub8991ad* we consider firms subsidised in the 1989-91 period (but not in the 1992-94) using Del Colle indicator which measures manufacturing employees concentration within a district (number of workers in the manufacturing sector per 1000 inhabitants).

All these indicators yield substantially equivalent results on the impact of district location on medium term effect of subsidised credit. Table 6 shows that district subsidised firms have significantly better differences in return on equity between the two periods than both non district subsidised and never subsidised firms.

Table 6. Impact of soft loans on firm performance. Dependent variable: Average (1992-1994) ROI/ Average (1989-1991) ROI

	Specification #1		Specification #2		Specification #3	
	Coeff.	T-stat	Coeff.	T stat	Coeff.	T-stat
Centre	2.996	2.101	2.965	2.078	2.976	2.086
North-West	3.067	2.398	3.070	2.399	3.039	2.375
North-East	3.095	2.391	3.076	2.376	3.053	2.357
Special	-0.179	-0.120	-0.172	-0.115	-0.180	-0.121
Traditional	0.030	0.022	0.048	0.034	0.038	0.027
Scale	1.028	0.729	1.039	0.737	1.026	0.728
Size	-0.001	-2.586	-0.001	-2.591	-0.001	-2.588
Birth	0.017	1.141	0.017	1.135	0.017	1.148
Sub8991d	2.714	2.611	-	-	-	-
Sub8991ul	-	-	0.313	2.520	-	-
Sub8991ad	-	-	-	-	0.064	2.566
Constant	-36.326	0.211	-36.155	0.214	-36.490	0.209

Table 7. Dependent variable: cost of bank debt

Variable	Coefficient	t-statistics
Centre	-0.108	-0.068
North-west	0.856	0.602
North-East	0.287	0.199
Special	-6.857	-4.005
Traditional	-6.983	-4.395
Scale	-6.869	-4.286
Size	0.000	-0.365
Birth	-0.039	-2.343
Bankcon	-0.990	-1.623
Constant	83.389	0.011

Note: The average balance sheet cost of bank debt is measured as the ratio of financial expenditure versus the banking system over total debt versus the banking system.

In the second estimate we verify whether the cost of bank debt is different between district and non district subsidised firms. Our aim is to assess whether relative changes in bank-firm bargaining power affect borrowing terms according to what implicitly predicted by the the Stiglitz-Weiss (1981) model under the assumption that relative changes in the number of the two counterparts are positively related with changes in relative bargaining strength.[7] The use in our estimates of a variable computing bank concentration within each district will proxy bank firm relative bargaining power.

To evaluate the impact bank-firm bargaining power on the cost of bank debt we run the following regression on the subsample including only district firms:

---

[7] This is not necessarily true as, with Bertrand competition, the simple passage from one to two firms may lead from monopoly to competitive equilibrium and any marginal increase in the number of firms may not change the Bertrand equilibrium. With the exception of this extreme case, though, changes in numbers may be thought as being roughly related to relative bargaining power. Geographical concentration of one of the two counterparts (banks or firms) may enhance their bargaining power if they collude (banks) or if they create formal coalitions to discuss borrowing conditions (firms as in the experience of Consorzi Fidi in Italy). It may otherwise reduce relative bargaining power by increasing counterpart's outside option. The hypothesis of the paper is that, within industrial districts, a higher concentration of banks increases their competition and then improves firm borrowing terms.

$$Cdeb = \alpha_0 + \sum_{i=1}^{3} \alpha_i Darea_i + \sum_{k=1}^{22} \theta_k Dset_k + \beta Size + \gamma Birth +$$

$$\delta Bankcon + \varepsilon$$

(2)

where regressors are defined as in (1) and *Bankcon* measures financial services concentration within a district (share of units providing financial services on total manufacturing sector in the district over the same share calculated on the whole industrial system). The dependent variable *Cdeb* is the cost of bank debt. Results are presented in table 7. It is noteworthy that *Bankcon* shows a slightly significant and negative coefficient indicating that the cost of bank debt is lower for firms belonging to an industrial district. This evidence suggests that firms located in an economic environment in which bargaining power between banks and firms is more balanced might obtain relative reductions in the cost of debt. As predicted from the implicit hypothesis of the Stiglitz-Weiss (1981) model if competition among banks and/or bargaining power of borrowers increase we may have non monopolistic solutions in which the subsidy rent is more equally shared among the counterparts and subsidised firms obtain better borrowing terms.

6   Conclusions

In times in which the focus of domestic economic policies is increasingly shifting from macropolicies to measures creating proper regulatory environment and enhancing endogenous and local mechanisms of development and self-employment, many economists wonder whether public intervention is more effective in ID where positive externalities within a geographically limited area may enhance and propagate benefits of limited state intervention.

This paper tries to provide an answer looking at the experience of the past and testing whether the recent policy of Italian credit subsidies has been more effective for district than for non district firms. Two are the main results obtained. First, district subsidised firms present in the medium run a relative improvement of their return on investment with respect to the control sample.

Second district subsidised firms seem to obtain better borrowing terms. According to some credit rationing models (Stiglitz-Weiss, 1981; De Meza-Webb, 1987), banks act as monopolist profit maximisers facing a multiplicity of firms with heterogeneous projects. However if we postulate relatively higher bank competition and, consequently, changes in bank-firm bargaining power we obtain a modification in the borrowing terms according to what implicitly predicted by the the Stiglitz-Weiss model (1981). This implicit assumption may explain why district subsidised firms seem to have lower cost of debt than non district firms.

Our empirical results even if not free from interpretative caveats and methodological limits shed light on the evaluation of the effects of subsidies at empirical level. The evidence supports the view that industrial policy may be more effective on "fertile grounds" where infrastructures and cooperation among firms are already developed. These findings also provide partial support to the new industrial policies promoted both by European Union and Italy aimed to increase services provided and to concentrate intervention on start-ups and innovation in targeted areas.

References

Abdel-Rahman H. and Fujita M., 1990, Product Variety Marshallian Externalities and City Sizes, *Journal of Regional Science*, 30.

Bagella M., and Becchetti L.,1998, The impact of subsidised credit on firm's short term and medium term performance: an empirical analysis with microdata, mimeo

Bagella M., Becchetti L. and Caggese A., 1996, Financial constraints on investments: evidence from direct revelation, *Rivista di Politica Economica*, 86.

Becattini G., 1987, *Mercato e Forze Locali: Il Distretto Industriale*, Bologna, Il Mulino.

Becattini G., 1991, The Marshallian Industrial District as a socioeconomic notion, in F. Pyke, G. Becattini and W. Sengenberger (eds.), *Industrial district and interfirm cooperation in Italy*, Geneva International Institute for Labour Studies.

Becchetti L., 1995, Finance, investment and innovation: a theoretical and empirical comparative analysis, *Empirica*, 22.

Becchetti L. and Rossi S.P.S., 1999a, EU and non EU Export Performance of Italian Firms. Is There an Industrial District Effect?, in *The Competitive advantage of Italian district: theoretical and empirical analysis*, M.Bagella (ed.) Physica Verlag, and *Quaderni di Politica Industriale*, N.19, Mediocredito Centrale.

Becchetti L. and Rossi S., 1999b, The positive effect of Industrial District on the export performance of Italian firms, *The Review of Industrial Organisation*, (forth.).

Bellandi M., 1996, Innovation and change in the Marshallian Industrial District, in *European Planning Studies*, Vol. 4, n. 3.

Bernanke B.S. and Gertler M., 1987, Financial fragility and economic performance, *NBER, Working Paper n. 2318*.

Besanko D. and Thakor A.V., 1993, Collateral and rationing: sorting equilibria in mopolistic and competitive credit markets, *International Economic Review*, 28.

Bester H., 1987, Screening vs. rationing in credit markets with imperfect information, *American Economic Review*, 75.

Bond S. and Meghir C., 1994, Dynamic Investment Models and the Firm's Financial Policy, *Review of Economic Studies*, 61.

De Cecco M. and Ferri G., 1997, Merchant Banks and Industrial Investment in Italy, paper presented at the 1997 Financial Conference in Venice.

De Meza D. and Webb D.C., 1987, Too Much Investment : A Problem of Asymmetric Information, *Quarterly Journal of Economics*,101.

Del Colle E. 1997, *Le aree produttive. Struttura economica dei sistemi regionali in Italia*, Franco Angeli.

Devereux M. and Schiantarelli F., 1989, Investment, financial factors, and cash flow: evidence from UK panel data, *NBER Working Paper 3116*, 1989.

Dobkins L.H., 1996, Location, Innovation and Trade: The Role of Localization and Nation-Based Externalities, *Regional Science and Urban Economics*, 26.

Fazzari S.M., Hubbard G.R. and Petersen B.C., 1988, Financing constraints and corporate investment, *Brooking Papers on Economic Activity*.

Gale W.G., 1991, Economic Effects of Federal Credit Programs, *American Economic Review*, 133-152.

Grossman G.M. and Helpman E., 1991, *Innovation and Growth in the Global Economy*, Cambridge, MA, MIT Press.

Hoshi T., Kashyap A. and Scharfstein D., 1992, Corporate structure, liquidity and investment: evidence from Japanese industrial groups, *Quarterly Journal of Economics* 90.

Innes R., 1992, Adverse Selection, investment and profit taxation, *European Economic Review*, 36.

Kashyap A.K., Lamont O.A. and Stein J.C., 1993, Credit conditions and the cyclical behaviour of inventories, *WP* N.7 Federal Reserve Bank of Chicago.

Milde H. and Riley J.G., 1988, Signalling in Credit Markets, *Quarterly Journal of Economics*, 103, 101-29.

Moran P.A.P., 1950, Notes on continuous stochastic phenomena, *Biometrika*, 37.

Pyke F. and Sengenberger W., 1992, *Industrial GA and local Economic Regeneration*, Geneva, International Institute for Labour Studies.

Pyke F., Becattini G. and Sengenberger W., 1991, *Industrial district and interfirm cooperation in Italy*, Geneva International Institute for Labour Studies.

Rivera-Batiz F.L., 1988a, Increasing Returns, Monopolistic Competition and Agglomeration Economies in Consumption and Production, *Regional Science and Urban Economics*, 18.

Rivera-Batiz F.L., 1988b, Modeling urban Agglomeration: Producer Services, Linkage Externalities and Specialisation Economies, in *Modeling and Simulation*, M.H. Mickel and V. Vogt (eds.), Instrument Society of America, Research Triangle Park, NC.

Schiantarelli F. and Georgoutsos D., 1990, Monopolistic Competition and the Q Theory of Investment, *European Economic Review*, 34.

Sforzi F., 1995, Sistemi Locali di Impresa e Cambiamento Industriale in Italia, *AGEI-Geotema* n. 2.

Stiglitz J., and Weiss A., 1981, Credit rationing in markets with imperfect information, *American Economic Review* 71.

Stiglitz J., and Weiss A., 1986, Credit Rationing and Collateral, in *Recent developments in corporate finance*, J.Edwards, J.Franks e S.Schaefer (*eds.*), Cambridge, Cambridge University Press.

Stiglitz J., and Weiss A., 1986, Credit rationing: reply, *American Economic Review*, 77, 228-31.

Stiglitz J., and Weiss A., 1992, Asymmetric Information in credit markets and its implications for macroeconomics, *Oxford Economic Papers*, 44.

Stiglitz J.E., 1993, The role of the state in financial markets, Proceedings of the World Bank Annual Conference on Development Economics.

Part II: Industrial Districts and Foreign Competitiveness: Export and Internationalisation Performance

The Positive Link Between Geographical Agglomeration and Export Intensity: The Engine of Italian Endogenous Growth?

Michele Bagella

University of Rome "Tor Vergata", Faculty of Economics, Department of Economics and Institutions, Via di Tor Vergata snc, 00133 Rome. E-mail: bagella@uniroma2.it

Leonardo Becchetti

University of Rome "Tor Vergata", Faculty of Economics, Department of Economics and Institutions, Via di Tor Vergata snc, 00133 Rome. E-mail: becchetti@uniroma2.it

Simona Sacchi

University of Rome "Tor Vergata", Faculty of Economics, Department of Economics and Institutions, Via di Tor Vergata snc, 00133 – Rome.

Abstract: The theoretical part of the paper presents a stylised model where geographical proximity is assumed to increase private firm benefits from generating export services. On these premises the model shows that export intensity is higher for firms agglomerated in "industrial districts" than for isolated firms. It also shows how this positive relationship between export intensity and geographical agglomeration may be univocally established only when competition on foreign markets among firms cooperating in export services is not too high. The validity of this conclusion is analysed under different frameworks such as infinitely repeated noncooperative and cooperative games. The empirical part of the paper provides partial support to this theoretical hypothesis showing that benefits from geographical agglomeration in terms of higher export intensity and higher export participation are decreasing in firm size and generally higher in sectors characterised by forms of competition based on horizontal product differentiation.

JEL Classification: R3

Keywords: Export performance, Geographical agglomeration.

1   Introduction*

A distinctive feature of the downsized Italian industrial system is the tendency of small-medium firms to cluster in "industrial districts". An "Industrial district" is generally intended as a network of small-medium firms concentrated in a delimited area, linked by input-output relationships and social organisational rules, in which geographical proximity among different units generates both positive and negative spillovers. From a theoretical point of view, the justification for the existence of industrial districts, composed by small-medium firms, and their survival together with large vertically integrated firms is based on the relative lower weight of transaction costs with respect to coordination costs for the same types of firms and products. According to some, this occurs when the final product may be decomposed into intermediate goods and services which are technically and contractually identifiable and when a division of labour among firms may be more efficient than a division of labour within a single firm (Bellandi, 1996). According to others, this is more likely to happen when dynamic learning economies of scale and economies of scale on the division of the production cycle prevail for certain activities over static economies of scale postulating average cost reduction when firm size increases (Sengenberger-Pyke, 1992; Pike-Becattini-Sengenberger, 1991).

Another relative advantage justifying the existence of "industrial districts" is their higher capacity of adapting to external shocks, given that their reduced dimension, their lower amount of sunk costs under the form of fixed investments and their higher input flexibility make it easier to reallocate labour and capital inputs after a shock. In addition, the relevant number of market transactions of intermediate goods and services occurring in an industrial district before the final product is obtained may be an efficient mechanism for quality control.

Industrial district development and operation is based on a complex mix of competitive and cooperative actions (Sengenberger-Pyke, 1992). The paradoxical coexistence of these two types of actions may be justified by the fact that competing firms may find a relative advantage in exchanging information (Pike-Becattini-Sengenberger, 1991) or in assuming the role of component producers and assembling "system companies" in the production of complex systemic products (Tani, 1996). In particular, about these advantages, it has been observed that the cooperative action of exchanging information on export markets among firms in the districts may generate important benefits in terms of cost reduction of real services.

---

* The paper is part of an empirical work on Italian industrial districts supported by Italian Center of National Research and has been presented at the 1997 Conference of the European Regional Studies Association (ERSA) and at the International Workshop on "Italian industrial districts: internationalisation and export performance", held at Istituto Tagliacarne in 1997. The authors thank M.Bellandi, R.Cappellin, C.Pietrobelli, F.Sforzi for helpful comments and suggestions.

Theoretical literature has only partially analysed the positive effects of the agglomeration of small-medium firms in industrial districts and the empirical literature is even more far behind in assessing the relative costs and benefits of geographically agglomerated firms vis-à-vis those which are not.

In particular, with regard to the exchange of export services, how exactly geographical agglomeration makes it easier this exchange? For which types of firms according to size and industrial sector this benefit is larger?

The aim of this paper is that of suggesting an answer to these two questions by providing a theoretical model which describes the effect of geographical agglomeration on private firm export intensity and by analysing the effects of geographical agglomeration on export intensity at microlevel on a sample of around 4000 small-medium Italian firms. The paper is organised as follows. The first section presents a simple model using a game theoretical approach and the second section provides results on export intensity and export participation for firms by macroarea, macrosectors and size class for the firms included in the Mediocredito sample.

2   The Partnership Stage Game

Consider the following game:

Fig. 1. The one stage export game.

		Player 2	
		e	ne
Player 1	e	$pq+\lambda-\gamma,\ pq+\lambda-\gamma$	$p-\gamma,\lambda$
	ne	$\lambda,p-\gamma$	$0,0$

In this stage game each player i (i=1,2) simultaneously chooses a (pure) action a_i from a finite set A_i with m_i elements, or a mixed action α_i. The two pure actions *(e,ne)* in this game represent respectively the decision to exert *(e)* or not *(ne)* effort in producing services for exports (acquiring all information needed to access foreign markets and to organise sales abroad). The effort in producing export services is assumed to increase player's percentage of net sales from exports over total net sales. This variable is the payoff of the game.

The game is based on four fundamental parameters:

which is the "stand-alone effort" contribution to player's payoff;

q which is the marginal effect of opponent effort in producing export services on an individual player payoff (for simplicity we assume that players have homogeneous skills and that $q_i=q_j=q$);

γ which is the effort cost; and iv) λ which is the no effort contribution to payoff. About this last parameter, a crucial assumption in the model is that the degree of geographical proximity among players *(gp)* increases the no effort contribution to payoff $\lambda'(gp)>0$. This is because part of the export service knowledge generated by an individual player is public good which may be appropriated by competitors according to their degree of geographical proximity to that player.

2.1 The Game for Small-Medium Firm Players and for Players in Sector Characterised by "Horizontal Product Differentiation"

We assume that the effect of opponent effort in producing export services on an individual player payoff is superadditive (q>1) in all cases in which benefits from joint production of services for access to foreign markets are higher than costs from having a competitor in these markets.[1] This is more likely to occur for small-medium firms with limit capacity and for firms in sectors with horizontal product differentiation.[2] In these two cases the impact of a competitor in export markets generates a relatively smaller reduction of individual player profits, given the relative size of firms with respect to market demand and given the type of competition.

In this case the one shot game has a trivial solution with a unique *(e,e)* Nash equilibrium when $\gamma \in [0, p]$.[3] In fact only two possible rankings among individual players payoff exist and are $pq+\lambda-\gamma>\lambda>p-\gamma$ and $pq+\lambda-\gamma>p-\gamma>\lambda$. The *(e,e)* strategy is also the unique equilibrium of the finitely and infinitely repeated game given that no player has incentives to deviate from that equilibrium.

Given that the payoff from the *(e,e)* strategy is increasing in λ, the conclusion is that for firms for which joint production of export services is superadditive *(q>1)* (small firms and firms in sectors with horizontal product differentiation) geographical agglomeration always generates a relatively higher payoff.

---

[1] This assumption could have been endogenised in the model by specifying firm's profit functions and the oligopolistic model of the market. We nonetheless think that this would not add much to the paper reducing instead clarity and simplicity of exposition of its main ideas.

[2] For horizontal product differentiation we mean those forms of competition where entry of new firms has only the effect of reducing incumbents market shares without pushing them out of the market. Typical models of horizontal product differentiation is that of Hotelling (1929) and D'Aspremont-Gabszewicz-Thisse (1979).

[3] γ cannot be higher than p as the game payoff is the share of export sales over total sales which can never be negative. In fact the maximum cost in producing effort services may at most generate a zero share of export sales over total net sales by orienting the firm only to domestic production.

2.2 The Game for Large Firm Players and for Players in Sector with Vertical Product Differentiation

We assume that the effect of opponent effort in producing export services on an individual player payoff is subadditive (q<1) in all cases in which benefits from joint production of services for access to foreign markets are lower than costs from having a competitor in these markets. This is more likely to occur for large firms with potentially unlimited capacity and for firms in sectors characterised by vertical product differentiation (Shaked-Sutton, 1983). In these two cases the impact of a competitor in export markets generates a relatively high reduction on individual player profits, given the relative size of firms with respect to market demand and given the type of competition.

Also in this case our assumption on nonnegative payoff (nonnegative share of export sales over total sales) implies that $\gamma \in [0, pq]$. In the game with q<1 we may consider three different rankings among different payoffs attainable in the game with equilibria in price strategies. In fact: i) when $\lambda \in [0, p(1-q)]$ we have $p-\gamma > pq + \lambda - \gamma > \lambda$; ii) when $\lambda \in [p(1-q), p-\gamma]$ we have $pq + \lambda - \gamma > p - \gamma > \lambda$; iii) when $\lambda \in [p-\gamma, \infty]$ we have $pq + \lambda - \gamma > \lambda > p - \gamma$. While case ii) and iii) give the same results of the previous section, case i) provides a different outcome with geographical agglomeration always increasing equilibrium payoffs when q>1.

Proposition 1. When joint effort to provide services for access to foreign markets has subadditive effects on individual player payoff (q<1) and when spillovers from geographical agglomeration are limited such that $\lambda \in [0, p(1-q)]$ a weaker relationship exists between geographical agglomeration and individual player payoff (the share of export sales over total sales).

Analysing equilibria in the one shot stage game it is clear that, with $q<1$, $\lambda \in [0, p(1-q)]$, and $\gamma \in [0, pq]$ the game described in Fig. 1 has a unique Nash equilibrium, (e,e), if $\gamma > pq$. The game has instead three Nash equilibria in the following strategies, (e,e), (e,ne) and (ne,e), if $\gamma = pq$. It is clear then that in two of the three last equilibria there is not an univocal relationship between geographical agglomeration and export intensity for one of the two players. The likelihood that $\gamma = pq$ cannot be considered too low with respect to all other possible values of γ in the admissible interval, so that in the one shot game, with q<1, the non univocal relationship between geographical agglomeration and export intensity must not be considered infrequent outcome. Two intuitions may be provided to explain this point: i) for many firms costs of individual access to foreign markets are prohibitively high (so that $\gamma = pq$) because γ is very high (this may be the case of firms in underdeveloped areas such as the South); ii) for firms in certain sectors competition on export markets may be so strong that opponent's effort in providing export services has a very negative effect on other player payoff and q is very low. A limiting case may be that with q=0 where we obtain $\gamma = pq$ and the non univocal relationship between geographical agglomeration and export intensity in a very large range of $\lambda \in [0, p]$. In these two explanations it is then argued that geographical agglomeration does not help export intensity if costs for accessing foreign markets are too high or competition among geographically agglomerated firms is too strong.

An analysis of the game when it is infinitely repeated may show that, even with $\gamma > pq$, we may obtain a weak relationship between geographical agglomeration and export intensity.

To evaluate which equilibria may be supported when the game is infinitely repeated consider that folk theorem applies only for those payoff vectors v with $v_i > \underline{v}_i$ for all players i, where:

$$\underline{v}_i = \min_{\alpha_{-i}} \left[\max_{\alpha i} g_i (\alpha, \alpha_{-i}) \right] \tag{1}$$

is the minmax of a player deviating from the equilibrium and also her reservation utility (Fudenberg-Tirole, 1992). In our game it is possible to show that, when $\gamma = pq$, $\underline{v}_i = \lambda$. When $\gamma < pq$ then: $\underline{v}_i = pq + \lambda - \gamma$.

As a consequence, in infinitely repeated games with $\gamma = pq$ the three equilibria in pure strategies of the one shot game are in the set of feasible strictly individually rational payoffs $\{v \in V | v_i > \underline{v}_i, \forall i\}$. When $\gamma < pq$ the set V is empty and *(e,e)* is the unique equilibrium giving the minmax payoff to both players.

It must be considered, however, that *(e,e)* may not be the only equilibrium if deviation from *(e,e)* of player i may be rewarded by her opponent. An alternative feasible equilibrium *(e,ne)* may be in fact devised when $(p-\gamma)-(pq+\lambda-\gamma) > (pq+\lambda-\gamma)-\lambda$ or $p(1-q)-\lambda > pq-\gamma$ and player 2 is compensated for her shirking by player 1 with a share of $((p-\gamma)-(pq+\lambda-\gamma))-((pq+\lambda-\gamma)-\lambda)$ equal to ε. We define this equilibrium as a *(e, ne|ε) equilibrium*.

Loosely speaking, considering admissible values for q, γ and λ, an *(e, ne|ε)* equilibrium is more likely to be feasible, the higher is γ and the lower are q and λ.

Two problems occur for the attainment of a *(e, ne|ε)* equilibrium. How the two counterparts decide about who is going to shirk and how the extra profit share is bargained? Do Folk Theorem results apply to the *(e, ne|ε)* equilibrium considering that player 1 may have an incentive to renegate side payments (see folk theorem)? To the first point we may reasonably assume that players bargaining strength (BS) is such that $BS_i = f(q_i, \lambda_i)$. If, as it is assumed in the basic stage game $q_i = q_{-i} = q$ and $\lambda_i = \lambda_{-i} = \lambda$, players have equal bargaining strength and a (½-½) division of extra profits is decided. In this case the two counterparts are indifferent to whom is going to shirk. To the second point we may apply folk theorem to see that there exists a $\underline{\delta} < 1$ such that:

$$(1-\underline{\delta}_i)\max_a g_i(a)+\underline{\delta}_i \underline{v}_i = v_i \qquad (2)$$

where (2) corresponds in this case to

$$(1-\underline{\delta}_i)(p-\gamma)+\underline{\delta}_i(pq+\lambda-\gamma)= p-\gamma-\varepsilon$$

with

$$\varepsilon =(1/2)((p\text{-}\gamma)\text{-}(pq+\lambda\text{-}\gamma))\text{-}((pq+\lambda\text{-}\gamma)\text{-}\lambda).$$

Then, for all $\delta \in [\underline{\delta}_i,1]$, the $(e,ne|\varepsilon)$ equilibrium can be supported in the infinitely repeated game described in Fig. 1.

The usual objection to this application of the Folk Theorem is that it is not subgame perfect as unrelenting punishment from player 2 when player 1 renegates side payments is a costly strategy for her. To overcome the objection we may check that (Aumann-Shapley, 1976) Perfect Folk Theorem may be applied to this type of game. In fact, if players evaluate sequences of stage-game utilities by the time-average criterion, the *(e,ne)* equilibrium with side payment of $\varepsilon =(1/2)((p\text{-}\gamma)\text{-}(pq+\lambda\text{-}\gamma))\text{-}((pq+\lambda\text{-}\gamma)\text{-}\lambda)$ from the non shirker to the shirker is a subgame perfect equilibrium of the game. To obtain the result just check that an N exists such that:

$$\max_a g_i(a)+N\underline{v}_i < \min_a g_i(a)+Nv_i \qquad (3)$$

if the deviating player is minmaxed with mixed strategies or check that an N exists such that:

$$\max_a g_i(a)+N\underline{v}_i < +Nv_i \qquad (4)$$

where the deviating player is minmaxed in pure strategies, where N is the number of periods for which player 1 is minmaxed if she deviates from the equilibrium. It is clear that, in our example, $N=(p\text{-}\gamma)/(p(1\text{-}q)\text{-}\lambda\text{-}\varepsilon)$. The intuition for this result is that for "infinitely patient" agents costs of punishing the deviating player are irrelevant. The assumption is quite unrealistic and it is interesting to see if subgame perfection of the Folk Theorem may be supported by relaxing it.

An alternative Perfect Folk Theorem moving in this direction allows us to say that the $(e,ne|\varepsilon)$ equilibrium may be shown to be subgame perfect by removing the extreme assumption of time-average criterion and assuming overtaking criterion and strategies in which punishment grows exponentially (Rubinstein, 1979).[4]

---

[4] The overtaking criterion represents a small departure from the "infinite patience". It establishes that, given two payoff sequences g=(g^0,g^1,...) and $\hat{g} = (\hat{g}^0,\hat{g}^1,..)$, the former

Perfect Folk Theorems confirm our proposition that, when joint effort to provide services for access to foreign markets has subadditive effects on individual player's payoff, geographical agglomeration does not univocally increase individual players' payoffs represented by export intensity. The rationale behind this result is that the advantage from geographical agglomeration in access to foreign markets arises only when both players are exerting their effort (cooperation in the provision of export services), while this may not be the case for those size classes and for those types of (vertical) product competition where joint effort has costs which are higher than benefits.

3   The Methodological Approach of the Empirical Analysis

The empirical analysis is carried on the Mediocredito database. The database includes a sample of more than 5000 firms drawn from the whole set of Italian manufacturing firms (64.463 firms at 1992 according to Cerved database). The sample is stratified and randomly selected (it reflects sector's geographical and dimensional distribution of Italian firms) for firms from 11 to 500 employees. It is by census for firms with more than 500 employees. For a subsample of 3852 firms both qualitative and quantitative data (balance sheets for the period 1989-1991) are collected. Qualitative data provide, among other things, information on firm property, degree of internationalisation, entitlement to state subsidies and conclusion of agreements with partners and competitors. Descriptive features of this sample illustrates some important features of Italian economy (Table 1): i) the strong specialisation in Traditional sectors compared with the very low specialisation in High-Tech sectors; ii) the relevant weight of very small firms (with no more than 50 employees) in a system where small-medium firms represent the large majority of the industrial system; iii) the striking difference between firms in the North and firms in the South which are smaller, younger and export less.

To classify firms in the sample according to their degree of geographical proximity we use a criterion of pure geographical agglomeration (Sforzi, 1995)

---

is preferred to the latter if and only if there exists a time T' such that, for all T>T', the partial sum $\sum_{t=0}^{T} g'$ strictly exceeds the partial sum $\sum_{t=0}^{T} \hat{g}^{t}$ (Fudenberg-Tirole, 1992).

Table 1. Macroregional features of the Mediocredito sample (values in %)

	North West	North East	Centre	South	Italy
Firms with 11-50 employees	31.9	37.8	46.1	49.7	37.5
Firms with 50-500 employees	53.8	54.0	45.0	43.7	51.7
Firms with more than 500 employees	14.4	8.2	8.9	6.6	10.8
	North West	North East	Centre	South	Italy
Firms with 0-10 billion liras net sales	35.1	38.7	47.7	55.7	40.0
Firms with 10-50 billion liras net sales	38.1	39.9	33.3	28.3	37.1
Firms with more than 50 billion liras net sales	26.7	21.4	18.9	16.0	22.9
	North West	North East	Centre	South	Italy
High-tech sectors	4.6	1.6	4.7	4.0	3.6
Specialised sectors	24.1	26.7	15.5	11.1	22.5
Scale sectors	28.8	27.7	27.1	28.6	28.2
Traditional sectors	40.1	42.0	49.4	53.4	43.3
Other non manufacturing	2.4	2.0	3.3	2.9	2.5
	North West	North East	Centre	South	Italy
Firm affiliated to groups	65.8	70.0	74.0	77.1	69.4
Firms participated for less than 50%	3.6	2.5	2.7	3.1	3.1
Firms participated for more than 50%	30.7	27.5	23.3	19.7	27.6
	North West	North East	Centre	South	Italy
Firms receiving subsidised credit	54.3	53.6	48.6	58.9	53.7
Firms non receiving subsidised credit	45.7	46.4	51.4	41.1	46.3
Exporting firms	77.3	73.1	61.4	40.9	70.3
Non exporting firms	22.7	26.9	38.6	59.1	29.7
Average size (n. of employees)	470	201	233	160	319
Average size (net sales in billion liras)	116	49	117	45	87
Share of exports sales on total sales	23	26	22	11	23
Average foundation year	1964	1971	1971	1974	1968

which calculates a coefficient of geographical concentration measured as the share of local employment in small medium firms in the manufacturing sector and it considers as a threshold the national average (firms are "geographically agglomerated" if they are localised in an area where the above mentioned ratio is higher than average and not otherwise). In particular geographical agglomeration (GA) is calculated as:

$$GA = (E_{m,ls} / E_{t,ls}) / (A_{m,i} / A_{t,i}) \qquad (5)$$

where $E_{m,ls}$ is the number of employees in firms with less than 250 employees for the manufacturing sector in the local system[5], $E_{t,ls}$ is the number of employees in

---

[5] For local system we simply mean the sum of adjoining councils (comuni) for which the indicator is higher than one.

the manufacturing sector in the local system, $_{Am,}i$ is the total number of employees in firms with less than 250 employees for the manufacturing sector in Italy and $_{At,}i$ is the total number of employees in the manufacturing sector in Italy.

3.1 Empirical Descriptive Results

The application of the first criterion to our sample shows that 47.7% of firms in the Mediocredito sample belong to an industrial district. Descriptive stastistics from Tab. 2 clearly show small firms' locational preference for industrial districts in all areas. Tab 3 shows a locational preference for industrial districts for firms in Traditional and Specialised sectors, but not for firms in High-Tech sectors. This is consistent with the hypothesis that some of the potential positive effects from geographical agglomeration, and specially those on export performance, are negatively related to firm size and to the degree of vertical product differentiation in the sector specific model of competition.

3.2 Descriptive Analysis of the Relationship Between Export Intensity and District Agglomeration

Tab. 4 presents descriptive evidence on differences in export intensity for firms which are geographically agglomerated and firms which are not and for firmshich belong to industrial district and firms which do not. At a national level geographical agglomeration and participation to industrial district increases average export intensity by 4 percentage points. The effect at a macroregional level ranges from 3 to 5 percentage points with the exception of the South of Italy where it is null or even slightly negative. At a macrosector level the effect is strong for Scale, Traditional and Specialised sectors, while it is negative for High-tech sectors. It seems that firms in the South and firms in High-Tech sectors correspond exactly to the two cases where $\gamma=pq$ and geographical agglomeration does not help to increase export intensity (firms in the South could have costs of access to foreign market which are too strong and High-Tech firms could suffer from too strong competition on foreign markets). Further descriptive evidence on the positive effect of geographical agglomeration is provided by Tab. 5 showing how participation to industrial district significantly increases access to EU markets.

Table 2. Sample firms by area, size and geographical agglomeration

Size	Firms belonging to GA in the North East area		Firms not belonging to GA in the North East area		Total	
	N°	%	N°	%	N°	%
Small	279	37%	203	38%	482	38%
Medium	413	56%	274	52%	687	54%
Large	50	7%	54	10%	104	8%
Total	**742**	**100%**	**531**	**100%**	**1273**	**100%**
	Firms belonging to GA in the North West area		Firms not belonging to GA in the North West area		Total	
	N°	%	N°	%	N°	%
Small	259	35%	276	29%	535	32%
Medium	420	57%	483	51%	903	54%
Large	52	7%	189	20%	241	14%
Total	**733**	**100%**	**948**	**100%**	**1679**	**100%**
	Firms belonging to GA in the Centre area		Firms not belonging to GA in the Centre area		Total	
	N°	%	N°	%	N°	%
Small	129	52%	124	42%	253	46%
Medium	121	47%	126	43%	247	45%
Large	3	1%	46	15%	49	9%
Total	**253**	**100%**	**296**	**100%**	**549**	**100%**
	Firms belonging to GA in the South area		Firms not belonging to GA in the South area		Total	
	N°	%	N°	%	N°	%
Small	32	64%	141	47%	174	50%
Medium	18	36%	135	45%	153	44%
Large	0	0	23	7%	23	6%
Total	**50**	**100%**	**299**	**100%**	**350**	**100%**

Note: small firms: firms with 0-50 employees; Medium firms: firms with 51-500 employees; Large firms: firms with more than 500 employees . To classify firms in the sample according to their degree of geographical proximity we use as an indicator of geographical agglomeration the concentration of local employment in small-medium sized manufacturing firms (Sforzi, 1995). In particular geographical agglomeration (GA) is calculated on 1991 Census data as:

$$GA = (E_{m,ls} / E_{t,ls}) / (A_{m,i} / A_{t,i})$$

where $E_{m,ls}$ is the number of employees in firms with less than 250 employees for the manufacturing sector in the local system, $E_{t,ls}$ is the number of employees in the manufacturing sector in the local system, $A_{m,i}$ is the total number of employees in firms with less than 250 employees for the manufacturing sector in Italy and $A_{t,i}$ is the total number of employees in the manufacturing sector in Italy . According to this indicator firms are classified as "geographically agglomerated" if they are localised in areas where the above mentioned ratio is higher than the national average and not otherwise.

Table 3. Locational choice by manufacturing macrosector

Sector by Pavitt classification	GA firms	NonGAfirms	Total
Scale sectors	24%	33.2%	28.8%
Specialised sectors	24.3%	21.8%	23%
Traditional sectors	50.2%	39.4%	44.6%
High-tech sectors	1.5%	5.5%	3.5%

Macroarea	NE GA	NE non GA	NW GA	NW non GA	C GA	C non GA	S GA	S non GA
Specialised	26.3%	30.6%	23.8%	34.4%	20.2%	35.0%	14.0%	33.1%
Scale	27.7%	27%	25.7%	23.0%	14.3%	17.9%	4.0%	12.7%
Traditional	44.9%	40.3%	48.8%	35.5%	64.0%	39,3%	78,0%	49.8%
High-Tech	1.109%	2.11%	1.7%	7.1%	1.6%	7.9%	4.0%	4.4%
Total n°	**742**	**531**	**731**	**948**	**253**	**296**	**51**	**299**

Note: to classify firms in the sample according to their degree of geographical proximity we use as an indicator of geographical agglomeration the concentration of local employment in small-medium sized manufacturing firms (Sforzi, 1995) . In particular geographical agglomeration (GA) is calculated on Census 1991 data as:

$$GA = (E_{m,ls} / E_{t,ls}) / (A_{m,i} / A_{t,i})$$

where $E_{m,ls}$ is the number of employees in firms with less than 250 employees for the manufacturing sector in the local system, $E_{t,ls}$ is the number of employees in the manufacturing sector in the local system, $A_{m,i}$ is the total number of employees in firms with less than 250 employees for the manufacturing sector in Italy and $A_{t,i}$ is the total number of employees in the manufacturing sector in Italy . According to this indicator firms are classified as *geographically agglomerated* if they are localised in areas where the above mentioned ratio is higher than the national average and not otherwise.

Table 4. Average export towards the EU/total sales

	ALL Firms		Firms with less than 250 employees		Firms with less than 100 employees	
	Obs.	Mean	Obs.	Mean	Obs.	Mean
All Non GA	2074	12.56*	1560	11.44*	1087	8.81*
All GA	1777	15.45*	1538	14.67*	1097	13.15*
Scale Non GA	658	12.59	462	9.85*	330	7.28*
Scale GA	421	14.51	340	12.33*	237	10.68*
Specialised Non GA	441	15.17*	349	14.40*	248	11.48*
Specialised GA	426	18.34*	377	17.65*	274	15.46*
Traditional Non GA	863	11.73*	694	11.17*	475	8.78*
Traditional GA	905	14.62*	803	14.33*	576	13.18*
North-East Non GA	531	15.57	425	14.24	306	10.74*
North-East GA	742	15.79	621	15.02	443	13.42*
North-West Non GA	948	13.07*	665	12.20*	434	9.60*

	ALL Firms		Firms with less than 250 employees		Firms with less than 100 employees	
	Obs.	Mean	Obs.	Mean	Obs.	Mean
North-West GA	731	15.76*	623	14.59*	427	13.04*
Centre Non GA	296	11.16*	221	10.01*	161	8.67*
Centre GA	253	15.07*	243	15.39*	186	14.30*
South Non GA	299	7.00	249	5.9*	186	3.89*
South GA	51	7.83	51	7.83*	41	5.96*

Table 4. Continuation.

*Subgroup means which are significantly different from each other at 99% are indicated with an asterisk.

Note: to classify firms in the sample according to their degree of geographical proximity we use as an indicator of geographical agglomeration the concentration of local employment in small-medium sized manufacturing firms (Sforzi, 1995) . In particular geographical agglomeration (GA) is calculated on 1991 Census data as:

$$GA = (E_{m,ls} / E_{t,ls}) / (A_{m,i} / A_{t,i})$$

where $E_{m,ls}$ is the number of employees in firms with less than 250 employees for the manufacturing sector in the local system, $E_{t,ls}$ is the number of employees in the manufacturing sector in the local system, $A_{m,i}$ is the total number of employees in firms with less than 250 employees for the manufacturing sector in Italy and $A_{t,i}$ is the total number of employees in the manufacturing sector in Italy . According to this indicator firms are classified as "geographically agglomerated" if they are localised in areas where the above mentioned ratio is higher than the national average and not otherwise.

Table 5. Effect of geographical agglomeration on average export intensity by macroareas and macrosectors

	Geographical agglomeration	
	No GA	GA
All Italy	21.08	25.61
North-East	24.91	27.21
North-West	22.53	25.17
Centre	19.26	24.29
South	11.45	12.01
Scale	18.84	23
Traditional	20.32	24.18
Specialised	28.85	32.7
High-Tech	16.55	14.88

4   Results from Econometric Analysis

Descriptive results do not provide conclusive evidence on the positive effect of geographical agglomeration on export intensity, as they are not controlled for dimensional sector and geographical effects. Longitudinal regressions performed try to provide a breakdown by size, macroarea and macrosector of the net effect of geographical agglomeration on export intensity and export participation. A synthetic description of the results is presented in Tables 6-7 while full results are presented in Appendix. Tab. 6 presents coefficients and T-statistics on the net impact of geographical agglomeration (GA) on export intensity from the following Tobit specification respectively testing for the impact of industrial district:

$$Exp/fatt = \alpha_0 + \sum_{i=1}^{22}\alpha_i Dset_i + \sum_{i=1}^{3}\gamma_k Darea_k + \beta_1 Size +$$

$$+ \beta_2 Consex + \beta_3 Subex + \beta_4 Birth + \beta_5 Group + \beta_6 GA + \varepsilon \qquad (6)$$

where *Exp/fatt* is the three year (1989-91) average of the share of export sales on total sales, *Dset* are 22 sector dummies, *Darea* are three macroarea dummies, *ID* is a dummy which takes value of 1 if the firm belongs to an industrial district and zero otherwise, *Size* is the three year (1989-91) average of firm's employees, *Birth* is the firm's foundation year, *Consex* and *Subex* are two dummies which pick up respectively firms participating to export "consortia"[6] and firms receiving export subsidies, *Group* is a dummy which takes value of one for firms affiliated to groups (subsidiaries or parent companies) and zero otherwise.

Table 6. Percentage of firms exporting toward EU by size and geographical agglomeration

Firms/ size	N°Obs	% exporters toward EU countries	Standard deviation	95% confidence interval
Small GA firms	700	35.34	41.21	32.28 - 38.40
Small non GA firms	696	27.94	39.99	24.96 - 30.92
Medium GA firms	972	54.92	35.77	52.67 - 57.17
Medium non GA firms	973	50.47	38.51	48.05 - 52.90
Large GA	105	62.03	30.76	56.08 - 67.99
Large nonGA firms	294	52.54	35.66	48.45 - 56.64
Total	3740	45.09	39.70	43.82 - 46.36

---

[6] Export consortia are contractual agreeements ruled by Italian Civil Law among firms which choose to cooperate, to provide common funds and to share information for the development of their exports. They may lead or not to the creation of an independent corporation even though constituents always maintain their independent identity. Consortia differ from cartels and are tolerated by antitrust authorities because their goal is not to restrict competition by altering prices or quantities but just to cooperate in order to improve their export performance. Consortia may then be considered a type of formal cooperation for export services, while geographical agglomeration represents a type of informal cooperation.

Table 7. The marginal impact of geographical agglomeration on export intensity -
Synthesis of empirical results

Sample	All firms	Firms with less than 500 employees	Firms with less than 300 employees	Firms with less than 100 employees
All firms	3.39	4.31	4.32	7.43
	(2.76)	(3.30)	(3.08)	(4.09)
North-East	4.53	4.42	5.93	9.58
	(2.14)	(2.02)	(2.47)	(3.10)
North-West	5.29	6.16	4.59	7.25
	(3.19)	(3.43)	(2.39)	(2.91)
Centre	11.61	11.61	13.39	11.06
	(2.73)	(2.73)	(2.84)	(1.85)
Traditional sectors	5.93	6.62	6.54	10.14
	(3.03)	(3.22)	(2.98)	(3.53)
Specialised sectors	6.54	7.77	8.02	9.87
	(2.72)	(3.22)	(3.15)	(3.03)
Scale sectors	3.88	4.30	3.93	4.33
	(1.67)	(1.68)	(1.39)	(1.17)

Note: The table reports magnitude and T-statistics (in parenthesis) for the district dummy coefficient, β_1, in the following regression:

$$Exp/\,fatt = \alpha_0 + \sum_{i=1}^{22}\alpha_i Dset_i + \sum_{i=1}^{3}\gamma_k Darea_k + \beta_1 Size + $$

(7)

$$\beta_2 Consex + \beta_3 Subex + \beta_4 Birth + \beta_5 Group + \beta_6 GA + \varepsilon$$

where *Exp/fatt* is the three year (1989-91) average of the share of export sales on total sales, *Dset* are 22 sector dummies, *Darea* are 3 macroarea dummies (North-East, North-West, Centre, South), *GA* is a dummy which takes value of 1 if the firm is located in an area where the coefficient of geographical agglomeration is higher than 1, *Size* is the three year (1989-91) average of firm's employees, *Birth* is firm's year of foundation, *Consex* and *Subex* are two dummies which pick up respectively firm's participation to export "consortia" and firm's obtainment of export subsidies, *Group* is a dummy which takes value of one for firms affiliated to groups (subsidiaries or parent companies) and zero otherwise.

Vertical and horizontal headers for any of table cells indicate the subsample on which the regression is performed. The table then provides the net impact of participation to industrial district on export intensity for 36 different subsamples discriminating the overall set of firms by macroareas, macrosectors and size classes.

The regression is longitudinal and the dependent variable is expressed in percentage points so that any significant coefficient of the industrial district effect on export intensity indicates a net effect in percentage points on the sample average export intensity. Full econometric results for any of the performed regressions are provided in the Appendix.

Empirical results seem to show that: i) geographical agglomeration significantly affects export intensity in the regression including all macroareas and in the regression for Scale and Traditional sectors for almost all classes (the net effect ranges between 3 and 5 percentage points); ii) the positive effect of geographical agglomeration is decreasing in firm's size (the difference may range from 3 to 7 points according to macroareas and macrosectors considered); iii) firms participating to export consortia and receiving export subsidies export significantly more. The first two results support the idea presented in the theoretical model that the advantage of cooperation for the access to foreign markets is significantly higher when costs of sharing the market with partners are low. This is more likely to occur for smaller firms and in sectors with horizontal product differentiation more than in sectors with vertical product differentiation.

Tab. 8 presents results on the impact of GA on "export participation" (a variable which takes value of one for exporters and zero for non exporters) from multivariate logits performed by macrosector, macroarea and size classes using the following specification for the analysis of the impact of geographical agglomeration:

$$Expart = \alpha_0 + \sum_{i=1}^{22} \alpha_i DSet_i + \sum_{k=1}^{3} \alpha_k Darea_k + \beta_1 GA +$$
$$+ \beta_2 Size + \beta_3 Consex + \beta_4 Subex + \varepsilon$$
(8)

where Export participation is a dummy which takes value of one if the firm exported in the period 1989-91 and zero otherwise, and other variables are defined as in the two Tobit regressions whose specification is described by (6) and (7).

Table 8. The marginal impact of geographical agglomeration on export participation-Synthesis of empirical results

Sample	All firms	Firms with less than 500 employees	Firms with less than 300 employees	Firms with less than 100 employees
All firms	0.35	0.35	0.32	0.35
	(15.65)	(13.84)	(10.98)	(10.02)
North-East	0.34	0.28	0.27	0.33
	(5.51)	(3.29)	(2.92)	(3.37)
North-West	0.27	0.29	0.21	0.24
	(3.53)	(3.81)	(1.86)	(1.72)
Centre	0.48	0.6	0.6	0.47
	(4.6)	(6.3)	(6.16)	(2.99)
Traditional sectors	0.32	0.32	0.29	0.37
	(6.87)	(5.98)	(4.91)	(5.75)
Specialised sectors	0.48	0.51	0.5	0.48
	(4.98)	(5.46)	(4.95)	(3.79)
Scale sectors	0.36	0.33	0.29	0.27
	(4.1)	(3.14)	(2.34)	(1.41)
High-tech sectors	0.42	0.21	0.33	1.55
	(0.38)	(0.08)	(0.2)	(0.82)

Note: The table reports coefficient and T-statistics for the geographical agglomeration dummy in a logit which controls for macrosector, size and other variables

$$Expart = \alpha_0 + \sum_{i=1}^{22} \alpha_i DSet_i + \sum_{k=1}^{3} \gamma_k Darea_k + \beta_1 GA + \beta_2 Size +$$

$$\beta_3 Consex + \beta_4 Subex + \varepsilon$$ (9)

where *Export participation* is a dummy which takes value of one if the firm has nonzero export sales on foreign markets as a three year (1989-91) average, *Dset* are 22 sector dummies, *Darea* are 3 macroarea dummies (North-East, North-West, Centre, South), *GA* is a dummy which takes value of 1 if the firm located in an area where the coefficient of geographical agglomeration is higher than 1, *Size* is the three year (1989-91) average of firm's employees, *Age* is firm foundation year, *Consex* and *Subex* are two dummies which pick up respectively firm's participation to export "consortia" and firm's obtainment of export subsidies.

Vertical and horizontal headers for any of table cells indicate the subsample on which the regression is performed. The table then provides the net impact of participation to industrial district on export intensity for 36 different subsamples discriminating the overall set of firms by macroareas, macrosectors and size classes.

Full econometric results are provided in the Appendix.

Results on Export participation are consistent with those on export intensity, even though geographical agglomeration and participation to industrial district have in this case significant effects on export participation also in macroareas (Centre and North-West) and macrosectors (Specialised sectors) where agglomeration did not affect firms in terms of export intensity.

5   Conclusions

Industrial districts are generally intended as geographical agglomerations of small-medium firms which decide to locate themselves next to each other when Marshallian externalities generated by proximity of potential competitors are higher than costs from increased competition.

It is general opinion among economists that one of the major benefits of this distinctive and well-established form of industrial development is the provision of export services for small-medium firms that may in this way overcome the fixed cost threshold that prevents their access to foreign markets. Very few empirical evidence at micro level demonstrated so far the validity of this hypothesis.

The paper investigates theoretically and empirically the validity of the positive relationship between participation to "Marshallian district" and access or intensity of firm's exports.

The theoretical section of the paper tackles the issue in a game theoretic framework in which the decision of small-medium firm players to cooperate or not in the provision of export services affects export performance in a different way according to the degree of their geographical proximity and to the model of product competition. The main result of this section is to show that geographical agglomeration may generate additional benefits only when firms find it advantageous to cooperate. This is more likely to occur for small firms and firms in sectors characterised by horizontal product differentiation. The rationale of this theoretical hypothesis is that the lower is the negative externality arising from the export activity of one's neighbour, the higher is the incentive to cooperate in the provision of export services. The empirical prediction stemming from this hypothesis is that gains from geographical proximity, in terms of export intensity or export participation, are inversely proportional to firm size and to the degree of vertical product differentiation in sector-specific competition.

Empirical findings presented in the paper are consistent with this prediction as they show that geographical agglomeration significantly increases export intensity and export participation of small medium firms. The result is robust when controlled for firm size, sector and geographical areas and for the separate and positive effects of export subsidies and export "consortia" on export intensity and export participation. In almost all cases geographical agglomeration benefits on export performance are higher for firms belonging to small size classes and to sectors in which horizontal product differentiation prevails over vertical product differentiation.

References

Aumann R. and Shapley L., 1976, Long Term Competition - a Game Theoretic Analysis, mimeo.

Bagella M. and Becchetti L., 1996, "Business Cycle and Growth in an Economy with Financial Market Imperfections", in E.Phelps, M.Baldassarri, L.Paganetto (eds.) "Finance, Research, Education and Growth" Mc Millan.

Bagella M., Becchetti L. and Caggese, A., 1996, "Finanza, Investimenti ed Innovazione in Italia: il divario Nord-South" in B.Quintieri (ed.) "Finanza, Istituzioni e sviluppo regionale: il problema del Mezzogiorno", Il Mulino.

Becattini G.,1987, *Mercato e Forze Locali: Il Distretto Industriale*, Bologna, Il Mulino.

Bellandi M., 1996, Innovation and Change in the Marshallian Industrial District, European Planning Studies, 4, 357-366.

Bianchi P., 1989, *Concorrenza Dinamica, Distretti Industriali e Interventi Locali*, In F. Gobbo Distretti Industriali e sistemi produttivi alla soglia degli anni '90, Milano, F. Angeli.

D'Aspremont C., Gabszewicz J.J., Thisse J.F., 1979, "On Hotelling's "stability in competition"", *Econometrica*, Vol.47.

Fudenberg D. and Tirole J.J., 1992, Game Theory, MIT Press, Cambridge Massachussets

Goffman E., 1988, *L'interazione Strategica*, Bologna, Il Mulino.

Mistri M., 1993, *Distretti Industriali e Mercato Unico Europeo,* Istituto G Tagliacarne, Milano, F. Angeli.

Hotelling. H., 1929, "Stability in competition", *Economic Journal*. Vol. 39.

Momigliano F. and Dosi G., 1983, *Tecnologia e organizzazione Industriale Internazionale*, Bologna, Il Mulino.

Nuti F., 1992, I Distretti Industriali Manifatturieri, Vol.1, CNR.

Onida F., Viesti G. and Falzoni A.M., 1992, *Distretti Industriali: Crisi o Evoluzione?,* CESPRI, Egea,1992.

Porter M., 1991, *Il vantaggio Competitivo delle Nazioni*, Milano, Mondadori.

Pyke F. and Sengenberger W., 1992, *Industrial District and local Economic Regeneration*, Geneva, International Institute for labour Studies.

Rubinstein A., 1979, Equilibrium in Supergames with the Overtaking Criterion, *Journal of Economic Theory*, 21, 1-9.

Sforzi F., 1991, Sistemi Locali di Piccola e Media Impresa, IRPET.

Sforzi F., 1995, *Sistemi Locali di Impresa e Cambiamento Industriale in Italia*, AGEI-Geotema n°2.

Shaked A. and Sutton J., 1983, "Natural oligopolies", *Econometrica*, Vol. 51.

Appendix: Extended Empirical Results

Export participation and geographical agglomeration model

The table reports magnitude and T-statistics (in parenthesis) for coefficients of the following regression:

$$Exp/fatt = \alpha_0 + \sum_{i=1}^{22} \alpha_i Dset_i + \sum_{i=1}^{3} \gamma_k Darea_k + \beta_1 Size +$$

$$+ \beta_2 Consex + \beta_3 Subex + \beta_4 Birth + \beta_5 Group + \beta_6 GA + \varepsilon$$

where $Exp/fatt$ is the three year (1989-91) average of the share of export sales on total sales, $Dset$ are 22 sector dummies, $Darea$ are 3 macroarea dummies (North-East, North-West, Centre, South), GA is a dummy which takes value of 1 if the firm is located in an area where the coefficient of geographical agglomeration is higher than 1 and zero otherwise, $Size$ is the three year (1989-91) average of firm's employees, $Birth$ is firm's year of foundation, $Consex$ and $Subex$ are two dummies which pick up respectively firm's participation to export "consortia" and firm's obtainment of export subsidies, $Group$ is a dummy which takes value of one for firms affiliated to groups (subsidiaries or parent companies) and zero otherwise.

Vertical headers for any of table cells indicate the subsample on which the regression is performed.

The regression is longitudinal and the dependent variable is expressed in percentage points so that any significant coefficient of the industrial district effect on export intensity indicates a net effect in percentage points on the sample average export intensity.

Legend of sector dummies:

Dset1: Non-metallic mineral products; Dset2: Chemicals; Dset2: Pharmaceuticals; Dset4: Artificial fibres; Dset5: Metal products; Dset6: Mechanical Equipment; Dset7: Office equipment and computers; Dset8: Electronics and electrical equipment; Dset 9: Vehicles and vehicle components; Dset10: Other means of transport; Dset11 Precision instruments and apparels; Dset12: Food; Dset13: Sugar, tobacco, etc...; Dset14: Textile; Dset15: Leather: Dset16: Shoes and clothing; Dset17: Wood and wooden furniture; Dset18: Paper and printing; Dset19: Rubber and plastics; Dset 20: Other manufacturing; dset21: Other non manufacturing; Dset22; Electrical measure, equipment and telecommunications; Dset23: Aerospace.

Table A.1 Tobit estimates on the determinants of export participation in Italy

	All firms		Firms with less than 500 employees		Firms with less than 250 employees		Firms with less than 100 employees	
	Coeff.	T stat	Coeff.	T stat	Coeff.	T stat	Coeff.	T stat
Birth	-0.12	-4.69	-0.09	-3.33	-0.08	-2.46	-0.10	-2.69
CONSEX (Export Consortia)	16.17	5.72	17.80	6.11	17.11	5.71	18.15	4.66
SUBEX (Export subsidies)	19.82	6.84	22.78	6.63	23.21	6.02	18.68	3.21
Size	0.00	2.72	0.07	10.92	0.14	12.36	0.36	10.61
Non-metallic mineral products	1.82	0.17	12.97	1.02	21.52	0.80	16.17	0.56
Chemicals	8.14	0.76	17.46	1.36	27.40	1.02	20.10	0.70
Pharmaceuticals	-1.17	-0.10	11.55	0.81	23.57	0.85	17.20	0.54
Artificial fibres	-3.96	-0.25	-21.91	-1.02	-34.81	-0.99	-192.14	-
Metal products	4.73	0.45	16.52	1.32	26.39	0.99	19.89	0.70
Mechanical Equipment	24.19	2.31	34.52	2.76	43.35	1.62	35.85	1.26
Office equipment, computers	-19.96	-1.47	-10.79	-0.62	-1.12	-0.04	2.18	0.07
Electronics, electrical equipment	10.79	1.03	20.29	1.61	31.30	1.17	25.17	0.88
Vehicles, vehicle components	12.85	1.15	13.64	1.01	23.48	0.86	19.06	0.64
Other means of transport	12.04	0.96	20.45	1.35	26.10	0.91	13.37	0.40
Precision instruments, apparels	14.59	1.28	23.69	1.75	35.70	1.30	28.65	0.97
Food	-6.80	-0.63	5.51	0.43	14.28	0.53	9.08	0.31
Sugar, tobacco, etc	-8.69	-0.77	2.08	0.16	13.37	0.49	20.23	0.69
Textile	5.96	0.57	15.13	1.21	24.63	0.92	17.03	0.59
Leather	29.24	2.59	41.04	3.11	50.77	1.88	43.06	1.48
Shoes, clothing	16.66	1.58	26.79	2.14	36.73	1.37	32.06	1.12
Wood, wooden furniture	8.35	0.78	19.87	1.56	28.63	1.07	17.56	0.61
Paper, printing	-17.22	-1.63	-5.80	-0.46	3.84	0.14	-3.92	-0.14
Rubber, plastics	11.36	1.07	23.33	1.84	33.77	1.26	24.87	0.87
Other manufacturing	14.10	1.32	25.97	2.05	35.66	1.33	32.87	1.14
Other non manufacturing	-23.46	-2.10	-24.55	-1.80	-10.18	-0.37	-28.97	-0.97
Electrical measure, equipment, telecommunications	-11.27	-0.90	5.76	0.39	15.07	0.53	15.82	0.51
Group	8.09	6.19	2.44	1.59	1.79	1.05	-1.44	-0.58
North-West	19.70	8.35	20.22	8.01	20.67	7.56	22.57	6.41
North-Easth	21.18	8.78	21.03	8.21	21.59	7.81	22.89	6.45
Centre	15.62	5.88	17.06	6.03	17.92	5.90	20.63	5.32
GA location	3.39	2.76	4.31	3.30	4.32	3.08	7.43	4.09
Constant	100.08	3.73	57.87	1.90	24.84	0.62	45.43	0.96
Left censored observations		1131		1083		1037		884
Uncensored observations		2550		2197		1918		1204
Right censored observations		15		15		15		8
χ^2		727.21		794.11		741.62		508.79
Log Likelihood		-13429.5		-11615.3		-10216.8		-6579.09

Note: The table reports magnitude and T-statistics of the following Probit estimate:

$$Expl\ fatt = \alpha_0 + \sum_{i=1}^{22} \alpha_i Dset_i + \sum_{i=1}^{3} \gamma_k Darea_k + \beta_1 Size +$$

$$+ \beta_2 Consex + \beta_3 Subex + \beta_4 Birth + \beta_5 Group + \beta_6 GA + \varepsilon$$

where *Expart* is a dummy variable which takes the value of zero if the firm has a nonzero three year (1989-91) average of the share of export sales on total sales. $Dset_i$ are 22 sector dummies, $Darea_k$ are 3 macroarea dummies (NEST, NOVEST, CENTRE), *GA* is a dummy which takes value of 1 if the firm is located in an area where the coefficient of geographical agglomeration is higher than 1 and zero otherwise, *Birth* is firm's year of foundation, *Size* is the three year (1989-91) average of firm's employees, *Consex* and *Subex* are two dummies which pick up respectively firms participating to export "consortia" and firms receiving export subsidies, *Group* is a dummy which takes value of one for firms affiliated to groups (subsidiaries or parent companies) and zero otherwise.

Vertical headers for any of table cells indicate the subsample on which the regression is performed. Coefficients significant at 99% are in bold. Estimate disturbances are controlled for normality and heteroskedasticity.

Table A.2 Dependent variable: export sales over total sales: North-East.

	All firms		Firms with less than 500 employees		Firms with less than 250 employees		Firms with less than 100 employees	
	Coeff.	T stat	Coeff.	T stat	Coeff	T stat	Coeff	T stat
Birth	-0.14	-2.38	-0.06	-0.88	-0.008	-0.10	-0.02	-0.17
CONSEX (Export Consortia)	21.81	4.63	24.19	5.13	23.16	4.71	25.85	4.06
SUBEX (Export subsidies)	21.36	4.38	19.66	3.63	22.17	3.56	18.67	2.09
Size	0.004	2.75	0.09	8.13	0.17	8.65	0.40	7.18
Special	28.95	3.46	26.79	2.72	27.75	2.63	18.43	1.35
Scale	7.44	0.89	4.73	0.48	6.04	0.57	-3.85	-0.28
Traditional	10.39	1.25	10.28	1.05	12.97	1.24	6.26	0.46
Group	4.59	1.99	-1.23	-0.48	-2.53	-0.89	-2.74	-0.70
GA location	4.53	2.14	4.42	2.02	5.93	2.47	9.58	3.10
Constant	130.36	2.35	45.35	0.73	-9.81	-0.14	-6.24	-0.07
Left censored observations	341		331		319		281	
Uncensored observations	871		778		671		432	
Right censored observations	6		6		6		4	
χ^2	158.23		197.07		123.12		123.12	
Log Likelihood	-4621.44		-4123.32		-2373.86		-2373.86	

Note: The table reports magnitude and T-statistics of the following Tobit estimate:

$$Exp/ fatt = \alpha_0 + \sum_{i=1}^{3} \alpha_i Dset_i + \beta_1 Size + \beta_2 Consex +$$

$$+ \beta_3 Subex + \beta_4 Birth + \beta_5 Group + \beta_6 GA + \varepsilon$$

where *Exp/fatt* is the three year (1989-91) average of the share of export sales on total sales. The dependent variable is left censored at 0 and righ censored at 1. *Dset_i* are 3 macrosector dummies, , GA is a dummy which takes value of 1 if the firm is located in an area where the coefficient of geographical agglomeration is higher than 1 and zero otherwise, *Birth* is firm's year of foundation, *Size* is the three year (1989-91) average of firm's employees, *Consex* and *Subex* are two dummies which pick up respectively firms participating to export "consortia" and firms receiving export subsidies, *Group* is a dummy which takes value of one for firms affiliated to groups (subsidiaries or parent companies) and zero otherwise.

Vertical headers for any of table cells indicate the subsample on which the regression is performed. Coefficients significant at 99% are in bold. Estimate disturbances are controlled for normality and heteroskedasticity.

Tabble A.3 Dependent variable: export sales over total sales: North-West

	All firms		Firms with less than 500 employees		Firms with less than 250 employees		Firms with less than 100 employees	
	Coeff.	T stat	Coeff.	T stat	Coeff.	T stat	Coeff	T stat
Birth	-0.07	-2.46	-0.08	-2.49	-0.06	-1.76	-0.09	-2.28
CONSEX (Export Consortia)	10.49	2.43	11.17	2.49	11.23	2.45	12.19	1.92
SUBEX (Export subsidies)	16.30	4.20	20.51	4.23	17.45	3.24	14.53	1.75
Size	0.0007	1.28	0.06	7.04	0.13	7.97	0.30	5.97
Special	8.89	2.10	0.50	0.09	-0.84	-0.14	1.18	0.15
Scale	18.17	4.33	13.63	2.58	12.31	2.11	10.92	1.39
Traditional	7.48	1.77	0.84	0.16	-0.59	-0.10	-2.29	-0.30
Group	8.34	4.71	2.63	1.23	1.71	0.73	0.53	0.15
GA location	5.29	3.19	6.16	3.43	4.59	2.39	7.25	2.91
Constant	70.16	2.52	79.67	2.51	57.52	1.71	80.29	2.00
Left censored observations	380		358		341		284	
Uncensored observations	1229		1024		895		539	
Right censored observations	3		3		3		3	
χ^2	102.59		149.59		143.73		84.86	
Log Likelihood	-6307.73		-5290.21		-4648.17		-2870.55	

Note: The table reports magnitude and T-statistics of the following Tobit estimate:

$$Exp/\ fatt = \alpha_0 + \sum_{i=1}^{3} \alpha_i Dset_i + \beta_1 Size + \beta_2 Consex +$$

$$+ \beta_3 Subex + \beta_4 Birth + \beta_5 Group + \beta_6 GA + \varepsilon$$

where *Exp/fatt* is the three year (1989-91) average of the share of export sales on total sales. The dependent variable is left censored at 0 and righ censored at 1. *Dset$_i$* are 3 macrosector dummies, , GA is a dummy which takes value of 1 if the firm is located in an area where the coefficient of geographical agglomeration is higher than 1 and zero otherwise, *Birth* is firm's year of foundation, *Size* is the three year (1989-91) average of firm's employees, *Consex* and *Subex* are two dummies which pick up respectively firms participating to export "consortia" and firms receiving export subsidies, *Group* is a dummy which takes value of one for firms affiliated to groups (subsidiaries or parent companies) and zero otherwise.

Vertical headers for any of table cells indicate the subsample on which the regression is performed. Coefficients significant at 99% are in bold. Estimate disturbances are controlled for normality and heteroskedasticity.

Table A.4 Dependent variable: export sales over total sales: Centre

	All firms		Firms with less than 500 employees		Firms with less than 250 employees		Firms with less than 100 employees	
	Coeff.	T stat	Coeff.	T stat	Coeff.	T stat	Coeff.	T stat
Birth	-0.08	-0.68	-0.08	-0.68	-0.02	-0.16	-0.01	-0.04
CONSEX (Export Consortia)	30.12	3.70	30.12	3.70	31.26	3.63	29.04	2.78
SUBEX (Export subsidies)	31.70	2.59	31.70	2.59	41.20	2.60	54.71	2.29
Size	0.004	1.58	0.004	1.58	0.21	5.06	0.59	4.96
Special	1.34	0.14	1.34	0.14	3.61	0.24	6.18	0.26
Scale	16.88	0.10	16.88	0.10	23.50	1.55	32.02	1.31
Traditional	10.86	1.14	10.86	1.14	19.77	1.37	28.80	1.21
Group	13.02	2.74	13.02	2.74	-0.48	-0.08	-20.33	-1.96
GA location	11.61	2.73	11.61	2.73	13.39	2.84	11.06	1.85
Constant	62.58	0.56	62.58	0.56	-12.19	-0.09	-45.77	-0.22
Left censored observations	211		201		193		165	
Uncensored observations	312		273		247		166	
Right censored observations	5		5		5		3	
χ^2	47.46		65.88		75.92		67.68	
Log Likelihood	-1770.21		-1557.63		-1415.79		-973.77	

Note: The table reports magnitude and T-statistics of the following Tobit estimate:

$$Expl\ fatt = \alpha_0 + \sum_{i=1}^{3} \alpha_i Dset_i + \beta_1 Size + \beta_2 Consex + \beta_3 Subex +$$

$$\beta_4 Birth + \beta_5 Group + \beta_6 GA + \varepsilon$$

where *Exp/fatt* is the three year (1989-91) average of the share of export sales on total sales. The dependent variable is left censored at 0 and righ censored at 1. *Dset_i* are 3 macrosector dummies, , GA is a dummy which takes value of 1 if the firm is located in an area where the coefficient of geographical agglomeration is higher than 1 and zero otherwise, *Birth* is firm's year of foundation, *Size* is the three year (1989-91) average of firm's employees, *Consex* and *Subex* are two dummies which pick up respectively firms participating to export "consortia" and firms receiving export subsidies, *Group* is a dummy which takes value of one for firms affiliated to groups (subsidiaries or parent companies) and zero otherwise.

Vertical headers for any of table cells indicate the subsample on which the regression is performed. Coefficients significant at 99% are in bold. Estimate disturbances are controlled for normality and heteroskedasticity.

Table A.5 Dependent variable: export sales over total sales: Traditional sectors

	All firms		Firms with less than 500 employees		Firms with less than 250 employees		Firms with less than 100 employees	
	Coeff.	T stat	Coeff.	T stat	Coeff.	T stat	Coeff.	T stat
Birth	-0.12	-3.48	-0.11	-2.80	-0.11	-2.69	-0.15	-3.09
CONSEX (Export Consortia)	21.33	4.96	21.69	4.86	20.37	4.47	20.92	3.53
SUBEX (Export subsidies)	29.61	5.29	36.34	5.49	38.00	5.31	42.85	3.92
Size	0.00	0.68	0.07	6.92	0.15	8.26	0.35	6.42
Special	15.81	4.56	15.03	4.16	15.52	3.98	14.22	2.87
Scale	16.86	4.74	16.89	4.57	18.74	4.73	19.06	3.79
Traditional	15.79	4.05	17.92	4.40	20.14	4.65	22.55	4.16
Group	5.18	2.32	0.70	0.28	0.38	0.14	0.61	0.15
GA location	5.93	3.03	6.62	3.22	6.54	2.98	10.14	3.53
Constant	111.97	3.20	87.58	2.34	83.66	2.09	111.70	2.33
Left censored observations	576		561		534		451	
Uncensored observations	1115		1016		897		559	
Right censored observations	13		13		13		6	
χ^2	127.4		169.41		190.57		131.18	
Log Likelihood	-6062.06		-5548.14		-4924.36		-3159.44	

Note: The table reports magnitude and T-statistics of the following Tobit estimate:

$$Exp/\ fatt = \alpha_0 + \sum_{i=1}^{3} \alpha_i Dset_i + \beta_1 Size + \beta_2 Consex + \beta_3 Subex +$$

$$\beta_4 Birth + \beta_5 Group + \beta_6 GA + \varepsilon$$

where *Exp/fatt* is the three year (1989-91) average of the share of export sales on total sales. The dependent variable is left censored at 0 and righ censored at 1. *Dset$_i$* are 3 macrosector dummies, , GA is a dummy which takes value of 1 if the firm is located in an area where the coefficient of geographical agglomeration is higher than 1 and zero otherwise, *Birth* is firm's year of foundation, *Size* is the three year (1989-91) average of firm's employees, *Consex* and *Subex* are two dummies which pick up respectively firms participating to export "consortia" and firms receiving export subsidies, *Group* is a dummy which takes value of one for firms affiliated to groups (subsidiaries or parent companies) and zero otherwise.

Vertical headers for any of table cells indicate the subsample on which the regression is performed. Coefficients significant at 99% are in bold. Estimate disturbances are controlled for normality and heteroskedasticity.

Table A.6 Dependent variable: export sales over total sales: Scale sectors

	All firms		Firms with less than 500 employees		Firms with less than 250 employees		Firms with less than 100 employees	
	Coeff.	T stat	Coeff.	T stat	Coeff.	T stat	Coeff.	T stat
Birth	0.02	0.33	0.04	0.53	0.12	1.44	0.02	0.22
CONSEX (Export Consortia)	15.59	2.44	21.64	3.17	19.52	2.76	30.50	2.99
SUBEX (Export subsidies)	7.63	1.28	9.39	1.21	9.06	1.01	6.93	0.58
Size	0.00	2.66	0.09	7.17	0.18	7.73	0.49	6.88
Special	22.16	5.04	23.16	4.71	24.67	4.63	29.80	4.07
Scale	18.94	4.15	19.47	3.85	19.94	3.63	19.77	2.65
Traditional	11.04	2.19	11.52	2.05	11.82	1.94	11.23	1.35
Group	12.57	5.44	1.81	0.61	-0.20	-0.06	-3.04	-0.61
GA location	3.88	1.67	4.30	1.68	3.93	1.39	4.33	1.17
Constant	-30.95	-0.57	-60.05	-0.86	-144.98	-1.81	-70.33	-0.63
Left censored observations	351		336		324		277	
Uncensored observations	678		520		438		261	
Right censored observations	1		1		1		1	
χ^2	101.29		119.65		113.09		95.41	
Log Likelihood	-3599.08		-2791.72		-2382.35		-1467.23	

Note: The table reports magnitude and T-statistics of the following Tobit estimate:

$$Expl\ fatt = \alpha_0 + \sum_{i=1}^{3} \alpha_i Dset_i + \beta_1 Size + \beta_2 Consex + \beta_3 Subex +$$

$$\beta_4 Birth + \beta_5 Group + \beta_6 GA + \varepsilon$$

where *Exp/fatt* is the three year (1989-91) average of the share of export sales on total sales. The dependent variable is left censored at 0 and righ censored at 1. *Dset$_i$* are 3 macrosector dummies, , GA is a dummy which takes value of 1 if the firm is located in an area where the coefficient of geographical agglomeration is higher than 1 and zero otherwise, *Birth* is firm's year of foundation, *Size* is the three year (1989-91) average of firm's employees, *Consex* and *Subex* are two dummies which pick up respectively firms participating to export "consortia" and firms receiving export subsidies, *Group* is a dummy which takes value of one for firms affiliated to groups (subsidiaries or parent companies) and zero otherwise.

Vertical headers for any of table cells indicate the subsample on which the regression is performed. Coefficients significant at 99% are in bold. Estimate disturbances are controlled for normality and heteroskedasticity.

Table A.7 Dependent variable:export sales over total sales. Specialised sectors

	All Firms		Firms with less than 500 employees		Firms with less than 250 employees		Firms with less than 100 employees	
	Coeff.	T stat	Coeff.	T stat	Coeff.	T stat	Coeff.	T stat
Birth	-0.17	-2.73	-0.05	-0.75	0.04	0.51	0.15	1.28
CONSEX (Export Consortia)	14.66	2.77	16.00	3.13	16.51	3.13	19.65	3.02
SUBEX (Export subsidies)	23.30	4.99	19.52	3.87	17.72	3.09	10.44	1.16
Size	0.01	2.60	0.10	7.34	0.19	8.08	0.42	6.88
Special	31.57	4.86	34.09	5.13	29.08	4.19	27.94	3.33
Scale	40.40	6.14	38.73	5.76	32.80	4.66	30.11	3.55
Traditional	25.76	3.52	28.63	3.85	22.62	2.91	22.89	2.44
Group	4.20	1.62	-1.84	-0.66	-3.62	-1.21	-7.59	-1.84
GA location	6.54	2.72	7.77	3.22	8.02	3.15	9.87	3.03
Constant	152.96	2.49	28.61	0.42	-62.05	-0.80	-178.55	-1.56
Left censored observations	166		159		154		139	
Uncensored observations	666		603		539		360	
Right censored observations	1		1		1		1	
χ^2	134.31		170.75		152.95		100.03	
Log Likelihood	-3417.34		-3072.58		-2756.4		-1878.09	

Note: The table reports magnitude and T-statistics of the following Tobit estimate:

$$Expl\ fatt = \alpha_0 + \sum_{i=1}^{3} \alpha_i Dset_i + \beta_1 Size + \beta_2 Consex + \beta_3 Subex +$$

$$\beta_4 Birth + \beta_5 Group + \beta_6 GA + \varepsilon$$

where *Exp/fatt* is the three year (1989-91) average of the share of export sales on total sales. The dependent variable is left censored at 0 and righ censored at 1. *Dset$_i$* are 3 macrosector dummies, , GA is a dummy which takes value of 1 if the firm is located in an area where the coefficient of geographical agglomeration is higher than 1 and zero otherwise, *Birth* is firm's year of foundation, *Size* is the three year (1989-91) average of firm's employees, *Consex* and *Subex* are two dummies which pick up respectively firms participating to export "consortia" and firms receiving export subsidies, *Group* is a dummy which takes value of one for firms affiliated to groups (subsidiaries or parent companies) and zero otherwise.

Vertical headers for any of table cells indicate the subsample on which the regression is performed. Coefficients significant at 99% are in bold. Estimate disturbances are controlled for normality and heteroskedasticity.

Export Participation and Geographical Agglomeration

The table reports coefficient and T-statistics for the geographical agglomeration dummy in a logit which controls for macrosector, size and other variables

$$Expart = \alpha_0 + \sum_{i=1}^{22} \alpha_i DSet_i + \sum_{k=1}^{3} \gamma_k Darea_k + \beta_1 GA +$$
$$+ \beta_2 Size + \beta_3 Consex + \beta_4 Subex + \varepsilon$$

where *Export participation* is a dummy which takes value of one if firms has nonzero export sales on foreign markets as a the three year (1989-91), *Dset* are 22 sector dummies, *Darea* are 3 macroarea dummies (North-East, North-West, Centre, South), *GA* is a dummy which takes value of 1 if the firm belongs to an geographical agglomeration and zero otherwise, *Size* is the three year (1989-91) average of firm's employees, *Consex* and *Subex* are two dummies which pick up respectively firm's participation to export "consortia" and firm's obtainment of export subsidies.

Vertical headers indicate the subsample on which the regression is performed. The table then provides the net impact of participation to industrial district on export intensity for 36 different subsamples discriminating the overall set of firms by macroarea, macrosector and size class.

Legend of sector dummies:

Dset1: Non-metallic mineral products; Dset2: Chemicals; Dset2: Pharmaceuticals; Dset4: Artificial fibres; Dset5: Metal products; Dset6: Mechanical Equipment; Dset7: Office equipment and computers; Dset8: Electronics and electrical equipment; Dset9: Vehicles and vehicle components; Dset10: Other means of transport; Dset11 Precision instruments and apparels; Dset12: Food; Dset13: Sugar, tobacco, etc...; Dset14: Textile; Dset15:

Leather: Dset16: Shoes and clothing; Dset17: Wood and wooden furniture; Dset18: Paper and printing; Dset19: Rubber and plastics; Dset 20: Other manufacturing; Dset21: Other non manufacturing; Dset22; Electrical measure, equipment and telecommunications; Dset23: Aerospace.

Table A.8 Dependent variable: Export participation: Italy

Variables	All firms	Firms with less than 500 employees	Firms with less than 300 employees	Firms with less than 100 employees
Constant	11.06 (19.61)	9.03 (11.01)	7.07 (6.19)	6.4 (3.38)
GA	0.35 (15.65)	0.35 (13.84)	0.32 (10.98)	0.35 (10.02)
Age	-0.01 (26.43)	-0.01 (17.48)	-0.009 (11.12)	-0.009 (6.7)
Addmed	0.001 (51.41)	0.006 (123.66)	0.01 (147.5)	0.02 (102.5)
Subsidies	0.61 (53.4)	0.47 (28.41)	0.39 (18.08)	0.28 (6.73)
Scale	0.5 (6.64)	0.64 (8.57)	0.47 (3.99)	0.26 (0.82)
Traditional	0.81 (18.35)	1.01 (22.53)	0.88 (14.72)	0.68 (5.93)
Specialised	1.17 (18.35)	1.35 (35.42)	1.26 (26.9)	0.97 (11.2)
Dset 3	0.41 (0.88)	0.07 (0.01)	-0.09 (0.02)	0.42 (0.17)
Dset 8	0.17 (1.08)	0.18 (1.07)	0.23 (1.55)	0.29 (1.83)
Dset 11	-0.26 (0.51)	-0.32 (0.61)	-0.26 (0.36)	-0.31 (0.36)
Centre	0.69 (19.1)	0.76 (20.07)	0.76 (18.56)	0.78 (14.11)
North East	1.22 (70.93)	1.24 (65.25)	1.22 (58.49)	1.16 (37.2)
North West	1.33 (87.63)	1.35 (78.52)	1.34 (71.67)	1.3 (46.74)

Note: The table reports magnitude and T-statistics (in parenthesis).

Table A.9 Dependent variable: Export participation: Centre

Variables	All firms	Firms with less than 500 employees	Firms with less than 300 employees	Firms with less than 100 employees
Constant	14.71 (5.09)	3.74 (0.25)	3.97 (0.27)	7.4 (0.63)
GA	0.48 (4.6)	0.6 (6.3)	0.6 (6.16)	0.47 (2.99)
Age	-0.01 (6.16)	-0.007 (0.96)	-0.007 (0.8)	-0.01 (1.26)
Addmed	0.0005 (4.35)	0.008 (27.31)	0.01 (30.28)	0.02 (18.91)
Subsidies	0.38 (3.29)	0.25 (1.23)	0.06 (0.08)	-0.03 (0.01)
Scale	1.01 (4.09)	2.13 (8.1)	1.39 (3.45)	1.15 (0.99)
Traditional	1.64 (11.3)	2.93 (15.97)	2.23 (9.38)	2.11 (3.47)
Specialised	1.59 (8.88)	2.83 (13.5)	2.12 (7.6)	1.96 (2.82)
Dset 3	2.66 (8.94)	2.66 (5.1)	3 (4.63)	2.25 (1.47)
Dset 8	0.86 (4.01)	0.6 (1.53)	0.51 (1.03)	0.27 (0.16)
Dset 11	5.46 (0.24)	5.96 (0.21)	6.08 (0.22)	5.78 (0.22)

Note: The table reports magnitude and T-statistics (in parenthesis).

124   M. Bagella, L. Becchetti and S. Sacchi

Table A.10 Dependent variable: Export participation: North-East

Variables	All firms	Firms with less than 500 employees	Firms with less than 300 employees	Firms with less than 100 employees
Constant	9.28 (3.53)	8.27 (2.43)	5.97 (1.23)	1.76 (0.08)
GA	0.34 (5.51)	0.28 (3.29)	0.27 (2.92)	0.33 (3.37)
Age	-0.01 (5)	-0.01 (3.85)	-0.008 (2.25)	-0.004 (0.43)
Addmed	0.003 (30.1)	0.008 (55.05)	0.01 (57.27)	0.02 (36.12)
Subsidies	0.46 (9.43)	0.25 (2.55)	0.19 (1.4)	0.12 (0.48)
Scale	1.21 (5.58)	1.31 (5.21)	1.14 (3.84)	0.94 (1.83)
Traditional	1.86 (13.47)	1.96 (12.13)	1.81 (10.07)	1.73 (6.43)
Specialised	2.63 (24.97)	2.72 (21.97)	2.55 (18.71)	2.37 (11.43)
Dset 3	0.76 (0.5)	0.26 (0.04)	-0.07 (0.003)	0.77 (0.2)
Dset 8	0.55 (3.34)	0.53 (2.86)	0.68 (4.36)	0.53 (2.28)
Dset 11	-1.06 (3.58)	-1.21 (3.98)	-1.25 (3.87)	-1.3 (3.42)

Note: The table reports magnitude and T-statistics (in parenthesis).

Table A.11 Dependent variable: Export participation: North-West

Variables	All firms	Firms with less than 500 employees	Firms with less than 300 employees	Firms with less than 100 employees
Constant	10.76 (9.68)	11.56 (8.82)	9.26 (5.09)	9 (3.02)
GA	0.27 (3.53)	0.29 (3.81)	0.21 (1.86)	0.24 (1.72)
Age	-0.01 (9.29)	-0.01 (8.95)	-0.01 (5.55)	-0.009 (3.39)
Addmed	0.001 (18.39)	0.005 (34.51)	0.01 (47.82)	0.02 (39.15)
Subsidies	0.68 (24.7)	0.56 (14.77)	0.54 (12.36)	0.35 (3.76)
Scale	0.3 (1.12)	0.27 (0.72)	0.3 (0.82)	0.03 (0.006)
Traditional	0.16 (0.33)	0.1 (0.12)	0.17 (0.29)	-0.35 (0.8)
Specialised	0.44 (2.15)	0.38 (1.4)	0.51 (2.32)	-0.08 (0.03)
Dset 3	-0.65 (1.28)	-0.55 (0.56)	-0.9 (1.37)	4.82 (0.12)
Dset 8	-0.18 (0.58)	-0.11 (0.16)	-0.13 (0.22)	0.18 (0.3)
Dset 11	-0.3 (0.26)	-0.36 (0.26)	-0.17 (0.04)	-0.46 (0.14)

Note: The table reports magnitude and T-statistics (in parenthesis).

Table A.12 Dependent variable: Export participation: South

Variables	All firms	Firms with less than 500 employees	Firms with less than 300 employees	Firms with less than 100 employees
Constant	25.53 (7.6)	22.29 (5.61)	21.47 (4.62)	27.48 (1.34)
GA	0.22 (0.32)	0.23 (0.33)	0.27 (0.44)	0.66 (1.78)
Age	-0.02 (0.32)	-0.02 (7.29)	-0.02 (6.1)	-0.04 (7.82)
Addmed	0.003 (12.74)	0.005 (13.84)	0.009 (17.02)	0.02 (10.63)
Subsidies	1.07 (15.68)	1.14 (16.44)	1.06 (13.07)	1.56 (15.52)
Scale	0.6 (1.02)	1.24 (2.9)	0.79 (0.86)	7.69 (0.15)
Traditional	1.22 (4.46)	1.84 (6.77)	1.56 (3.58)	8.73 (0.2)

Variables	All firms	Firms with less than 500 employees	Firms with less than 300 employees	Firms with less than 100 employees
Specialised	1.04 (2.4)	1.77 (4.93)	1.78 (3.86)	9.06 (0.21)
Dset 3	-	-	-	-
Dset 8	0.4 (0.46)	0.31 (0.27)	0.57 (0.78)	1.05 (1.8)
Dset 11	0.44 (0.1)	0.47 (0.12)	0.38 (0.08)	0.89 (0.38)

Table A.12 Continuation.

Note: The table reports magnitude and T-statistics (in parenthesis).

Table A.13 Dependent variable: Export participation specialised

Variables	All firms	Firms with less than 500 employees	Firms with less than 300 employees	Firms with less than 100 employees
Constant	13.37 (3.55)	9.82 (1.78)	5.62 (0.5)	10.17 (1.2)
GA	0.48 (4.98)	0.51 (5.46)	0.5 (4.95)	0.48 (3.79)
Age	-0.01 (4.33)	-0.01 (2.33)	-0.007 (0.81)	-0.01 (1.63)
Addmed	0.002 (11.95)	0.005 (14.74)	0.01 (30.41)	0.02 (19.92)
Subsidies	1.02 (23.84)	0.89 (17.62)	0.73 (10.43)	0.61 (5.99)
Centre	1.01 (4.53)	0.89 (3.39)	0.57 (1.25)	0.54 (0.92)
North East	1.95 (20.42)	1.8 (16.77)	1.47 (10.28)	1.33 (6.81)
North West	1.47 (12.2)	1.34 (9.7)	1.1 (5.93)	0.86 (2.93)

Note: The table reports magnitude and T-statistics (in parenthesis).

Table A.14 Dependent variable: Export participation: Traditional sectors

Variables	All firms	Firms with less than 500 employees	Firms with less than 300 employees	Firms with less than 100 employees
Constant	19.66 (24.14)	18.68 (17.92)	15.45 (11.76)	19.04 (10.74)
GA	0.32 (6.87)	0.32 (5.98)	0.29 (4.91)	0.37 (5.75)
Age	-0.02 (26.18)	-0.02 (20.27)	-0.01 (13.95)	-0.02 (12.77)
Addmed	0.001 (15.5)	0.007 (57.31)	0.01 (68.25)	0.02 (38.62)
Subsidies	0.41 (10.97)	0.29 (4.97)	0.25 (3.49)	0.21 (1.81)
Centre	0.75 (11.8)	0.82 (13.03)	0.84 (12.86)	0.85 (9.86)
North East	1.13 (31.93)	1.09 (27.63)	1.11 (27.06)	1.07 (18.32)
North West	1.03 (27.41)	0.94 (20.82)	1 (21.89)	0.82 (10.84)

Note: The table reports magnitude and T-statistics (in parenthesis).

Table A.15 Dependent variable Export participation. Scale sectors

Variables	All firms	Firms with less than 500 employees	Firms with less than 300 employees	Firms with less than 100 employees
Constant	0.6 (0.01)	-0.88 (0.03)	-2.15 (0.19)	-5.29 (0.79)
GA	0.36 (4.1)	0.33 (3.14)	0.29 (2.34)	0.27 (1.41)
Age	-0.002 (0.21)	-0.001 (0.04)	0.0001 (0.0007)	0.002 (0.19)

Variables	All firms	Firms with less than 500 employees	Firms with less than 300 employees	Firms with less than 100 employees
Addmed	0.002 (27.9)	0.008 (52.95)	0.01 (47.92)	0.03 (42.54)
Subsidies	0.57 (12.9)	0.41 (5.68)	0.37 (4.47)	0.17 (0.65)
Centre	0.7 (5.02)	0.73 (4.53)	0.74 (4.35)	0.75 (2.62)
North East	1.13 (16.2)	1.19 (15.07)	1.28 (15.95)	1.2 (8.31)
North West	1.76 (39.49)	1.85 (36.4)	1.93 (36.53)	2.18 (26.91)

Table A.15: Continuation

Note: The table reports magnitude and T-statistics (in parenthesis).

Table A.16 Dependent variable: Export participation: High tech sectors

Variable	All firms	Firms with less than 500 employees	Firms with less than 300 employees	Firms with less than 100 employees
Constant	20.27 (2.79)	20.39 (2.4)	18.54 (1.9)	-11.99 (0.06)
GA	0.42 (0.38)	0.21 (0.08)	0.33 (0.2)	1.55 (0.82)
Age	-0.02 (2.96)	-0.02 (2.64)	-0.01 (2.04)	0.001 (0.006)
Addmed	0.001 (4.41)	0.003 (2.24)	0.002 (0.31)	0.02 (1.21)
Subsidies	0.87 (3.55)	0.79 (2.19)	0.63 (1.31)	0.72 (0.57)
Centre	0.07 (0.008)	0.22 (0.05)	-0.17 (0.02)	7.35 (0.02)
North East	0.43 (0.23)	1.02 (0.88)	0.74 (0.37)	9.33 (0.04)
North West	0.74 (0.96)	1.19 (1.58)	0.83 (0.58)	10.04 (0.05)

Note: The table reports magnitude and T-statistics (in parenthesis).

EU and Non EU Export Performance of Italian Firms. Is There an Industrial District Effect?[1]

Leonardo Becchetti

Università Tor Vergata, Roma, Facoltà di Economia, Dipartimento di Economia e Istituzioni, Via di Tor Vergata snc, 00133 Roma. E-Mail: Becchetti@uniroma2.it

Stefania P.S. Rossi

Istituto Universitario Navale, Facoltà di Economia, Istituto di Studi Economici, Via Medina 40, 80133 Napoli, E-Mail: Rossiste@cds.unina.it

Abstract: Geographical agglomeration of productive units is expected to affect positively cooperation in "multiple winners" games in which costs from increased neighbour competition are not too high. Small-medium firm export activity is a typical game with these features. Economies of scale in the provision of export services and informal face-to-face exchanges of information about export markets may in fact facilitate participation to export activity without threatening potential profits due to productive capacity constraints and the large scale of the market. The current paper carries an empirical test and finds that geographical agglomeration of small-medium firms in a delimited area significantly affects their export intensity and their probability of becoming exporters. The effect is stronger for exports towards non EU markets and is negatively related to firm size. The significance of geographical agglomeration persists in spite of all controls included in the estimate which show how the dependent variable is also (positively) affected by export subsidies, formal export cooperation among firms, size and age. Paper results suggest that geographical agglomeration, by shifting firms from domestic to foreign markets, may then be - if technological benefits from more competition are relatively higher on foreign markets - an important engine for endogenous growth in a downsized system, such as Italy, with a strong specialisation in Traditional and Specialised sectors.

JEL Classification: R3

Keywords: Industrial districts, Technological innovation, Export performance.

---

[1] A previous version of this paper has been presented at the International Workshop on "Italian industrial districts: internationalisation and export performance". The authors thank M.Bagella, M. Bellandi, G.Dei Ottati, G.Esposito, K.Kaiser, G. Pellegrini, G. Scanagatta, S. Sacchi for useful comments and suggestions. The usual disclaimer applies. Although this paper is a common research work sections 1 and 4 have been written by S.Rossi and sections 2, 3 and 5 have been written by L.Becchetti.

1   Introduction

The agglomeration of small-medium sized enterprises in geographically delimited areas, known as industrial "district", is the most relevant form of economic development and industrial organization developed in Italy in the last decades.

The literature has widely analysed the distinctive features of this particular form of Italian industrial development. According to Becattini (1991) an industrial district is "a socio-territorial entity, characterised by the active presence of both a community of people and a population of firms in one naturally and historically bounded area", which generates both positive and negative spillovers. The homogeneous system of values shared by this community of people produce a sense of belonging to the district which stimulates high work mobility and allows an easy transmission of skills.

Industrial district firms are generally characterised by input-output interlinks, high degree of specialisation in one or few complementary industries; highly flexible division of labour; horizontal competition and vertical cooperation. The innovative capacity and creativity enhanced by geographical proximity allows frequent and unplanned face-to-face contacts which are an effective mean for communicating practical knowledge. Moreover, the interaction of different production approaches and know-how favour original combinations of ideas about products, processes and markets (Bellandi, 1996).

Among the features described above two of them may positively affect export performance of small firms located in the industrial district. First, an efficient system of formal and informal exchange of complementary information can substitute for the lack of internal resources (an export division within the firm) needed to overcome fixed informational costs and to provide services necessary to enter foreign markets (Pyke-Becattini-Senegenberger, 1991). Second, tighter competition, fostered by geographical proximity, may improve product quality of district *vis-a-vis* non-district firms. This may allow the district firms to have a better performance in large segmented foreign markets and, particularly, in Traditional sectors characterised by horizontal product differentiation[2] and in Specialised sectors where strong product complementarities turn neighbour technological improvement into a positive externality.

Theoretical literature has only partially analysed the positive effects of the agglomeration of small-medium firms in industrial districts and the empirical literature is even further behind in assessing the relative advantages of geographically agglomerated (from now on GA) firms vis-à-vis those which are not.

---

[2] For horizontal product differentiation we mean those forms of competition in which entry of new firms has only the effect of reducing incumbents' market shares without pushing them out of the market. Typical models of horizontal product differentiation are those of Hotelling (1929) and D'Aspremont-Gabszewicz-Thisse (1979).

In this paper we provide empirical evidence for the hypothesis that small-medium firms' export performance may be improved by location in a GA area. We further test whether the impact of geographical agglomeration on export intensity is different for firms exporting towards European and non European markets. In particular, we analyze whether the district effect is higher for those firms which export towards non EU countries, where access is more difficult and requires more services and information.

The paper is organised as follows: the second section outlines the methodological approach adopted for identifying geographically agglomerated firms and non GA firms. The third section presents some descriptive evidence from the selected sample on the higher export intensity of GA firms towards EU and non EU markets. The forth section presents results from econometric analysis on the district effect on EU and non EU export performance of small firms. In our paper we show that this positive effect : i) is stronger on export performance towards non EU markets where access is more difficult and requires more services and information ; ii) is decreasing in firm size as smaller firms are those which cannot afford internal export divisions ; iii) does not disappear when size, age, export consortia and export subsidies, which also have relevant impact on export performance, are introduced as control variables.

2   The Methodological Approach of the Empirical Analysis

The empirical analysis is carried out on the Mediocredito database. This database includes a sample of more than 5,000 firms drawn from the whole set of Italian manufacturing firms (64,463 firms in 1992 according to Cerved database). The sample is stratified and randomly selected (according to the sector's geographical and dimensional distribution of Italian firms) for firms from 11 to 500 employees. It reflects census data for firms with more than 500 employees. For a subsample of 3,852 firms both qualitative and quantitative data (balance sheets for the period 1989-1991) are collected. Qualitative data provide, among other things, information on firm property, degree of internationalisation, entitlement to state subsidies and agreements with partners and competitors. Descriptive analysis of this sample illustrate some important features of Italian economy (Tab. 1): i) the relative specialisation in Traditional sectors compared with the despecialisation in High-Tech sectors; ii) the relevant weight of very small firms (with no more than 50 employees) in a country where small-medium firms represent the large majority of the industrial system[3]; iii) the striking difference between firms in the North and firms in the South which are smaller, younger and export less.

---

[3] Downsizing is a typical feature of Italian industrial system. De Cecco-Ferri (1997) show how institutional features of the domestic financial institutions (underdevelopment of merchant banking, abundance of state subsidies to small-medium firms, lobbying pressure of Italian tax consultants ('commercialisti') whose services are demanded mainly by small firms) contributed to downsizing. Bagella-Becchetti-Caggese (1996, 1997a) show how

Table 1. Macroregional features of the Mediocredito sample (values in %)

	North West	North East	Centre	South	Italy
Firms with 11-50 employees	31.9	37.8	46.1	49.7	37.5
Firms with 50-500 employees	53.8	54.0	45.0	43.7	51.7
Firms with more than 500 employees	14.4	8.2	8.9	6.6	10.8
Firms with 0-10 billion liras net sales	35.1	38.7	47.7	55.7	40.0
Firms with 10-50 billion liras net sales	38.1	39.9	33.3	28.3	37.1
Firms with more than 50 billion liras net sales	26.7	21.4	18.9	16.0	22.9
High-tech sectors	4.6	1.6	4.7	4.0	3.6
Specialised sectors	24.1	26.7	15.5	11.1	22.5
Scale sectors	28.8	27.7	27.1	28.6	28.2
Traditional sectors	40.1	42.0	49.4	53.4	43.3
Other non manufacturing	2.4	2.0	3.3	2.9	2.5
Firm affiliated to groups	65.8	70.0	74.0	77.1	69.4
Firms participated for less than 50%	3.6	2.5	2.7	3.1	3.1
Firms participated for more than 50%	30.7	27.5	23.3	19.7	27.6
Firms receiving subsidised credit	54.3	53.6	48.6	58.9	53.7
Firms non receiving subsidised credit	45.7	46.4	51.4	41.1	46.3
Exporting firms	77.3	73.1	61.4	40.9	70.3
Non exporting firms	22.7	26.9	38.6	59.1	29.7
Average size (n. of employees)	470	201	233	160	319
Average size (net sales in billion liras)	116	49	117	45	87
Share of exports sales on total sales	23%	26%	22%	11%	23%
Average foundation year	1964	1971	1971	1974	1968

To classify firms in the sample according to their degree of geographical proximity we use as an indicator of geographical agglomeration the concentration of local employment in small-medium sized manufacturing firms (Sforzi, 1995). In particular geographical agglomeration (GA) is calculated on 1991 Census data as:

$$GA = (E_{m,ls} / E_{t,ls})/(A_{m,i} / A_{t,i}) \tag{1}$$

where $E_{m,ls}$ is the number of employees in manufacturing firms with less than 250 employees in a town council[4], $E_{t,ls}$ is the number of employees in the manufacturing sector in a town council, $A_{m,i}$ is the total number of employees in manufacturing firms with less than 250 employees in Italy and $A_{t,i}$ is the total number of employees in the manufacturing sector in Italy. According to this

downsizing generates extra costs for small-medium firms in terms of higher cost of debt and higher probability of credit rationing.

[4] The index of geographical agglomeration is computed for any town council or "comune" (Italian administrative unit smaller than the province and corresponding to a town and its small surroundings). A sum of adjoining "comuni" makes a local system or a GA area.

indicator firms are classified as "geographically agglomerated" if they are localised in town councils in where the above mentioned ratio is higher than the national average and not otherwise.[5]

3   Empirical Descriptive Results

The application of the Sforzi (1995) criterion to the Mediocredito sample shows that almost one half of all firms (47.7 per cent) in the dataset is located in GA areas. Descriptive statistics from table 2 clearly indicate the location preference of small firms for industrial districts in all areas. Table 3 shows that firms in Traditional and Specialised sectors, with the exception of those in High-Tech and Scale sectors, prefer location in GA areas. This is consistent with the hypothesis that some of the potential positive effects from geographical agglomeration, and specially those on export performance, are negatively related to firm size and to the degree of vertical product differentiation (Shaked- Sutton, 1983) in the sector specific model of competition.

Tables 4 and 5 compare mean values of the export/total sales ratio for different sample subgroups indicating when the difference between GA and non GA firms is statistically significant. These tables show that location in a GA area increases by around one half the firm's export towards EU countries (8.81 against 13.15) and doubles the firm's export towards non EU countries (0.41 against 0.84) when only firms with less than 100 employees are considered. Descriptive analysis does also reveal that Traditional and Specialised sectors benefit more than Scale sectors from GA. This result may be intuitively explained by the features of these sectors. In Traditional sectors technological innovation is relatively less important as a competitive factor and competition is similar to that described in models of "horizontal product differentiation". As a consequence, costs from increased competition are lower than gains from increased cooperation when firms are located in GA areas. In Specialised sectors technological competition is relatively more relevant, but segmented demand and strong complementarity of mechanical components in integrated products still make gains from cooperation higher than costs from competition for Specialised sector firms located in GA areas (Bellandi, 1996).

---

[5] This criterion, based on geographical employment concentration, deliberately abstracts from product considerations. In fact any attempt to define a "Marshallian district" on the product side is much more difficult and ambiguous as in all these areas we find a relative specialisation in at least two or three sectors with a mix of "horizontal" (multiple industrial units producing exactly the same) and "vertical" features (multiple units which are upstream and downstream integrated). Theoretical literature highlights how, in spite of its obvious limitations, this is the dominant, widely followed criterion for defining district and non district firms (Bellandi, 1996).

Table 2. Sample firms by area, size and geographical agglomerations (GAs)

Size	Firms belonging to GAs in the North East area		Firms not belonging to GAs in the North East area		Total	
	N°	%	N°	%	N°	%
Small	279	37%	203	38%	482	38%
Medium	413	56%	274	52%	687	54%
Large	50	7%	54	10%	104	8%
Total	**742**	**100%**	**531**	**100%**	**1273**	**100%**

Size	Firms belonging to GAs in the North West area		Firms not belonging to GAs in the North West area		Total	
	N°	%	N°	%	N°	%
Small	259	35%	276	29%	535	32%
Medium	420	57%	483	51%	903	54%
Large	52	7%	189	20%	241	14%
Total	**733**	**100%**	**948**	**100%**	**1679**	**100%**

Size	Firms belonging to GAs in the Centre area		Firms not belonging to GAs in the Centre area		Total	
	N°	%	N°	%	N°	%
Small	129	52%	124	42%	253	46%
Medium	121	47%	126	43%	247	45%
Large	3	1%	46	15%	49	9%
Total	**253**	**100%**	**296**	**100%**	**549**	**100%**

Size	Firms belonging to GAs in the South area		Firms not belonging to GAs in the South area		Total	
	N°	%	N°	%	N°	%
Small	32	64%	141	47%	174	50%
Medium	18	36%	135	45%	153	44%
Large	0	0	23	7%	23	6%
Total	**50**	**100%**	**299**	**100%**	**350**	**100%**

Note: small firms: firms with 0-50 employees; Medium firms: firms with 51-500 employees; Large firms: firms with more than 500 employees . To classify firms in the sample according to their degree of geographical proximity we use as an indicator of geographical agglomeration the concentration of local employment in small-medium sized manufacturing firms (Sforzi, 1995). In particular geographical agglomeration (GA) is calculated on 1991 Census data as:

$$GA = (E_{m,ls} / E_{t,ls}) / (A_{m,i} / A_{t,i})$$

where $E_{m,ls}$ is the number of employees in firms with less than 250 employees for the manufacturing sector in the local system, $E_{t,ls}$ is the number of employees in the manufacturing sector in the local system, $A_{m,i}$ is the total number of employees in firms with less than 250 employees for the manufacturing sector in Italy and $A_{t,i}$ is the total number of employees in the manufacturing sector in Italy . According to this indicator firms are classified as "geographically agglomerated" if they are localised in areas where the above mentioned ratio is higher than the national average and not otherwise.

Table 3. Locational choice by manufacturing macrosector

Sector by Pavitt classification	GA firms	Non GA firms	Total
Scale sectors	24%	33.2%	28.8%
Specialised sectors	24.3%	21.8%	23%
Traditional sectors	50.2%	39.4%	44.6%
High-tech sectors	1.5%	5.5%	3.5%

Macroarea	NE GA	NE non GA	NW GA	NW non GA	C GA	C non GA	S GA	S non GA
Specialised	26.3%	30.6%	23.8%	34.4%	20.2%	35.0%	14.0%	33.1%
Scale	27.7%	27%	25.7%	23.0%	14.3%	17.9%	4.0%	12.7%
Traditional	44.9%	40.3%	48.8%	35.5%	64.0%	39,3%	78,0%	49.8%
High-Tech	1.109%	2.11%	1.7%	7.1%	1.6%	7.9%	4.0%	4.4%
Total n°	**742**	**531**	**731**	**948**	**253**	**296**	**51**	**299**

Note: GA firms are classified according to their degree of geographical proximity using the Sforzi indicator.

Table 4. Average export towards the EU/total sales

	All Firms		Firms with less than 250 employees		Firms with less than 100 employees	
	Obs.	Mean	Obs.	Mean	Obs.	Mean
All Non GA	2074	12.56*	1560	11.44*	1087	8.81*
All GA	1777	15.45*	1538	14.67*	1097	13.15*
Scale Non GA	658	12.59	462	9.85*	330	7.28*
Scale GA	421	14.51	340	12.33*	237	10.68*
Specialised Non GA	441	15.17*	349	14.40*	248	11.48*
Specialised GA	426	18.34*	377	17.65*	274	15.46*
Traditional Non GA	863	11.73*	694	11.17*	475	8.78*
Traditional GA	905	14.62*	803	14.33*	576	13.18*
North-East Non GA	531	15.57	425	14.24	306	10.74*
North-East GA	742	15.79	621	15.02	443	13.42*
North-West Non GA	948	13.07*	665	12.20*	434	9.60*
North-West GA	731	15.76*	623	14.59*	427	13.04*
Centre Non GA	296	11.16*	221	10.01*	161	8.67*
Centre GA	253	15.07*	243	15.39*	186	14.30*
South Non GA	299	7.00	249	5.9*	186	3.89*
South GA	51	7.83	51	7.83*	41	5.96*

Table 4. Continuation.

*Subgroup means which are significantly different from each other at 99% are indicated with an asterisk.

Note: GAs firms are classified according to their degree of geographical prximity using the Sforzi indicator.

Table 5. Export towards non EU/total sales

	All Firms		Firms with less than 250 employees		Firms with less than 100 employees	
	Obs.	Mean	Obs.	Mean	Obs.	Mean
All	2074	0.56*	1560	0.49*	1087	0.41*
All GA	1777	0.84*	1538	0.86*	1097	0.84*
Scale	658	0.58	462	0.54	330	0.57
Scale GA	421	0.44	340	0.35	237	0.33
Specialised Non GA	441	0.96	349	0.77*	248	0.43*
Specialised GA	426	1.53	377	1.46*	274	1.45*
Traditional Non GA	863	0.35*	694	0.29*	475	0.26*
Traditional GA	905	0.72*	803	0.79*	576	0.76*
North-East non GA	531	0.55*	425	0.49*	306	0.50
Norht-East GA	742	1.17*	621	1.20*	443	1.12
North-West GA	948	0.74	665	0.68	434	0.50
North-West Non GA	731	0.56	623	0.57	427	0.59
Centre Non GA	296	0.30	221	0.22	161	0.26
Centre GA	253	0.88	243	0.91	186	0.90
South Non GA	299	0.24	249	0.23	186	0.18
South GA	51	0.01	51	0.01	41	0

*Subrgoup means which are significantly different from each other at 99% are indicated with an asterisk.

Note: GA firms are classified according to their degree of geographical proximity using the Sforzi indicator.

4   Results from Econometric Analysis

Descriptive results do not provide conclusive evidence for the positive effect of GA on export intensity of small-medium firms towards EU and non EU countries, because subgroup average export/total sales ratios incorporate dimensional, sector and geographical biases. This is why this section of the paper measures the net effect of GA on export intensity and export participation of small-medium firms towards EU and non EU countries with Tobit and Probit estimates. Tables 6 and 7 present results of two Tobit maximum likelihood estimates[6] on the net impact GA

---

[6] The export/total sales variable has a large number of observations reaching its lower limit (non exporting firms) and fewer observations reaching its upper limit (firms whose net sales are all from exports). When the dependent variable has more left censored than right censored observations, OLS parameter estimates are downward biased. This is because observations with negative disturbances are more likely to be left censored than those with positive disturbances so that average error term in an estimate with uncensored observations is likely to be positive. We therefore adopt a MLE which is consistent, asymptotically efficient and asymptotically normal under conditions described by Amemiya (1973).

on export intensity (respectively towards EU and towards non EU countries) using the following specifications:

$$_{EU}Exp/fatt = \alpha_0 + \sum_{i=1}^{22} \alpha_i Dset_i + \sum_{i=1}^{3} \gamma_k Darea_k + \beta_1 Size + \beta_2 Consex +$$ (2)

$$+ \beta_3 Subex + \beta_4 Birth + \beta_5 Group + \beta_6 District + \varepsilon$$

$$_{NON-EU}Exp/fatt = \alpha_0 + \sum_{i=1}^{22} \alpha_i Dset_i + \sum_{i=1}^{3} \gamma_k Darea_k + \beta_1 Size +$$ (3)

$$+ \beta_2 Consex + \beta_3 Subex + \beta_4 Birth + \beta_5 Group + \beta_6 District + \varepsilon$$

where $_{EU}Exp/fatt$ ($_{NON-EU}Exp/fatt$) are respectively three year (1989-91) average of the share of export sales towards EU (non EU) countries on total sales[7]. $Dset_i$ are 22 sector dummies, $Darea_k$ are three macro areas dummies (North-East, North-West, Centre), $Size$ is the three year (1989-91) average of the number of employees in the firm, $Consex$ and $Subex$ are two dummies which refer respectively to the firms participating in export "consortia"[8] and to the firms receiving export subsidies, $Birth$ is the firm's foundation year, $Group$ is a dummy which takes the value of one for firms affiliated to groups (subsidiaries or parent companies) and zero otherwise, $District$ is a dummy which takes the value of one if firms are located in GA areas, measured with the Sforzi criterion, and zero otherwise.

---

[7] We also perform estimates using export sales per employees as a dependent variable. Estimates results, reported in the Appendix, are not qualitatively different from those obtained from (2) and (3), see tables 6 and 7.

[8] Export consortia are contractual agreements, ruled by Italian Civil Law, among firms which choose to cooperate, in order to provide common funds and share information for the development of export activity. They may lead or not to the creation of an independent corporation even though constituents always maintain their independent identity. Consortia differ from cartels and are tolerated by antitrust authorities because their goal is not to restrict competition by altering prices or quantities but just to cooperate in the provision of services to improve export performance. Consortia may then be considered a type of formal cooperation, while geographical agglomeration represents a type of informal cooperation.

Table 6. The determinants of export intensity toward EU countries

Dep. variable: export towards EU/total sales	All firms		Firms with less than 250 employees		Firms with less than 100 employees	
	Coeff.	T stat	Coeff.	T stat	Coeff.	T stat
Non-metallic mineral products	1.54	(0.19)	9.79	(0.47)	7.11	(0.31)
Chemicals	4.21	(0.52)	12.50	(0.60)	6.93	(0.31)
Pharmaceuticals	-2.88	(-0.33)	8.16	(0.38)	-3.70	(-0.14)
Artificial fibres	1.32	(0.11)	-26.04	(-0.96)	-15.00	(-0.14)
Metal products	4.00	(0.50)	14.15	(0.69)	10.94	(0.49)
Mechanical equipment	12.28	(1.55)	21.76	(1.05)	18.05	(0.80)
Office equipment and computers	-14.93	(-1.43)	-10.99	(-0.48)	-10.56	(-0.40)
Electronics and electrical equipment	8.41	(1.05)	17.01	(0.82)	14.73	(0.65)
Vehicles and vehicle components	11.29	(1.33)	14.73	(0.70)	11.79	(0.50)
Other means of transport	13.90	(1.47)	19.85	(0.89)	13.41	(0.51)
Precision instruments and apparels	6.64	(0.77)	17.54	(0.83)	14.13	(0.61)
Food	-3.99	(-0.49)	5.94	(0.29)	4.60	(0.20)
Sugar, tobacco, etc	-5.18	(-0.61)	3.59	(0.17)	10.25	(0.44)
Textile	6.90	(0.86)	14.57	(0.71)	11.91	(0.53)
Leather	**21.18**	**(2.47)**	31.29	(1.50)	28.96	(1.26)
Shoes and clothing	11.83	(1.48)	20.96	(1.01)	20.41	(0.91)
Wood and wooden furniture	8.31	(1.02)	17.54	(0.85)	9.44	(0.42)
Paper and printing	-10.29	(-1.28)	-1.79	(-0.09)	-6.21	(-0.28)
Rubber and plastics	10.75	(1.33)	21.17	(1.02)	16.50	(0.73)
Other manufacturing	10.16	(1.26)	18.84	(0.91)	16.46	(0.73)
Other non manufacturing	**-24.16**	**(-2.80)**	-20.41	(-0.96)	-25.05	(-1.06)
Electrical measure, equipment, telecommunications	-4.76	(-0.50)	9.22	(0.42)	11.79	(0.49)
North-West	**14.72**	**(8.07)**	**14.75**	**(6.95)**	**16.08**	**(5.73)**
North-Easth	**15.11**	**(8.11)**	**15.09**	**(7.04)**	**16.23**	**(5.75)**
Centre	**10.83**	**(5.29)**	**11.88**	**(5.04)**	**13.61**	**(4.40)**
Size	**0.001**	**(2.88)**	**0.10**	**(11.56)**	**0.26**	**(9.64)**
CONSEX (Export Consortia)	**11.44**	**(5.32)**	**12.08**	**(5.26)**	**12.58**	**(4.09)**
SUBEX (Export subsidies)	**5.45**	**(2.46)**	**8.20**	**(2.76)**	**9.48**	**(2.06)**
Birth	**-0.07**	**(-3.52)**	-0.04	(-1.87)	**-0.08**	**(-2.69)**
Group	**5.85**	**(5.86)**	1.72	(1.32)	-0.06	(-0.03)
District	**1.79**	**(1.91)**	**2.12**	**(1.97)**	**4.10**	**(2.84)**
Constant	**51.13**	**(2.51)**	10.12	(0.33)	39.58	(1.07)
N. of observations	3696	-	2970	-	2096	-
χ^2	518.9	-	575.08	-	309.53	-
Log likelihood	-11979.5	-	-9076.77	-	-5779.48	-
Left censored obs.	1311	-	1186	-	997	-
Right censored obs.	6	-	6	-	6	-

Note: The table reports magnitude and T-statistics (in parenthesis) of the following Tobit estimate:

$$_{EU}Exp/\,fatt = \alpha_0 + \sum_{i=1}^{22}\alpha_i Dset_i + \sum_{i=1}^{3}\gamma_k Darea_k + \beta_1 Size + \beta_2 Consex +$$

$$+ \beta_3 Subex + \beta_4 Birth + \beta_5 Group + \beta_6 District + \varepsilon$$

where *Exp/fatt* is the three year (1989-91) average of the share of export sales versus EU countries on total sales. The dependent variable is left censored at 0 and righ censored at 1. *Dset$_i$* are 23 sector dummies, *Darea$_k$* are 3 macroarea dummies (NEST, NOVEST, CENTRE), *District* is a dummy which takes value of 1 if the firm is located in an area where the cofficient of geographical agglomeration is higher than one and takes the value of zero otherwise, *Birth* is firm's year of foundation, *Size* is the three year (1989-91) average of firm's employees, *Consex* and *Subex* are two dummies which pick up respectively firms participating to export "consortia" and firms receiving export subsidies. *Group* is a dummy which takes value of one for firms affiliated to groups (subsidiaries or parent companies) and zero otherwise.

Vertical headers for any of table cells indicate the subsample on which the regression is performed. Coefficients significant at 99% are in bold. Estimate disturbances are controlled for normality and heteroskedasticity.

Table 7. The determinants of export intensity toward non-EU countries

Dep. Variable: Export toward non EU countries /total sales	All Firms		Firms with less than 250 employees		Firms with less than 100 employees	
	Coeff.	T stat	Coeff.	T stat	Coeff.	T stat
Non-metallic mineral products	-0.93	(-0.13)	7.87	(0.43)	3.14	(0.16)
Chemicals	5.03	(0.67)	13.21	(0.72)	8.37	(0.43)
Pharmaceuticals	-5.06	(-0.45)	-22.13	(-0.92)	-13.11	(0.60)
Artificial fibres	-1.24	(-0.15)	10.96	(0.58)	13.05	(0.60)
Metal products	-1.07	(-0.15)	7.63	(0.42)	1.72	(0.09)
Mechanical equipment	14.33	(1.95)	21.41	(1.18)	15.58	(0.80)
Office equipment and computers	-11.99	(-1.25)	1.51	(0.08)	2.08	(0.10)
Electronics and electrical equipment	2.85	(0.39)	12.21	(0.67)	6.62	(0.34)
Vehicles and vehicle components	-0.98	(-0.11)	3.70	(0.19)	-12.48	(-0.51)
Other means of transport	0.13	(0.02)	4.94	(0.27)	2.08	(0.10)
Precision instruments and apparels	10.78	(1.35)	18.86	(1.02)	13.28	(0.66)
Food	-5.49	(-0.72)	2.59	(0.14)	-3.51	(-0.18)
Sugar, tobacco, etc	-4.51	(-0.57)	6.33	(0.34)	8.61	(0.43)
Textile	-1.21	(-0.16)	6.46	(0.36)	-1.59	(-0.08)
Leather	11.71	(1.48)	20.76	(1.13)	13.82	(0.70)
Shoes and clothing	5.93	(0.80)	13.42	(0.74)	7.34	(0.38)
Wood and wooden furniture	-0.24	(-0.03)	8.10	(0.45)	1.68	(0.09)
Paper and printing	-14.49	(-1.94)	-5.11	(-0.28)	-12.50	(-0.64)
Rubber and plastics	0.24	(0.03)	10.33	(0.57)	3.28	(0.17)
Other manufacturing	4.12	(0.55)	14.56	(0.80)	14.09	(0.72)
Other non manufacturing	-11.35	(-1.44)	-9.20	(-0.49)	-39.99	(-1.80)
Electrical measure, equipment, telecommunications	-11.28	(-1.27)	-0.60	(-0.03)	-3.78	(-0.18)
North-West	**11.11**	**(6.46)**	**12.48**	**(6.10)**	**13.41**	**(5.02)**
North-Easth	**12.27**	**(7.00)**	**12.89**	**(6.25)**	**13.40**	**(4.99)**
Centre	**9.35**	**(4.86)**	**11.35**	**(5.03)**	**13.02**	**(4.45)**

Dep. Variable: Export toward non EU countries /total sales	All Firms		Firms with less than 250 employees		Firms with less than 100 employees	
	Coeff.	T stat	Coeff.	T stat	Coeff.	T stat
Size	0.001	(2.41)	0.09	(10.17)	0.24	(9.50)
CONSEX (Export Consortia)	9.21	(4.75)	10.24	(4.92)	11.85	(4.37)
SUBEX (Export subsidies)	17.51	(8.89)	18.24	(6.86)	12.86	(3.15)
Birth	-0.10	(-5.60)	-0.06	(-2.85)	-0.05	(-1.77)
Group	4.77	(5.19)	0.57	(0.46)	-1.33	(-0.74)
District	2.28	(2.63)	3.31	(3.28)	4.93	(3.72)
Constant	81.09	(4.33)	29.42	(1.04)	14.53	(0.42)
N. of observations	3696	-	2970	-	2096	-
χ^2	641.41	-	578.06	-	416.95	-
Log Likelihood	-10192.4	-	-7626.76	-	-4764.44	-
Left censored obs.	1669	-	1476	-	1191	-
Right censored obs	4	-	-4	-	1	-

Table 7. Continuation.

Note: The table reports magnitude and T-statistics (in parenthesis) of the following Tobit estimate:

$$_{NON-EU}Exp/\,fatt = \alpha_0 + \sum_{i=1}^{22}\alpha_i Dset_i + \sum_{i=1}^{3}\gamma_k Darea_k + \beta_1 Size+$$

$$+ \beta_2 Consex + \beta_3 Subex + \beta_4 Birth + \beta_5 Group + \beta_6 District + \varepsilon$$

where *Exp/fatt* is the three year (1989-91) average of the share of export sales versus non EU countries on total sales . The dependent variable is left censored at 0 and righ censored at 1 . $Dset_i$ are 23 sector dummies, $Darea_k$ are 3 macroarea dummies (NEST, NOVEST, CENTRE), *District* is a dummy which takes value of 1 if the firm is located in an area where the cofficient of geographical agglomeration is higher than one and takes the value of zero otherwise, *Birth* is firm's year of foundation, *Size* is the three year (1989-91) average of firm's employees, *Consex* and *Subex* are two dummies which pick up respectively firms participating to export "consortia" and firms receiving export subsidies.*Group* is a dummy which takes value of one for firms affiliated to groups (subsidiaries or parent companies) and zero otherwise.
Vertical headers for any of table cells indicate the subsample on which the regression is performed. Coefficients significant at 99% are in bold . Estimate disturbances are controlled for normality and heteroskedasticity.

Another relevant question for the empirical analysis of the effects of GA on export performance is the amount by which location in Marshallian district may increase the probability of accessing foreign markets (EU and non EU) net of other control variables. To answer this question we propose two Probit estimates specified as follows:

$$_{EU}Expart = \alpha_0 + \sum_{i=1}^{22}\alpha_i Dset_i + \sum_{i=1}^{3}\gamma_k Darea_k + \beta_1 Size+$$

(4)

$$\beta_2 Consex + \beta_3 Subex + \beta_4 Birth + \beta_5 Group + \beta_6 District + \varepsilon$$

$$NON-EU \, Expart = \alpha_0 + \sum_{i=1}^{22} \alpha_i Dset_i + \sum_{i=1}^{3} \gamma_k Darea_k +$$
$$+ \beta_1 Size + \beta_2 Consex + \beta_3 Subex + \beta_4 Birth + \qquad (5)$$
$$+ \beta_5 Group + \beta_6 District + \varepsilon$$

where regressors are defined as in 2 and 3 and $_{EU}Expart$ ($_{NON-EU}Expart$) is a dummy which takes the value of one if the firm has nonzero export sales towards EU (non EU) countries over total sales and zero otherwise. Tables 8 and 9 present the results of the two Probit estimates showing the effect of a marginal increase in the regressor on the probability of being an exporter.

Empirical evidence confirms that geographical agglomeration significantly affects export performance towards EU and non EU markets. This effect seems to be larger when we consider the export performance towards non EU markets, presumably because the marginal positive effect of agglomeration (and of informal exchange of information) is higher where fixed costs for accessing foreign markets are higher. In the EU, the impact of the district location variable on export intensity gets higher and more significant as far as we reduce the sample to firms of smaller size (Tables 6-7). Probit estimes confirm this result showing that belonging to a GA increases the probability of becoming an exporter, expecially for small firms. In particular, the probability of being an exporter towards EU countries for GA firms is significantly increased by 5 percent when we consider all firms or the subsample of firms with less than 250 employees and is significantly increased by 7 percent among firms with less than 100 employees (Tab. 8). The positive effect of GA on the probability of being an exporter towards non EU countries is slightly higher: 6 percent more chances for all firms and 9 percent more chances for firms with less than 100 employees (Tab. 9).

The dataset provides the opportunity to isolate the impact of the GA effect from the effect of organised cooperation of firms which associate themselves to promote export (the *Consex* variable) and the effect of export subsidies on the export performance.

Empirical results from tables 6-9 show that "formal cooperation" among firms (export consortia) and export subsidies have a very strong impact on export intensity towards EU and non EU countries. It is much more difficult here to infer the causality link given that participating to an "export consortium" is much more a choice variable than the decision of locating in a certain area. It is then likely that a firm enters a consortium because it is already an exporter and not viceversa. Another strong result which is also subject to the endogeneity problem is the significant association between export subsidies and export performance towards EU and non EU countries. Firms demand export subsidies because they are already exporters while it is more difficult to understand if export subsidies significantly contributed to their export intensity. In any case, the high degree of association between participation to export consortia and export subsidies, on one side, and export performance, on the other, indicates that these two variables are very important controls which may help to find the net impact of district location on export performance. A result which is common to both variables is that institutional (inter-firm, through consortia, or public, through subsidies) support to export activity has a stronger impact on markets which are more difficult to access (those of non-EU countries).

Table 8. The determinants of the probability of being an exporter toward EU countries

	All firms		Firms with less than 250 employees		Firms with less than 100 employees	
	(dF/dX)*	T stat	(dF/dX)*	T stat	(dF/dX)*	T stat
Non-metallic mineral products	-0.24	(-1.24)	0.01	(0.04)	-0.02	(-0.05)
Chemicals	-0.14	(-0.73)	0.07	(0.20)	0.01	(0.01)
Pharmaceuticals	-0.29	(-1.44)	-0.07	(-0.20)	-0.12	(-0.29)
Artificial fibres	-0.40	(-1.57)	-0.55	(-1.56)	-	-
Metal products	-0.18	(-0.96)	0.07	(0.21)	0.02	(0.06)
Mechanical equipment	-0.01	(-0.05)	0.22	(0.74)	0.20	(0.60)
Office equipment and computers	**-0.53**	**(-2.56)**	-0.25	(-0.64)	-0.20	(-0.51)
Electronics and electrical equipment	-0.14	(-0.74)	0.10	(0.30)	0.08	(0.23)
Vehicles and vehicle components	-0.12	(-0.59)	0.10	(0.29)	-0.10	(-0.27)
Other means of transport	-0.03	(-0.13)	0.12	(0.35)	-0.06	(-0.15)
Precision instruments and apparels	-0.07	(-0.35)	0.14	(0.45)	0.10	(0.27)
Food	-0.21	(-1.10)	0.03	(0.09)	0.01	(0.04)
Sugar, tobacco, etc	-0.22	(-1.08)	0.00	(0.00)	0.16	(0.46)
Textile	-0.17	(-0.90)	0.05	(0.16)	0.01	(0.02)
Leather	0.15	(0.91)	0.31	(1.24)	0.33	(1.09)
Shoes and clothing	-0.06	(-0.32)	0.13	(0.42)	0.14	(0.39)
Wood and wooden furniture	-0.08	(-0.45)	0.14	(0.43)	0.03	(0.08)
Paper and printing	**-0.38**	**(-2.03)**	-0.14	(-0.40)	-0.19	(-0.54)
Rubber and plastics	-0.03	(-0.17)	0.21	(0.71)	0.17	(0.51)
Other manufacturing	-0.08	(-0.42)	0.11	(0.34)	0.11	(0.31)
Other non manufacturing	**-0.59**	**(-3.46)**	-0.44	(-1.34)	-0.42	(-1.37)
Electrical measure, equipment, telecommunications	-0.26	(-1.20)	0.10	(0.29)	0.20	(0.56)
North-West	**0.28**	**(9.69)**	**0.28**	**(8.16)**	**0.27**	**(6.13)**
North-Easth	**0.23**	**(8.03)**	**0.23**	**(6.61)**	**0.22**	**(5.11)**
Centre	**0.14**	**(4.55)**	**0.16**	**(4.34)**	**0.17**	**(3.48)**
Size	**0.0001**	**(5.84)**	**0.002**	**(13.15)**	**0.005**	**(11.75)**
CONSEX (Export Consortia)	**0.23**	**(5.68)**	**0.27**	**(5.88)**	**0.29**	**(4.88)**
SUBEX (Export subsidies)	**0.19**	**(3.95)**	**0.19**	**(2.97)**	**0.24**	**(2.53)**
Birth	**-0.002**	**(-5.95)**	**-0.002**	**(-3.90)**	**-0.002**	**(-3.46)**
Group	**0.13**	**(6.98)**	**0.05**	**(2.07)**	0.03	(0.73)
District	**0.05**	**(2.90)**	**0.05**	**(2.54)**	**0.07**	**(2.67)**
N. of observations	3696	-	2970	-	2095	-
χ^2	668.67	-	692.88	-	483.46	-
Log Likelihood	-2069.65	-	-1651.59	-	-1207.87	-

Note: The table reports estimates of the following Probit estimate:

$$_{EU}Expart = \alpha_0 + \sum_{i=1}^{22} \alpha_i Dset_i + \sum_{i=1}^{3} \gamma_k Darea_k + \beta_1 Size + \beta_2 Consex+$$

$$+ \beta_3 Subex + \beta_4 Birth + \beta_5 Group + \beta_6 District + \varepsilon$$

where *Expart* is a dummy variable which takes the value of zero if the firm has a nonzero three year (1989-91) average of the share of export sales versus EU countries on total sales . *Dset$_i$* are 23 sector dummies, *Darea$_k$* are 3 macroarea dummies (NEST, NOVEST, CENTRE), *District* is a dummy which takes value of 1 if the firm is located in an area where the cofficient of geographical agglomeration is higher than one and takes the value of zero otherwise, *Birth* is firm's year of foundation, *Size* is the three year (1989-91) average of firm's employees, *Consex* and *Subex* are two dummies which pick up respectively firms participating to export "consortia" and firms receiving export subsidies . *Group* is a dummy which takes value of one for firms affiliated to groups (subsidiaries or parent companies) and zero otherwise.

Vertical headers for any of table cells indicate the subsample on which the regression is performed. Coefficients significant at 99% are in bold . Estimate disturbances are controlled for normality and heteroskedasticity.

*The table reports in the first column the effect on the probability of being an exporter of a marginal increase in the regressor (dF/dX) and, in the second column, the T-test measuring the statistical significance of this effect.

Table 9. The determinants of the probability of being an exporter toward non-EUcountries

	All Firms		Firms with less than 250 employees		Firms with less than 100 employees	
	(dF/dX)*	T stat	(dF/dX)*	T stat	(dF/dX)*	T stat
Non-metallic mineral products	0.03	(0.21)	0.32	(1.63)	0.03	(0.10)
Chemicals	0.19	(1.58)	**0.42**	**(2.45)**	0.22	(0.75)
Pharmaceuticals	0.01	(0.05)	0.33	(1.60)	0.34	(0.99)
Artificial fibres	-	-	-	-	-	-
Metal products	0.02	(0.13)	0.31	(1.56)	-0.03	(-0.09)
Mechanical Equipment	0.23	(1.92)	**0.46**	**(2.64)**	0.20	(0.67)
Office equipment and computers	-0.25	(-1.42)	0.27	(1.11)	0.07	(0.19)
Electronics and electrical equipment	0.09	(0.74)	**0.37**	**(2.01)**	0.09	(0.29)
Vehicles and vehicle components	0.04	(0.27)	0.31	(1.54)	0.02	(0.07)
Other means of transport	0.12	(0.73)	0.36	(1.59)	-0.16	(-0.47)
Precision instruments and apparels	0.18	(1.29)	**0.42**	**(2.35)**	0.16	(0.50)
Food	-0.01	(-0.06)	0.27	(1.31)	-0.04	(-0.14)
Sugar, tobacco, etc	0.10	(0.75)	0.36	(1.91)	0.25	(0.80)
Textile	0.05	(0.36)	0.31	(1.56)	-0.04	(-0.15)
Leather	0.25	(1.93)	**0.44**	**(2.63)**	0.23	(0.75)
Shoes and clothing	0.14	(1.16)	0.37	(1.99)	0.10	(0.32)
Wood and wooden furniture	0.10	(0.76)	0.36	(1.92)	0.04	(0.13)
Paper and printing	-0.19	(-1.49)	0.14	(0.64)	-0.19	(-0.69)
Rubber and plastics	0.11	(0.83)	**0.39**	**(2.12)**	0.09	(0.30)
Other manufacturing	0.07	(0.58)	0.34	(1.77)	0.11	(0.37)

	All Firms		Firms with less than 250 employees		Firms with less than 100 employees	
	(dF/dX)*	T stat	(dF/dX)*	T stat	(dF/dX)*	T stat
Other non manufacturing	**-0.34**	**(-2.55)**	-0.11	(-0.48)	**-0.40**	**(-2.01)**
Electrical measure, equipment and telecommunications	-0.10	(-0.63)	0.23	(0.98)	-0.01	(-0.04)
North-West	**0.25**	**(7.72)**	**0.26**	**(6.96)**	**0.26**	**(5.59)**
North-Easth	**0.25**	**(7.41)**	**0.26**	**(6.62)**	**0.24**	**(5.23)**
Centre	**0.15**	**(4.17)**	**0.19**	**(4.42)**	**0.19**	**(3.70)**
Size	**0.0001**	**(6.51)**	**0.002**	**(2.76)**	**0.005**	**(10.91)**
CONSEX (Export Consortia)	**0.30**	**(6.81)**	**0.35**	**(7.14)**	**0.37**	**(6.06)**
SUBEX (Export subsidies)	**0.31**	**(6.07)**	**0.31**	**(4.54)**	**0.21**	**(2.29)**
Birth	**-0.002**	**(-5.83)**	**-0.001**	**(-2.86)**	-0.0008	(-1.69)
Group	**0.11**	**(5.59)**	0.02	(0.62)	-0.02	(-0.47)
District	**0.06**	**(3.11)**	**0.07**	**(3.55)**	**0.09**	**(3.60)**
N. of observations	3696	-	2970	-	2096	-
χ^2	647.43	-	637.04	-	445.41	-
Log Likelihood	-2220.79	-	-1740.07	-	-1210.55	-

Table 9. Continuation.

Note: The table reports estimates of the following Probit estimate:

$$NON\text{-}EU Expart = \alpha_0 + \sum_{i=1}^{22}\alpha_i Dset_i + \sum_{i=1}^{3}\gamma_k Darea_k + \beta_1 Size +$$

$$+ \beta_2 Consex + \beta_3 Subex + \beta_4 Birth + \beta_5 Group + \beta_6 District + \varepsilon$$

where *Expart* is a dummy variable which takes the value of zero if the firm has a nonzero three year (1989-91) average of the share of export sales versus non EU countries on total sales. *Dset*$_i$ are 23 sector dummies, *Darea*$_k$ are 3 macroarea dummies (NEST, NOVEST, CENTRE), *District* is a dummy which takes value of 1 if the firm is located in an area where the cofficient of geographical agglomeration is higher than one and takes the value of zero otherwise, *Birth* is firm's year of foundation, *Size* is the three year (1989-91) average of firm's employees, *Consex* and *Subex* are two dummies which pick up respectively firms participating to export "consortia" and firms receiving export subsidies. *Group* is a dummy which takes value of one for firms affiliated to groups (subsidiaries or parent companies) and zero otherwise.

Vertical headers for any of table cells indicate the subsample on which the regression is performed. Coefficients significant at 99% are in bold. Estimate disturbances are controlled for normality and heteroskedasticity.

*The table reports in the first column the effect on the probability of being an exporter of a marginal increase in the regressor (dF/dX) and, in the second column, the T-test measuring the statistical significance of this effect.

Regional location, age, and size are other variables that affect significantly the export performance of Italian firms. The strong association between regional location and export performance is consistent with descriptive evidence from table 1, which shows how the share of exporters drops from around 77 percent in the

North-East to around 41 percent in the South of Italy. This justify why location in the Nort-East or in the North-West is associated in the Probit estimate with an almost ¼ higher likelihood of access to foreign markets. Age (which inversely related to of the regressor *Birth*) is positively related to export intensity and export participation towards EU countries. Its positive impact is increasing in size for trade towards non EU countries so that experience is no more significant when we look at small firm export towards non EU. The marginal impact of size on export performance and on the probability of being an exporter is obviously higher and more significant in subsamples including only small-medium firms. For firms with less than 100 employees and more than 10 workers imply an upsizing process which increases by 5-6 per cent the likelihood of becoming an exporter both on EU and non EU markets.

5   Conclusions

Industrial districts have a relative advantage over other forms of industrial organisation when product complementarities prevail over substitution effects. In this case district firm's product quality improvements, stimulated by enhanced spatial competition, may represent a positive (and not a negative) externality for the neighbour. Along this path district firms may improve their chances vis-a-vis those of non district firms in a multy-winner contest for the conquest of foreign markets. We therefore expect advantages from geographical agglomeration to be decreasing in firms size, higher on export performance towards markets which are more difficult to access, and more relevant in Traditional and Specialised sectors where complementarities and small scale production prevail.

Empirical results of the paper show that benefits on export performance from geographical agglomeration are higher for smaller firms and for firms belonging to Traditional and Specialised sectors. Econometric findings indicate that geographical agglomeration significantly increases export intensity and export participation and that the effect is larger when only firms with less than 100 employees are considered. The results is robust when controlled for firm size, sector and geographical areas and for the separate and positive effects on export intensity of export subsidies and export "consortia". Geographical agglomeration (but also export consortia and export subsidies) has a stronger impact on export performance towards non EU than EU countries.

The empirical analysis also evaluates the impact of a discrete change in the "district" dummy on the probability of being an exporter towards the EU (non EU) countries and finds that geographical agglomeration increases by 5 percent (7 percent) the likelihood of being an exporter when all firms (firms with less than 100 employees) are considered. The marginal impact of GA on the probability of being an exporter towards non EU countries rises to 6 percent (9 percent) when all firms (firms with less than 100 employees) are considered.

These results highlights an important source of domestic growth. When in fact geographical agglomeration and participation to industrial districts shift small-medium firms production from domestic to foreign markets, and when these markets are characterised by higher technological spillovers because they are more competitive, higher export intensity of small-medium firms may have significant effects on growth.

References

Amemiya T., 1973, Regression analysis when the dependent variable is truncated normal, in *Econometrica* 41.

Aumann R. and Shapley L., 1976, Long Term Competition: a Game Theoretic Analysis, *mimeo*.

Bagella M., Becchetti L. and Caggese A., 1996, Financial constraints on investments: evidence from direct revelation, in *Rivista di Politica Economica*.

Bagella M., Becchetti L. and Caggese A., 1996, Finanza, Investimenti ed Innovazione in Italia: il divario Nord-South in B.Quintieri (ed.) *Finanza, Istituzioni e sviluppo regionale: il problema del Mezzogiorno*, Il Mulino.

Bagella M. and Becchetti L., 1998, Geographical agglomeration in R&D games: theoretical and empirical evidence, in *The Competitive advantage of Italian district: theoretical and empirical analysis*, M.Bagella (*ed.*) Physica Verlag, and *Quaderni di Politica Industriale*, N.19, Mediocredito Centrale.

Bagella M. and Pietrobelli C., 1995, Distretti industriali e internazionalizzazione. Presupposti teorici ed evidenza empirica dell'America Latina, in *Economia e Politica Industriale* 86,2.

Becattini G.,1987, *Mercato e Forze Locali: Il Distretto Industriale*, Bologna, Il Mulino.

Becattini G., 1991, Il distretto industriale marshalliano come concetto socio-economico, in Pyke F., Becattini G., W. Sengenberger (*eds.*), *Distretti industriali e cooperazione tra imprese in Italia*, Quaderno n. 34 di Studi e Informazione della Banca Toscana

Becchetti L. and Rossi S.P.S., 1998, Distretti industriali e destinazione dell'export: quali le determinanti?, in *Quaderni di Politica Industriale*, N.19, Mediocredito Centrale.

Becchetti L. and Rossi S., 1999, The positive effect of Industrial District on the export performance of Italian firms, *The Review of Industrial Organisation*, (forth.).

Bellandi M., 1996, Innovation and change in the Marshallian Industrial District, in *European Planning Studies*, Vol. 4, n. 3.

Bianchi P., 1989, Concorrenza Dinamica, Distretti Industriali e Interventi Locali, in F. Gobbo, *Distretti Industriali e sistemi produttivi alla soglia degli anni '90*, F. Angeli, Milano.

Brusco S., 1991, La genesi dell'idea del distretto industriale, in Pyke F., Becattini G., W. Sengenberger (eds.), *Distretti industriali e cooperazione tra imprese in Italia*, Quaderno n. 34 di Studi e Informazione della Banca Toscana.

De Cecco M., and Ferri G., 1997, Merchant Banks and Industrial Investment in Italy, paper presented at the 1997 Financial Conference in Venice.

Fudenberg D., and Tirole J.J., 1992, *Game Theory*, MIT Press, Cambridge Massachusetts.

D'Aspremont C., Gabszewicz J.J. and Thisse J.F., 1979, On Hotelling's stability in competition, in *Econometrica*, Vol.47.

Del Colle E., 1997, *Le aree produttive. Struttura economica dei sistemi regionali in Italia*. Franco Angeli.

Kirsty Hughes, 1996, *Export and technology*, Cambridge University Press.

Momigliano F. and Dosi G., 1983, *Tecnologia e organizzazione Industriale Internazionale*, Bologna, Il Mulino.

Moran P.A.P., 1950, Notes on continuous stochastic phenomena, in *Biometrika*, 37.

Nuti F., 1992, *I Distretti Industriali Manifatturieri*, Vol.1, CNR.

Onida F., Viesti G. and Falzoni A.M., 1992, *Distretti Industriali: Crisi o Evoluzione?*, CESPRI, Egea.

Porter M., 1991, *Il vantaggio Competitivo delle Nazioni*, Milano, Mondadori.

Pyke F. and Sengenberger W., 1992, *Industrial GA and local Economic Regeneration*, Geneva, International Institute for Labour Studies.

Rubinstein A., 1979, Equilibrium in Supergames with the Overtaking Criterion, in *Journal of Economic Theory*, 21, 1-9.

Sforzi F., 1991, *Sistemi Locali di Piccola e Media Impresa*, IRPET.

Sforzi F., 1995, *Sistemi Locali di Impresa e Cambiamento Industriale in Italia*, AGEI-Geotema n°2.

Shaked A. and Sutton J., 1983, Natural oligopolies, in *Econometrica*, Vol. 51.

Appendix

Table A.1. The determinants of export intensity towards EU countries

Dep. Variable: Export per employees towards EU	All firms		Firms with less than 250 employees		Firms with less than 100 employees	
	Coeff.	T stat	Coeff.	T stat	Coeff.	T stat
Birth	-0.13	-1.86	-0.09	-1.03	-0.21	-1.65
CONSEX (Export Consortia)	**33.16**	**4.16**	**35.43**	**4.01**	**48.45**	**3.79**
SUBEX (Export subsidies)	**17.93**	**2.19**	**31.08**	**2.72**	**41.42**	**2.17**
Size	**0.00**	**2.11**	**0.29**	**8.25**	**0.93**	**8.18**
Non-metallic mineral products	1.18	0.04	17.48	0.22	6.39	0.07
Chemicals	29.94	0.99	44.45	0.56	24.87	0.27
Pharmaceuticals	1.55	0.05	26.15	0.32	-12.01	-0.11
Artificial fibres	2.37	0.05	-88.53	-0.86	-647.03	-
Metal products	9.26	0.31	29.78	0.38	16.58	0.18
Mechanical Equipment	31.99	1.09	52.73	0.67	41.21	0.44
Office equipment and computers	-39.20	-1.02	-46.72	-0.53	-51.52	-0.47
Electronics and electrical equipment	21.40	0.72	41.97	0.53	31.07	0.33
Vehicles and vehicle components	37.55	1.19	35.33	0.44	14.79	0.15
Other means of transport	27.08	0.77	44.88	0.53	29.19	0.27
Precision instruments and apparels	12.97	0.40	33.33	0.41	22.65	0.24
Food	15.36	0.50	36.22	0.46	25.93	0.28
Sugar, tobacco, etc	10.41	0.33	31.81	0.39	61.30	0.64
Textile	30.26	1.02	49.01	0.62	42.68	0.46
Leather	81.05	2.55	104.47	1.30	83.92	0.89
Shoes and clothing	44.29	1.49	63.55	0.80	62.95	0.68
Wood and wooden furniture	30.59	1.01	49.98	0.63	24.79	0.27
Paper and printing	-25.96	-0.87	-11.49	-0.15	-32.90	-0.35
Rubber and plastics	37.33	1.25	63.38	0.80	51.24	0.55
Other manufacturing	49.63	1.66	68.25	0.86	56.05	0.60
Other non manufacturing	-50.09	-1.58	-74.05	-0.91	-109.04	-1.11
Electrical measure, equipment, telecommunications	-8.96	-0.26	24.10	0.29	26.84	0.27
North-West	**53.39**	**7.77**	**56.43**	**6.79**	**63.63**	**5.36**
North-Easth	**54.47**	**7.76**	**57.38**	**6.83**	**63.89**	**5.35**
Centre	**43.63**	**5.67**	**49.99**	**5.43**	**60.14**	**4.61**
Group	**26.36**	**7.11**	**17.08**	**3.39**	**16.82**	**2.08**
District	4.29	1.23	5.51	1.32	**12.06**	**2.00**
Constant	54.85	0.72	-33.07	-0.28	43.94	0.29
N. of observations	3696	-	2970	-	2096	-
χ^2	362	-	397.32	-	298.25	-
Log Likelihood	-14945	-	-11364	-	-7272.4	-
Left censored obs.	1326	-	1196	-	1002	-

Note: The table reports magnitude and T-statistics of the following Tobit estimate:

$$_{EU}Expadd = \alpha_0 + \sum_{i=1}^{22} \alpha_i Dset_i + \sum_{k=1}^{3} \gamma_k Darea_k + \beta_1 Size +$$

$$\beta_2 Consex + \beta_3 Subex + \beta_4 Birth + \beta_5 Group + \beta_6 District + \varepsilon$$

where $_{EU}Expadd$ is the three year (1989-91) average of the share of export sales per employees towards EU countries. The dependent variable is left censored at 0. $Dset_i$ are 22 sector dummies, $Darea_k$ are three macro areas dummies (North-East, North-West, Centre), $Size$ is the three year (1989-91) average of the number of employees in the firm, $Consex$ and $Subex$ are two dummies which refer respectively to the firms participating in export "consortia"[9] and to the firms receiving export subsidies, $Birth$ is the firm's foundation year, $Group$ is a dummy which takes the value of one for firms affiliated to groups (subsidiaries or parent companies) and zero otherwise, $District$ is a dummy which takes the value of one if firms are located in GA areas, measured with the Sforzi criterion, and zero otherwise.

Vertical headers for any of table cells indicate the subsample on which the regression is performed. Coefficients significant at 95% are in bold. Estimate disturbances are controlled for normality and homoskedasticity .

Table A.2. The determinants of export intensity towards non EU countries

Dep. Variable: Export per employees towards non EU countries	All firms		Firms with less than 250 employees		Firms with less than 100 employees	
	Coeff.	T stat	Coeff.	T stat	Coeff.	T stat
Birth	**-0.35**	**-3.72**	-0.22	-1.78	-0.15	-0.96
CONSEX (Export Consortia)	**41.47**	**4.12**	**48.57**	**4.28**	**60.24**	**4.43**
SUBEX (Export subsidies)	**77.56**	**7.61**	**95.20**	**6.59**	**50.63**	**2.47**
Size	0.00	0.95	**0.37**	**8.08**	**1.04**	**8.32**
Non-metallic mineral products	5.39	0.14	19.56	0.20	-11.81	-0.12
Chemicals	43.33	1.10	60.07	0.61	29.75	0.30
Pharmaceuticals	20.15	0.47	41.10	0.40	47.82	0.44
Artificial fibres	-4.77	-0.08	-107.33	-0.83	-655.70	.
Metal products	4.25	0.11	15.40	0.16	-18.19	-0.19
Mechanical equipment	55.00	1.42	65.89	0.67	32.72	0.34
Office equipment and computers	-37.46	-0.75	-7.74	-0.07	-5.54	-0.05
Electronics and electrical equipment	30.90	0.80	53.47	0.54	24.22	0.25

[9] Export consortia are contractual agreements, ruled by Italian Civil Law, among firms which choose to cooperate, to provide common funds and to share information for the development of export activity. They may lead or not to the creation of an independent corporation even though constituents always maintain their independent identity. Consortia differ from cartels and are tolerated by antitrust authorities because their goal is not to restrict competition by altering prices or quantities but just to cooperate in the provision of services to improve export performance. Consortia may then be considered a type of formal cooperation, while geographical agglomeration represents a type of informal cooperation.

Dep. Variable: Export per employees towards non EU countries	All firms		Firms with less than 250 employees		Firms with less than 100 employees	
	Coeff.	T stat	Coeff.	T stat	Coeff.	T stat
Vehicles and vehicle components	13.48	0.33	17.11	0.17	-7.60	-0.07
Other means of transport	7.40	0.16	10.30	0.10	-64.36	-0.53
Precision instruments and apparels	32.05	0.76	47.61	0.47	18.40	0.18
Food	14.17	0.35	23.97	0.24	-11.73	-0.12
Sugar, tobacco, etc	15.66	0.38	37.81	0.38	39.05	0.39
Textile	10.65	0.27	20.60	0.21	-19.70	-0.20
Leather	67.51	1.62	84.24	0.84	35.30	0.36
Shoes and clothing	35.79	0.92	44.34	0.45	7.96	0.08
Wood and wooden furniture	18.48	0.47	32.09	0.32	-7.33	-0.08
Paper and printing	-43.53	-1.11	-30.89	-0.31	-66.97	-0.69
Rubber and plastics	17.27	0.44	39.15	0.40	1.69	0.02
Other manufacturing	41.42	1.05	64.62	0.65	60.84	0.62
Other non manufacturing	27.70	0.68	29.41	0.29	-194.69	-1.76
Electrical measure, equipment, telecommunications	-26.86	-0.58	-9.90	-0.09	-29.78	-0.28
North-West	**58.62**	**6.44**	**67.96**	**5.98**	**62.13**	**4.55**
North-Easth	**60.35**	**6.51**	**67.01**	**5.84**	**65.47**	**4.77**
Centre	**44.54**	**4.38**	**54.46**	**4.34**	**56.60**	**3.79**
Group	**27.33**	**5.71**	11.99	1.80	-1.39	-0.15
District	5.32	1.18	**11.21**	**2.02**	**19.55**	**2.91**
Constant	**220.60**	**2.25**	40.99	0.26	-25.38	-0.14
N. of observations	3696	-	2970	-	2096	-
χ^2	375.4	-	367	-	305	-
Log Likelihood	-13347	-	-10025	-	-5143	-
Left censored obs.	1680	-	1483	-	1193	-

Table A.2. Continuation

Note: The table reports magnitude and T-statistics of the following Tobit estimate:

$$_{NON-EU}Expadd = \alpha_0 + \sum_{i=1}^{22}\alpha_i Dset_i + \sum_{k=1}^{3}\gamma_k Darea_k + \beta_1 Size +$$

$$\beta_2 Consex + \beta_3 Subex + \beta_4 Birth + \beta_5 Group + \beta_6 District + \varepsilon$$

where $_{NON-EU}Expadd$ is the three year (1989-91) average of the share of export sales per employees towards non EU countries. The dependent variable is left censored at 0. $Dset_i$ are 22 sector dummies, $Darea_k$ are three macro areas dummies (North-East, North-West, Centre), $Size$ is the three year (1989-91) average of the number of employees in the firm, $Consex$ and $Subex$ are two dummies which refer respectively to the firms participating in export "consortia" and to the firms receiving export subsidies, $Birth$ is the firm's foundation year, $Group$ is a dummy which takes the value of one for firms affiliated to groups (subsidiaries or parent companies) and zero otherwise, $District$ is a dummy which takes the value of one if firms are located in GA areas, measured with the Sforzi criterion, and zero otherwise.

Vertical headers for any of table cells indicate the subsample on which the regression is performed. Coefficients significant at 95% are in bold. Estimate disturbances are controlled for normality and homoskedasticity.

Industrial Districts, Horizontal and Vertical Integration and Export Performance

Simona Sacchi

University of Rome "Tor Vergata", Faculty of Economics, Department of Economics and Institutions, Via di Tor Vergata snc, 00133 – Rome. E-mail sisac@tin.it

Abstract: The degree of integration among firms is one of the most relevant features which discriminate among different types of agglomeration. Collaboration and cooperation relationships in production and marketing, division of labour coming from the disintegration of production process, supply relationships and research agreements, generate a feeling of solidarity among firms that little by little turns into necessity of hierarchy and organization. In this framework the chapter studies export performance of geographical agglomerated firms which presumably turn out to be integrated among them by the mean of formal or tacit agreements of cooperation. The chapter finds support for the existence of positive externalities coming from localization; such externalities, in turn, come from spillover effects, from a faster circulation of information flows and from firms imitation processes that accelerate the pace of innovations.

JEL Classification: R3

Keywords: Industrial districts, Horizontal and vertical integration, Export performance.

1   Introduction

During the '70s the Fordist mass-productive system started to show some weaknesses, since it was no longer able to react promptly to demand changes. Flexibility and agility, considered key factors for an effective adaptation of the productive system to technological and demand changes in production, seemed to be the answer to the necessity of a renewal of such system. These two elements are present in productive systems characterised by specialization of the structures and by concentration in certain productive sectors and also by the presence of networks of firms in continuous evolution. These networks result to be sensitive to external changes and able to answer readily to demand shocks. The higher flexibility of small-medium firm networks with respect to the Fordist system fostered a process of spatial concentration in a framework of increasing economic uncertainty. This phenomenon is known as "localisation" and it is characterised by thick networks of economic relationships among firms of a certain geographic area. These firms are linked among them by particular relationships of cooperation[1] stimulated by the features of new technological paradigms and by market globalisation.

The synergistic action of those factors has multiplied challenges and opportunities for productive systems, accelerating the pace of innovation. This leads firms to outsource rather than to develop internally some production phases, generating in this way intense relationships of trade with the neighbours.

Agglomeration economies are characterised by: a) a strong boost towards division of labour among firms throughout a phase specialization and the existence of intense interfirm trade links that generate a reduction in total costs; b) the accumulation of knowledge and the diffusion of abilities concerning a certain sector of activity; c) the reduction of transaction costs among productive units in a certain area, due to the proximity and frequency of personal relationships; d) the wide availability of goods and services provided by other firms located in the proximity; e) the faster introduction of innovations and the significant improvement of the organizational and productive techniques, due to the intensity of informational flows. The functioning of local systems is regulated by two opposite and, at the same time, complementary mechanisms: competition and cooperation. Competition takes place among firms operating in the same phase of the productive process and contributes to give a remarkable dynamism to the system. Cooperation, instead, results from the complementary relation existing among units placed at different levels of the productive cycle. It allows firms to

---

[1] Rullani e Vaccà "Scienza e tecnologia nello sviluppo industriale", Economia e Politica Industriale, N° 53, 1987.

benefit of the external economies connected to networks dimension, but mainly it assures an effective activity of collaboration.

These connections among firms foster the creation of vertical type relationships (among producer and users firms of a certain good or service) and horizontal type relationships (among firms producing the same goods and services) corresponding respectively to a "speciality decentralisation" and "capability decentralisation" (Nuti, 1992). Firms are inclined to develop cooperative relations and not to reduce the intensity of competition among them, in order to increase their own competitive abilities by the mean of access to complementary resources. Following this set up, cooperative relationships turn out to be essential to uphold the "counting competition"[2], "the concentrated structure is the result of competition and not the sign of its lack" (Shaked and Sutton, 1983).

In such framework the aim of this paper is that of studying export performances of a sample of small-medium Italian firms belonging to local systems. The underlying hypothesis is that geographically agglomerated firms, which have developed integration agreements, record a better export performance with respect to other firms (agglomerated and not agglomerated).

2   The Localisation Indicator

The empirical analysis is carried on the Mediocredito database. Sample data concern qualitative and quantitative information about 3852 small-medium firms of the Italian manufacturing system, for the years 1989-1991.

To identify local systems we use the Sforzi classification method. Sample firms are divided into two classes: GA (geographically agglomerated) and Other Firms. In the former class a further classification has been created in order to identify firms that present a certain degree of integration. For this proposal it has been used an index worked out by Del Colle which takes into account a localisation ratio, comparable to a specialization index. It expresses the different incidence of each economic activity on the economy of a given area. Such index is given by the ratio between the employees share in a certain economic activity of the area[3] and the analogous share computed at region level. Index values greater than 1 signal some form of specialization.

[2] Gambardella, Torrisi, Zanfei *"Concorrenza dinamica e cooperazione fra imprese. Elementi per una teoria dei fallimenti delle reti"*, In Prospettive degli studi di economia e politica industriale in Italia, A cura di G. Becattini e S. Vaccà.

[3] To work out the areas see Del Colle, 1997.

Among GA firms it is possible to identify those firms with a localisation index greater than 1. Such firms are said to be "specialized" or likely integrated among them by vertical or horizontal relationships, while firms belonging to GA group with a specialization index less than 1 are said to be "not specialized".

3   Empirical Descriptive Results

3.1 Size

Firms with a number of employees ranged between 1 and 250 are considered small; firms with a number of employees ranged between 251 and 500 are considered medium sized and firms with more than 500 employees are large. The small firms' class is the largest (80.4% of the sample); while the most densely populated area is the North West (43.6% of firms), North East follows with 33.1%.

From table 1 comes out that small firms are particularly present in traditional sectors and in general where less sophisticated productions are realised; essentially their presence is detected in industrial sectors with low technological standard and with low demand of capitals. If on one hand, it is true that small-medium firms can benefit of external economies coming from industrial environment relationships, on the other hand a reason of their limited development can be brought about the difficulties to have access to different financing sources (Bagella-Becchetti-Caggese, 1996).

3.2 Geography

The Country can be considered as virtually divided into four main areas (macroareas): North West characterised by the presence of large firms, North East and Centre populated by small-medium firms and South where there are few large firms.

Different kinds of productive process organization depend on the relationship between economic activity and territory. The most complex phenomenon is given by the Marshallian industrial district, where territory, social and economic relationships among the participants are the characterizing and distinguishing elements. The main feature of industrial district resides in the territorial dimension subordinated to the thick network of social and economic intra-relations set up among firms and the local community.

The question is if this kind of model has reached an adult stage and if it requires an evolution by the light of an increasing international economic integration and of technological change boost, bringing into question the districts' "best" borders. It is interesting to see if districts are changing their structure towards broader network type system advantage, since networks represent very often the local productive system consolidation.

3.3 Horizontal and Vertical Integration

Integration among firms geographically agglomerated is revealed by the set of formal and informal agreements arranged by them, concerning production and marketing of their own products and exchange of services. To gain flexibility, in order to be able to adjust to market changes, firms need some strategies of coordination and redefinition of the internal tasks.

Stigler (1951) shows that firm vertical disintegration is higher where industrial concentration is stronger, taking into account the relationship between industry concentration and production facilities dimension. Such hypothesis is supported by various studies which highlight the higher degree of vertical integration for firms placed in less developed areas: Scott and Angel (1987), for the semiconductor industry, Florio (1982) for the furniture sector, Del Monte and Martinelli (1988) for the telecommunications and pressed circuit sectors, Giunta (1993) for footwear sector. These studies highlight some regularities concerning the relationships among firms and concerning the degree of vertical integration in certain areas: 1) the more a firm is technologically innovative, the higher is its degree of vertical integration, if it is located in an area not much developed; 2) a negative relationship between vertical integration and spatial industry concentration of (Del Monte 1994). Data reported in tables 1 and 2 support these hypothesis, showing how sample firms are distributed throughout the territory among GA firms, Other Firms (OF) and specialized GA firms. The highest concentration of specialized GA firms (mainly small firms) is present in the North east, 28.8%; it follows Centre with 24.1% and at last the North West and South.

The reason for the scarce development of firms' agreements in the South is due not only to the presence of high transaction costs, but also to other elements such as the degree of trust among agents. The degree of confidence among entrepreneurs is one of the factor that contributes to the development of the cooperative bonds among firms. Intense subsidisation in the South of Italy, matched with a lower quality of labour and to less industrial concentration, reduced the incentive to the creation of trust relationships.

3.4 Production Sectors

Following Pavitt' sector classification, four economic sectors are identifiable: Traditional, Special, Scale, High technology. Specialized GA firms turn out to operate mainly in the Traditional sectors (56.5%) and in the Special one (27.8%), while GA firms operate mainly in Scale (29.6%) and Traditional sectors (46.9%) (Table 3, appendix 1).

4   A Descriptive Analysis of the Positive Link Between Geographical Agglomeration, Specialization and Export Intensity

Table 4 shows that Specialized GA firms realised a share of export sales proceeds significantly higher than other GA firms (the difference is around 6 percentage points). This is true for all size classes and more significant for small firms (table 5). Such result is consistent with the hypothesis that some potential positive effects, coming from geographical agglomeration, are negatively related to firm dimension and to the degree of vertical differentiation (Shaked-Sutton, 1983). Also at macroregional level, empirical evidence shows a higher export share among Specialized GA firms, more significantly in the North, less in the Centre-South; this is likely due to the scant number of observations for those areas (table 6). The strongest difference between specialized GA and GA firms can be found in the North West (around 8%), it follows the North East (7 percentage points). In particular the matter is brought out in the North, where firms cooperation to gain access to foreign markets is likely more favourable, because of the lower costs of market sharing with partners.

At last, table 7 shows that for each Pavitt' macrosectors Specialized GA share of export sales proceeds is greater than the other in; particularly "special" sector has been an increase in the difference for 6.8% with respect to not Specialized GA firms.

5   Results from the Econometric Analysis

The descriptive results presented above do not provide conclusive evidence on the positive effect of specialized geographical agglomeration on export intensity, as they are not controlled for dimensional, sector and geographical effect. Therefore the econometric analysis carried out intends to isolate the net effect of geographical agglomeration on export intensity, using control variables for firm size, sector, geographic location, belonging to group and consortia. In table 8 are shown the coefficients and T statistics concerning the net effect of specialized geographical agglomeration on export intensity; equation (1) has been used for three sub-samples: 1) all firms, 2) firms with less than 250 employees; 3) firms with less than 100 employees.

$$Exp/s.p. = \alpha_0 + \sum \alpha_i DSett + \sum_{k=1}^{3} \beta_k Area + \gamma GA + \gamma_1 GA_s + \beta_4 Cons$$
$$+ \beta_5 Group + \beta_6 Dimen + \varepsilon \qquad (1)$$

Where $Exp/s.p.$ is the dependent variable, it is the three years (1989-1991) average of the share of export sales on total sales; $Dsett$ are 23 sector dummies; GA is a dummy which takes the value of 1 if the firm belongs to a local system, and the value of 0 otherwise; GA_s is a dummy that takes the value of 1 if it belongs to a local system and if the localisation index is greater than 1; $Dimen$ is the three years (1989-1991) average of firm's employees; $Cons$ is a dummy indicating consortium participation; $Group$ points out the belonging to a group of firms; at last, $Area$ indicates the four regions in which the territory is subdivided for the analysis.

Evidence from empirical results shows that: 1) specialized geographical agglomeration generates a positive effect on export and it is decreasing in firm size; 2) non specialized geographical agglomeration effect on export is decreasing in firm' size; 3) firms participating to export consortia obtain a higher share of export sales; 4) participation to the mechanical sector, footwear and clothing sector, leather sector generates a positive effect on export intensity; 5) firms located in the North of the Country present a higher share of export sales than firms located in other areas.

The first result seems to show that cooperation among firms generates a double positive effect: it allows firms to enjoy positive externalities linked to spillovers and to get rid of negative externalities coming from expenditure duplication that should be borne without cooperation. This result should confirm that the set up of cooperation relationships has the goal of reinforcing firms' competitive ability, rather than of reducing competition intensity. Furthermore, there is evidence that benefits from cooperation increase as firm size decreases, also for "non specialized GA firms", because small firms are likely to obtain higher benefits from imitating competitors. Taking part to an export consortium may be considered an aspect of cooperation, it affects positively the export performance. Point 4 highlights that in the years 1989-1991 Italian industry continued to be strongly characterised towards traditional consume sectors, (Onida, 1993). At last, from the analysis it is evident that firms located in the North export more than the others, confirming again the idea that cooperation advantage in entering foreign markets is significantly higher when sharing markets with competitors costs less.

Further analysis has been carried out in order to study the impact on export participation of variables like size, sector and area by using the following probit specification:

$$Expart = \alpha_0 + \sum \alpha_i DSett + \sum_{k=1}^{3} \beta_k Area + \gamma GA + \gamma_1 GA_s + \beta_4 Cons$$

$$+ \beta_5 Group + \beta_6 Dimen + \varepsilon$$

(2)

Where *Expart* is a dummy which takes the value of 1 when the sample firm realises sales proceeds from export, and the value of 0 otherwise; the other regressors are the same as in equation (1).

Empirical evidence gives us results which are similar to those obtained with equation (1): In particular the probability to export results to be a decreasing function of firm' size, such inverse relation is particularly true for not specialized GA firms and for firms located in the North of the Country.

6   Conclusions

During the '70s the production system based on large firms revealed itself obsolete and unable to answer promptly to market changes. In that period we assist to the birth of a system of small-medium firms that today constitutes the framework of Italian economy. There is a passage from a production in bulk (Ford type) to a widespread production (flexible type), where small-medium firms substituted large firms through a process of labour division. This new set up seemed to be more sensitive to market changes, following nimbly what is indicated by the environmental forces.

This scenario is characterised by a process of firms geographical agglomeration, known as "localisation". There exist different types of firms geographical agglomeration that imply different distinctive features. Industrial districts represent an example of this phenomenon, where socio-cultural elements permeate the overall activity carried out in the district; close relationships among entrepreneurs and with the whole local community allow to define the district's borders, such that we can recognise its peculiar feature: the capability of being self-containing, since labour force is endogenous to the system.

Geographical agglomeration phenomenon can be identified not only by industrial district; alternative shapes can be found in: 1) networks made up around large firms with strong local connotations; 2) networks coming from the joint disintegration of large firms; 3) networks in some areas which tend to a productive specialization; 4) networks of firms producing the same good; 5) system areas.

The degree of integration among firms is one of the most important features to distinguish among different types of agglomeration. Collaboration and cooperation relationships in production and marketing, labour division coming from the disintegration of production process, supply relationships and research agreements, generate a feeling of solidarity among firms that little by little turns into necessity of a hierarchy and organization. In this framework the chapter studies export performance of geographical agglomerated firms which presumably turn out to be integrated among them by the mean of formal or tacit agreements of cooperation. The chapter finds an evident existence of positive externalities coming from localisation; such externalities, in turn, come from spillover effects, from a faster circulation of information flows and from firms imitation processes that accelerate the pace of innovations.

Appendix 1

Table 1. Firms classified by dimension (percentages)

Firms	Small	Medium	Large	Total
Other firms	50.2	56.9	74.8	2068
GA	29.3	19.3	14.9	1036
GA specialised	20.5	21.1	13.4	747
N° observations	3098	337	417	3852

GA are those firms belonging to a local system (according to Sforzi's classification); GA specialised are those firms that belong to a local system and also present a localisation index greater than 1 (according with Del Colle classification); Other firms are those firms not geographically agglomerated.

Table 2. Firms present in the macroareas (percentages)

Firms	North-West	North-East	Centre	South
Other firms	56	41.8	53.9	85.4
GA	30.6	29.4	22	7.7
GA specialised	13.4	28.8	24.1	6.9
N° observations	1679	1274	549	350

GA are those firms belonging to a local system (according to Sforzi's classification); GA specialised are those firms that belong to a local system and also present a localisation index greater than 1 (according with Del Colle classification); Other firms are those firms not geographically agglomerated.

Table 3. Firms per macrosectors (percentages)

Firms	Other firms	GA	GA specialised	Total firms of the sector
Traditional	41.6	50.2	56.5	45.9
Special	21.3	24.3	27.8	22.5
Scale	31.7	24.1	15.5	28
High-Tech	5.4	1.5	0.1	3.6
N° observations	2068	1036	747	100

Table 4: Export sales proceeds (percentage)

Firms	Export average sales proceeds	Standard deviation	Confidence Interval	N° ob.
GA	23.08	27.20	21.24 to 24.73	1036
GA specialized	29.10	28.6	27.04 to 31.16	747
Other Firms	20.71	26.52	19.57 to 21.86	2068

GA are those firms belonginig to a local system (according to Sforzi's classification); GA specialized are those firms that belong to a local system and also present a localisation index greater than 1 (according with Del Colle classification); Other firms are those firms not geographically agglomerated.

Table 5: Export sales proceeds (percentage) for firms GA and GA specialized by dimension

Firms	Export average sales proceeds	Standard deviation	Confidence Interval			N° ob.
Small GA Special.	27.42	28.75	25.17	to	29.66	633
Small GA	22.03	27.34	20.53	to	23.81	909
Medium GA Special.	36.74	25.63	30.67	to	42.81	71
Medium GA	30	24.33	23.97	to	36.09	65
Large GA Special.	41.23	27.29	32.83	to	49.63	43
Large GA	31.17	25.89	24.60	to	37.75	62
total	25.64	27.96	24.30	to	26.90	1783

GA are those firms belonginig to a local system (according to Sforzi's classification); GA specialized are those firms that belong to a local system and also present a localisation index greater than 1 (according with Del Colle classification); Other firms are those firms not geographically agglomerated.

Table 6: Export sales proceeds (percentage) per Macroareas

Firms	Export average sales proceeds	Standard deviation	Confidence Interval			N° ob.
North West GA Special.	30.61	27.24	27.02	to	34019	224
North West GA	22.78	25.85	20.54	to	25.026	513
North Est GA Special.	30.90	27.89	28.04	to	33.77	367
North Est GA	23.60	27.42	20.81	to	26.38	375
Centre GA Special.	24.15	32.23	18.60	to	29.70	132
Centre GA	25.73	32.34	19.91	to	31.55	121
Soth GA special	14.70	26.19	3.64	to	25.76	24
South GA	9.62	20.75	1.41	to	17.84	27
Total	25.60	27.96	24.30	to	26.90	1783

GA are those firms belonginig to a local system (according to Sforzi's classification); GA specialized are those firms that belong to a local system and also present a localisation index greater than 1 (according with Del Colle classification); Other firms are those firms not geographically agglomerated.

Table 7: Export sales proceeds (percentage) per Macrosector

Firms	Export average sales proceeds	Standard deviation	Confidence Interval			N° ob.
Traditional GA Special.	24.86	28.4	25.14	to	27.58	422
Traditional GA	21.84	27.2	18.59	to	23.45	486
Specialized GA Special.	39.25	28.4	35.35	to	43.14	208
Specialized GA	32.47	29.14	28.59	to	36.35	219

Firms	Export average sales proceeds	Standard deviation	Confidence Interval	N° ob.
Scale GA Special.	26.5	25.2	21.94 to 31.24	116
Scale GA	19.6	24.2	16.88 to 22.34	307

Table 7. Continuation.

GA are those firms belonginig to a local system (according to Sforzi's classification); GA specialized are those firms that belong to a local system and also present a localisation index greater than 1 (according with Del Colle classification); Other firms are those firms not geographically agglomerated.

Appendix 2

Table 8: Tobit Regression; Independent variable: export sales proceeds/total sales proceeds for the years 1989-1991

Variable	All Firms		Firms with less than 250 employes		Firms with less than 100 employes	
	Coefficient	T Statistic	Coefficient	T Statistic	Coefficient	T Statistic
N° employed	0.000182	0.771618	.1574603	13.822	0.3780	11.340
Duset1	3.36865	0.261	-4.392714	-1.294	-2.164984	-0.500
Duset2	9.993958	0.772	2.176939	0.558	1.757194	0.352
Duset3	-.8278829	-0.061	-5.190999	-0.621	-6.880286	-0.488
Duset6	26.48835	2.080	17.94142	7.308	16.0855	5.104
Duset7	-18.56316	-1.208	-27.90225	-2.170	-20.57293	-1.299
Duset8	12.20217	0.955	5.153753	1.733	16.0855	1.658
Duset9	14.03433	1.051	-3.204277	-0.493	0.2514472	0.026
Duset10	16.25542	1.122	3.192853	0.298	-1.000133	-0.064
Duset11	14.85079	1.098	7.6554	1.190	5.630097	0.682
Duset12	-5.760857	-0.442	-12.78297	-3.189	-10.31245	-1.899
Duset13	-5.913347	-0.443	-11.84077	-2.105	0.5548715	0.076
Duset14	6.637382	0.519	-2.638291	-0.915	-4.436303	-1.191
Duset15	31.19087	2.316	25.04543	4.959	23.73804	3.699
Duset16	18.43402	1.439	11.05328	3.942	12.70993	3.594
Duset17	10.80925	0.835	3.592224	1.047	-1.582902	-0.357
Duset18	-16.1554	-1.259	-22.40093	-7.313	-23.10681	-6.140
Duset19	12.14627	0.944	7.713722	2.413	5.547715	1.454
Duset20	15.33241	1.189	8.816546	2.540	12.87487	2.780
Duset21	-20.49722	-1.539	-37.32058	-5.888	-50.91371	-5.483
Duset22	-5.341085	-0.372	-9.637952	-1.076	-3.552738	-0.318
North West	22.53731	9.563	22.54238	8.278	25.02205	7.159
North Est	22.84745	9.442	22.38581	8.087	23.9378	6.785
Centre	17.90241	6.736	19.99922	6.597	23.22393	6.040
Consortia	4.26943	2.362	7.509427	3.849	7.607834	3.107
Group	9.081464	7.057	1.374863	0.815	-1.808865	-0.743
GA Special	5.168525	3.170	6.480895	3.495	9.966055	4.214
GA no Special	1.326784	0.949	2.690374	1.706	5.458724	2.696
Constant	-18.02548	-1.402	-25.02841	-8.117	-38.15005	-9.474

$$Exp/s.p. = \alpha_0 + \sum \alpha_i DSett + \sum_{k=1}^{3} \beta_k Area + \gamma GA + \gamma_1 GA_s + \beta_4 Cons$$
$$+ \beta_5 Group + \beta_6 Size + \varepsilon \tag{A.1}$$

Where Exp/s.p. represents the export sales proceeds for the years 1989-1991; Dsett is a dummy for 23 sectors; GA is a dummy which takes the value of 1 if the firm belongs to a local system, and 0 otherwise; Ga$_s$ is a which takes the value of 1 if the firm belongs to a local system and also presents a localisation index (Del Colle) greater than 1; Size is the average number of employed in the years 89-91 for sample firms; Cons is a dummy which points out if a firm takes part to an export consortium, Group indicates if a firm belongs to a group of firms; Area points out the 4 regions in which the territory has been divided for the analysis.

Table 9: Probit Regression; export participation for the years 1989-1991

Variable	All Firms		Firms with less than 250 employes		Firms with less than 100 employes	
	Coefficient	T Statistic	Coefficient	T Statistic	Coefficient	T Statistic
N° employed	5.83e-07	0.234	0.0026761	15.340	0.0060598	12.714
Duset1	-0.246722	-1.397	0.0095948	0.031	-0.0286117	-0.083
Duset2	-0.078848	-0.467	0.1234587	0.444	0.1106393	0.337
Duset3	-0.149961	-0.806	0.110134	0.034	0.0460499	0.121
Duset4	-0.392053	-1.591	-0.5998637	-1.588	-	-
Duset5	-0.192141	-1.131	0.0723996	0.245	-0.0023804	-0.007
Duset6	0.0080181	0.052	0.2203399	0.862	0.1949681	0.622
Duset7	-0.465756	-2.291	-0.2180994	-0.590	-0.1704962	-0.432
Duset8	-0.150666	-0.886	0.0967884	0.337	0.047041	0.140
Duset9	-0.049726	-0.286	0.0550923	0.181	-0.1220529	-0.331
Duset10	-0.068481	0.350	0.06997	0.219	-0.1080018	-0.271
Duset11	-0.176268	-0.954	0.549434	0.181	-0.0223137	-0.062
Duset12	-0.213096	-1.200	0.0342718	0.113	-0.0048029	-0.014
Duset13	-0.190789	-1.050	0.46239	0.153	0.136933	0.418
Duset14	-0.239796	-1.375	-0.0063894	-0.021	-0.0884375	-0.254
Duset15	0.0964455	0.626	0.2489307	1.143	0.2443605	0.826
Duset16	-0.069117	-0.422	0.1283096	0.459	0.1155517	0.354
Duset17	-0.087607	-0.521	0.1419121	0.522	0.0599853	0.179
Duset18	-0.412128	-2.336	-0.1262494	0.386	-0.1963388	-0.526
Duset19	-0.044793	-0.273	0.1999086	0.799	0.1770294	0.564
Duset20	-0.116772	-0.685	0.0822859	0.283	0.0483369	0.143
Duset21	-0.556530	-3.204	-0.4248063	-1.249	-0.4923882	-1.583
Duset22	-0.248740	-1.252	0.0137101	0.042	0.07832979	0.219
North West	0.311732	12.211	0.3044698	10.018	0.3250239	8.223
North Est	0.2386503	9.424	0.2370883	7.758	0.2622351	6.522
Centre	0.1521727	5.668	0.1661652	5.162	0.1972284	4.587
Consortia	0.0070778	3.017	0.1203705	4.629	0.1198825	3.602
Group	0.1488517	8.931	0.0150733	0.636	-0.0122467	-0.364
GA Special	0.0679368	3.179	0.0929325	3.736	0.1156352	3.649
GA no Special	0.0269076	1.486	0.0414481	1.997	0.0769279	2.873

$$Expart = \alpha_0 + \sum \alpha_i DSett + \sum_{k=1}^{3} \beta_k Area + \gamma GA + \gamma_1 GA_s + \beta_4 Cons$$

$$+ \beta_5 Group + \beta_6 Size + \varepsilon \qquad (A.2)$$

Where **Expart** is a dummy with value of 1 if the firm exported its products for the years 1989-1991 and it takes value 0 if it has not ; Dsett is a dummy for 23 sectors; GA is a dummy which takes the value of 1 if the firm belongs to a local system, and 0 otherwise; Ga$_s$ is a which takes the value of 1 if the firm belongs to a local system and also presents a localisation index (Del Colle) greater than 1; Size is the average number of employed in the years 89-91 for sample firms; Cons is a dummy which points out if a firm takes part to an export consortium, Group indicates if a firm belongs to a group of firms; Area points out the 4 regions in which the territory has been divided for the analysis.

References

Amemiya T., *Regression analysis when the dependent variable is truncated normal,* Econometrica, 41, 1973.

Aumann R. and Shapely L., "Long term competition- a game theoretic analysis", mimeo.

Balducci M.- Pieri M.- Vannucchi R., *Le piccole imprese e le aree sistema,* Franco Angeli, Milano, 1992.

Becattini G., "Dal settore industriale al distretto industriale", in Economia e Politica industriale, n.1, 1979.

Bellandi M. "Il distretto industriale in Alfred Marshall"in L'Industria, n.3, 1982.

Dobkins L. H., *Location, Innovation and trade, The Role of Localisation and Nation-Based Externalities,* Regional Science and Urban Economics, 26, 1996.

Futia C., *Shumpeterian Competition,* Quarterly journal of Economics, 93, 1980.

Del Colle E., Le aree produttive, struttura economica dei sistemi regionali in Italia, 1997, Franco Angeli, Milano, 1985.

Del Monte A. and Martinelli F., "Gli ostacoli alla divisione tecnica e sociale del lavoro nelle aree depresse: il caso delle piccole imprese elettroniche in Italia", in L'Industria, n.3, 1988.

Florio M., Il falegname e l'economia politica, Il Mulino, Bologna, 1982.

Gaspar J. and Glaser E. L., *Information technology and the future of cities,* NBER Working paper n. 5562, 1996.

Marshall A., 1920, Priciples of Economics, 8th edition, (Procupine Press, Philadelphia, 1982).

Nuti F., I distretti dell'industria manifatturiera in Italia, Vol.1, Franco Angeli, Milano, 1992.

Pike F. and Sengeberger W., "Industrial GA and local economic regeneration, Geneva, International Institute for Labour Studies.

Scott A. J. and Angel D., "The US semiconductur Industry: a location Analysis", Enviroment and Planning, 1987.

Shaked A. and Sutton J., "Natural Oligopolies", Econometrica, vol. 51, 1983.

Sforzi F., "L'identificazione spaziale", in G. Becattini, Mercato e forze locali: il distretto industriale, Il Mulino, Bologna 1987.

Stigler G. J., "Trends in employement in the services industries, Princeton University Press, 1956.

The District Advantage in Small-Medium Firm Internationalisation[*]

Michele Bagella
University of Rome Tor Vergata, Faculty of Economics, Department of Economics and Institutions, Via di Tor Vergata snc, 00133 Rome. E-mail: bagella@uniroma2.it

Abstract: Studies on the internationalisation of Small and Medium Enterprises (SME) emphasise difficulties that these firms have in making direct investment abroad due to high transaction and information costs and to an equally high investment risk [Bagella, Pietrobelli 1995]. The recent Italian economic history has been characterised by the development of "industrial districts" [Becattini 1979]. The fact that SMEs in Italy are often members of a "district", prompts us to ask if this membership is an advantage to operate successfully not only on internal markets, but also on foreign markets. More specifically, we argue that the "district" may generate in some activities economies of scale, which reduce barriers to internationalisation. A district SME, especially if the district has strong product specialisation, may have greater access to a wide range of information on foreign markets, alternative products, technologies and sources of finance. Conversely, when it comes to making productive investments abroad, whatever the form and nature, such an advantage decreases substantially. The SME needs to invest in acquiring quantitative and qualitative information and "relational goods"[Brunetta R., Tronti 1995; Scandizzo 1995] in countries in which it wants to operate. The investment considerably increases not only internationalisation costs but also the variance of expected returns from the project. The realisation of the project within a district may help SME to dampen the above mentioned negative effects through risk sharing. Another potential advantage for small medium firms in a district is the opportunity of sharing the project with an enterprise that belongs to a district and is considered a market leader. This firm may have more experience, well established relationships and trading activities with the foreign market to which the foreign investment is directed. The aim of this paper is to investigate this second hypothesis by using a financial investment portfolio approach. The first section analyses the investment choice on the basis of a standard risk-return approach; the second section specifies conditions under which the SME will find the investment profitable. The third section outlines some policy implications of the paper.

JEL Classification: R3

Keywords: Small firm internazionalisation, Industrial districts.

---

[*] Translated from "Internazionalizzazione della piccolo e media impresa in America Latina", M.Bagella (ed.), il Mulino, Bologna, 1996.

1   The Internationalisation of SME

In this model we assume that a firm, which is considered to be a "market leader", decides to make a direct investment abroad under two possible scenarios:

-   the "market leader" firm intends to maintain total control on project management;

-   in order to operate the project the "market leader" firm creates a specific corporate entity, called "consorzio", which includes in it several firms located in the district. By choosing this second option the firm decides to share control, return and risk of the project with those SMEs being part of the "consortio".

In case 1, one or more district firms would contribute to the realisation of the project as suppliers of machinery and/or technologies required by the "market leader". Their internationalisation would be only indirect in this case as they would not be directly involved in the project.

These firms would assume only commercial risks with respect to the leader, and not entrepreneurial risks which would result from the productive collaboration outlined in case 2. Under this second hypothesis, one or more enterprises of the "district" would jointly contribute with the leader to the realisation of the project, assuming risks and participating to expected benefits.

In this scenario, one can also assume that the project will include a contractual agreement with a foreign counterpart from the "target" country (the foreign country in which the firm is directly investing) for the provision of goods and technology and/or technical assistance, maintenance and consulting activities related to the project. Alternatively, the agreement could include the creation of a joint company for the management of the plant and equipment, the internal and external sales of products, and the supply of services to firms in the sector.

Whatever the form of agreement, the problem for each enterprise participating in the joint-venture can be expressed as one of maximisation of return of the financial equivalent of the participation in the society that arranges the project and that will realize the investment. The outcome of such a maximisation would depend for large part on:

-   the transaction costs related to the investment given that such costs are presumably higher than those envisaged for a similar investment in the domestic market;

-   the level of risk and its allocation based on the total return expected from investment (point β on the ordinate of fig. 1).

2   The Optimum Level of Participation of the SME

The optimal participation level for the SME can be determined, by assuming that the SME participation in the project occurs through the purchase of a portion of the shares of the new society created to operate the project. Alternatively, one can assume the SME purchasing shares of a society, which is already operating, for instance, in other markets in which the leader holds a majority interest.

In such a case there would be the problem of how to calculate the marginal impact of expected profits from the internationalisation, net of expected proceeds from activities existing prior to the new project. In order to simplify, let's consider the first hypothesis.

The problem for the SME can be represented as a problem of portfolio selection in which the financial investor, in this case the SME, would estimate the return and risk of the stock on the basis of his expectations. Contrary to the case of a strictly financial investment in which the return is determined by market factors, not easily influenced by a small buyer, the investment would be in this case dependent on the outcome of the productive investment which is affected by the SME. On other terms the share of profits from the decision to participate to the venture is dependent not only on the efficiency of the new society (and therefore also on the efficiency of the leader enterprise), but also on the efficiency of the same participating SME.

An important point to consider is that there might not be an official secondary market to liquidate the holdings or that members may reach an agreement to transfer shares tied to one or more options in favour of the enterprise leader. Under these conditions the return on the shares corresponds to the return on the productive investment. The shares being non-transferable, except by explicit agreement, due to their poor liquidity, have a *pro quota* value corresponding to the value of the investment.

Keeping in mind these conditions, one can analyse the choice of the SME by taking a financial approach to the investment decision as suggested by Dixit and Pindyck (1994) and basing the analysis on a model of portfolio selection that consists of focusing on the yield-risk relation (Sharpe 1994).

168   M. Bagella

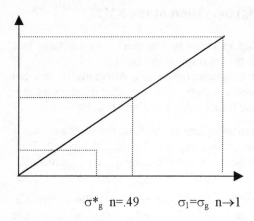

σ^*_g n=.49 $\sigma_1=\sigma_g$ n→1

Fig. 1

The horizontal axis in Fig. 1 measures risk, expressed by the standard deviation of the average expected return which is measured on the vertical axis. Given that n represents the participation share, if the investment is made by only one enterprise, $n = 1$. If, on the other hand, there are at least 2 enterprises, $n < 1$. In this case, the risk rises with the increase of n in an interval between 0 and 1. Assuming that the sum of the investment is Io and that the alternative investment of financial resources (i.e., bank deposit) has no risk and zero return, risk and return will increase in the participation share. The slope of the risk-return line is $\pi Io/\sigma_g$ and is determined considering that:

$$E(R)= \pi I_o n \qquad (1)$$
where $n=\sigma_i/\sigma_g$.

Substituting n in (1) we get:

$$E(R)= \pi I_o \sigma_i/\sigma_g \qquad (2)$$

Where $E(R)$ is the expected return of the investment I_o, π the expected profit in the investment Io corresponding to point β, σ_1 the portfolio risk, σ_g the risk related to the SME participation share. Consequently, if $\sigma_1=n\sigma_g$ (3) for n=1 we get $\sigma_1=\sigma_g$ (4)

Consequently, if there is a single financier with a participation share of 100% portfolio risk is at maximum risk and equal to σ_g, which is the risk of an individual share based on the variance of the expected net returns; if there are two or more financiers the risk that each assumes could be determined by (3).

Point α in fig. 1 indicates the equilibrium position for the SME financier, given that indifference curves express its risk-return preferences from an utility function $U(E(R), \sigma)$ with $U'(E(R),\sigma)>0$ and $U''(E(R),\sigma)<0$ which implies risk aversion.

The point α determines the share n that corresponds to:

$$dE(R)/d\sigma_i = \pi I o /\sigma_g \tag{5}$$

The equilibrium participation share determined by equation (5) assumes that the other firm, the leader, would not set any limit to the new firm's shareholding interest. If in fact indifference curves would shift further to the right, the equilibrium share n for the participating firm would increase for a given σ_g approaching $\sigma_i = \sigma_g$ for $n=1$.

Nevertheless, this hypothesis does not appear to have strong foundations for two reasons. The leader enterprise, being the promoter of the project, would most likely want to maintain control of the society with a majority shareholding. It is equally possible that the participating firm would have no interest in running the entire investment risk if the project is effectively directed by the leader enterprise. Under these considerations it is convenient to assume that the leader enterprise would accept only a minority participation to the project from another enterprise. A consequence of this is that the participating firm would participate to the venture only if its indifference curves are tangent to the risk-return line in an area whose right boundary is the vertical line at point σ_g^* marking the "barrier of proprietary control". σ_g^* corresponds to a participation share conventionally considered lower than 50%, that is $n < 50\%$, as in this way it is ensured that the leader enterprise will exert a maximum effort to make the investment successful.

One should take into account that the function of the leader enterprise, as perceived by the SME, is that of increasing the slope of the risk-return line, namely to increase π for given I and σ_g. This can be obtained, coeteris paribus, by minimising costs and particularly those related to the organisation of the new society and the start-up of the project, which may be generally considered as transaction costs. The incentive for the participating SME would derive principally from this advantage: in the absence of services offered by the project leader in project material and information, p could be considered insufficient in relation the negative investment risk. In this case the slope of the line would decrease.

3   The Constrained Choice

The constrained choice may be found by assuming that the profit function is given by $\pi_I = (D, \theta, X, C_T)$ where D represents leverage, O project quality, X the demand for the product, Ct the transaction cost with $\partial\pi_I/\partial D < 0$, $\partial\pi_I/\partial\theta > 0$, $\partial\pi_I/\partial X > 0$, $\partial\pi_I/\partial C_T > 0$ [Bagella, Becchetti 1996].

If the cost function is such that $\pi > 0$ and if the cost is the sum of the investment cost $C1$ and the transaction cost Ct, the total cost will be defined as $C = C1 + Cr$, where $Cr = a + b1$. Substituting we have:

$$C = C1 + a$$

where $a + bI$ represents transaction cost, formed by one fixed component equal to α, and by a variable component which is a function of the investment size (larger investments involve higher transaction costs). If the investment is given, Ct will also be determined. In the case under examination the lower Ct, the more the SME would be induced to enter the project, as the advantage of operating with a leader enterprise with grater market expertise translates into lower Ct.

In general the return realized by each SME, $E(R)$, will be positively related to the participation share n, negatively related to the risk σg, and positively related to the total profit realised from the investment πI, subject to the constraint $n < 0,5$ (Fig. 2).

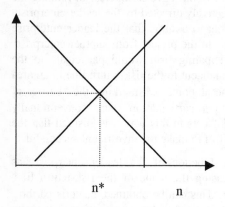

$\sigma_I E(R)$

Fig. 2

The expected yield function can be specified in the following terms:

$$E(R) = e^{\alpha n - \beta \overline{\sigma}_g + \gamma \overline{\pi}_I (D, X, \theta, C_T)} \tag{6}$$

subject to $n < n^*$.

The maximisation problem can be resolved by using the non-negativity constraint on coefficients so that $\alpha, \beta, \gamma \geq 0$ and by considering as given the level of risk of the individual share σ_g and the expected profit from the investment π. The problem to solve is the following:

$$\max_n E(R) = e^{\alpha n - \beta \overline{\sigma}_g + \gamma \overline{\pi}_I (D, X, \theta, C_T)} \tag{7}$$

s.t. $0 \leq n < n^*$; $\sigma_g, \pi_I > 0$; $\alpha, \beta, \gamma \geq 0$

By solving this problem (see Appendix) we find that:

$$n = \frac{-\ln \alpha n - \beta \overline{\sigma_g} + \gamma \overline{\pi}_I (D, X, \theta, C_T)}{\alpha} \qquad (8)$$

The participation share is inversely related to risk. σ_g and is directly proportional to the profit realised from the investment πI.

4   Conclusions

The results obtained in the chapter suggest the following policy considerations.

If SME's participation to productive internationalisation projects needs to be supported, it must be considered that, according to our risk-return approach:

-   transaction costs are more likely to be lower if the project is supported by a leader enterprise. An alternative to the leader enterprise would be a consortium of enterprises being part of an industrial district,

-   the project sharing between the leader and the SME does not necessarily imply that the SME's capital investment in the new enterprise is proportional to its contribution to the project. The SME can supply goods and services under the form of subforniture with a share of investment not necessarily corresponding to the participation share;

-   the SME's participation share is inversely related to its level of risk aversion for a given yield;

-   the "proprietary barrier of control (less than 50%)" leaves to the SME the possibility of a minority participation;

-   the return is inversely related to transaction costs that for the most part are connected to acquisition, information and consultancy costs.

Public policies aimed at supporting productive internationalisation can offer incentives for equity risk sharing, either by reducing transaction costs (more services to the enterprises), or investment risk (credit insurance) or, as well, by easing participation of public financial intermediaries to the capital of the new venture with the explicit role of ensuring transparency for all venture members.

Appendix

(by Luisa Corrado)

Given the (7), the constrained maximisation will be given by:

$$L = e^{an - \beta \overline{\sigma}_g + \gamma \overline{\pi}_I (D,X,\theta,C_T)} + \gamma (n* - n) = f(n, \overline{\sigma}_g, \overline{\pi}_I) + \lambda g(n) \quad (A.1)$$

Conditions describing the solutions are:

a) $0 = n \dfrac{\partial L}{\partial n}$, $n \geq 0$, $n \dfrac{\partial L}{\partial n} \geq 0$ (A.2)

b) $0 = \lambda g(n)$ $\lambda \geq 0$ $g(n) \geq 0$.   (A.3)

These conditions applied to our problem give the following relations:

a) $0 = n(\alpha e^{an - \beta \overline{\sigma}_g + \gamma \overline{\pi}_I (D,X,\theta,C_T)} - \lambda)$ $n \geq 0$ (A.4)

b) $0 = (n*-n)$ $\lambda \geq 0$ $(n*-n) \geq 0$ (A.5)

The problem may be solved in this way if we take into account of the condition on the participation constraint according to which n<n* or n*-n<0.

By assumption the participation share must respect the constraint n*-n>0. Given the transversality condition $0 = \lambda(n*-n)$ in b) we get $\lambda = 0$.

Starting from this result on the Lagrange multiplier we may assume the following solution:

$\lambda = 0$, n>0. We already explained why at optimum $\lambda = 0$. In addition. If n>0, from condition a) for $0 = n(\alpha e^{an - \beta \overline{\sigma}_g + \gamma \overline{\pi}_I (D,X,\theta,C_T)} - \lambda)$ to be valid it must be true that $\alpha e^{an - \beta \overline{\sigma}_g + \gamma \overline{\pi}_I (D,X,\theta,C_T)} - \lambda \leq 0$. If $\lambda = 0$ it follows that $\alpha e^{an - \beta \overline{\sigma}_g + \gamma \overline{\pi}_I (D,X,\theta,C_T)} \leq 0$. But, given the nonnegativity constraint on coefficients, this condition cannot be satisfied.

Uncertainty on the level of realised profits and on expected return

In this section we define the relationship between expected return E(R) and the participation share n when project profits π_I are uncertain.

Let's assume that profit dynamics is described by the following relationship:

$$\frac{d\pi_I}{\pi_I} = Rdt + s_\pi dz \quad (A.6)$$

where $\pi_{I=\pi_I}$ (D, θ,X, C_T), R is the deterministic project return, *dz* is a Wiener process (the continuous time limit of a discrete time random walk) and sπ is the process standard deviation.

The expected return grows exponentially in the participation share and in profits from investment.

$$F = f(n, \overline{\sigma}_g, \pi_I) = e^{\alpha n - \beta \overline{\sigma}_g + \gamma \overline{\pi}_I(D,X,\theta,C_T)} \tag{A.7}$$

where individual share risk $\overline{\sigma}_g$ is assumed as given.

By applying Ito's lemma we obtain:

$$dF = \frac{\partial F}{\partial t}dt + \frac{\partial F}{\partial n}dn + \frac{\partial F}{\partial \pi_I}d\pi_I +$$
$$\frac{1}{2}\left(\frac{\partial^2 F}{\partial n}(dn)^2 + \frac{\partial^2 F}{\partial \pi_I}(d\pi_I)^2 + 2\frac{\partial^2 F}{\partial \pi_I \partial n}\partial \pi_I \partial n\right) \tag{A.8}$$

or:

$$dF = \alpha e^{\alpha n - \beta \overline{\sigma}_g + \gamma \overline{\pi}_I(D,X,\theta,C_T)}dn + \gamma e^{\alpha n - \beta \overline{\sigma}_g + \gamma \overline{\pi}_I(D,X,\theta,C_T)}d\pi_I +$$
$$\frac{1}{2}\alpha^2 e^{\alpha n - \beta \overline{\sigma}_g + \gamma \overline{\pi}_I(D,X,\theta,C_T)}(dn)^2 \gamma^2 e^{\alpha n - \beta \overline{\sigma}_g + \gamma \overline{\pi}_I(D,X,\theta,C_T)}d(\pi_I)^2 \tag{A.9}$$
$$+ 2\gamma\alpha e^{\alpha n - \beta \overline{\sigma}_g + \gamma \overline{\pi}_I(D,X,\theta,C_T)}dnd\pi_I$$

Considering that $F = e^{\alpha n - \beta \overline{\sigma}_g + \gamma \overline{\pi}_I(D,X,\theta,C_T)}$ (A.9) may be rewritten in the following way:

$$dF = \alpha Fdn + \gamma Fd\pi_I +$$
$$\frac{1}{2}\left(\alpha^2 F(dn)^2 + \gamma^2 F(d\pi_I)^2 + 2\alpha\gamma Fdnd\pi_I\right) \tag{A.10}$$

In other terms:

$$dF = \alpha Fdn + \gamma Fd\pi_I +$$
$$\frac{1}{2}\left(\alpha^2 F(dn)^2 + \gamma^2 F(d\pi_I)^2 + 2\alpha\gamma Fdnd\pi_I\right) \tag{A.11}$$

According to rules of stochastic calculus, $(dz)^2=dt$; $dtdz=0$; $(dt)^2=0$. So $(d\pi_I)^2 = s_\rho^2 dt$.(A.12)

Moreover, considering (A.6), we may rewrite (A.11) as:

$$\frac{dF}{F} = \alpha dn + \gamma\pi_I(D,X,C_T,\theta)Rdt + \gamma\pi(D,X,C_T,\theta) +$$
$$\frac{1}{2}(\alpha^2 F(dn)^2 + \gamma^2 s_\pi^2 dt + 2\alpha\gamma\pi_I(D,X,C_T,\theta)dn(Rdt + s_\pi dz)) \tag{A.13}$$

and by putting dn=0 we get:

$$\frac{dF}{F} = \gamma \pi_I(D,X,C_T,\theta)R dt +$$

$$\gamma \pi_I(D,X,C_T,\theta)s_\pi dz + \frac{1}{2}\gamma^2 s_\pi^2 dt$$

(A.14)

Changes in expected returns crucially depend on the participation share (which defines the F function in A.7), on the level of realised profits π_I and on project risk measured by the variance of the stochastic process s_ρ^2.

References

Bagella M. and Pietrobelli, C, 1992, Distretti industriali e internazionalizzazione: presupposti teorici ed evidenza empirica dell'Ameria Latina, *Economia e Politica Industriale*, n.86.

Bagella M. and Becchetti L., 1997, The impact of the Italian system of subsidised credit: effects on leverage, firm's performance and bankruptcy risk, *El Credit Public a Europa* Freixas X. and Caminal R. (eds.)

Becattini G., 1979, "Dal settore industriale al distretto industriale. Alcune considerazioni sull'unità d'indagine dell'economia industriale", *Economia e Politica Industriale*, 1.

Brunetta R. and Tronti L., 1995, *Beni relazionali e crescita endogena*, Fondazione Brodolini.

Dixit A.K. and Pindick R.S., 1994, *Investment under uncertainty*, Princeton, Princeton University Press.

Sharpe A., 1990, *Investment*, Englewood Cliffs, Prentice Hall.

Scandizzo P.L. *Il Mezzogiorno e la crescita endogena*, Fondazione Brodolini.

From SMEs to Industrial Districts in the Process of Internationalisation: Theory and Evidence[+]

Michele Bagella

University of Rome "Tor Vergata", Faculty of Economics, Department of Economics and Institutions, Via di Tor Vergata snc, 00133 Rome. E-mail: bagella@uniroma2.it

Carlo Pietrobelli

University of Rome "Tor Vergata", Dipartimento di Economia e Istituzioni, via di Tor Vergata snc, 00133 Rome, Italy, Ph. +39.6.72595700-16, Fax: +39.6.2020500, E-Mail: carlo.pietrobelli@uniroma2.it

Abstract: Following the approach that emphasises the existence of a continuum of forms in firms' international expansion, ranging from exports of goods and services to foreign direct investment, many studies showed that Italian small and medium-size enterprises (SMEs) have recently been prone to international involvement, but only in the simplest form of exporting. The absence of a more complex internationalisation strategy has been explained with the existence of numerous obstacles of technological, informative and financial nature. The aim of this paper is to analyse the hypothesis that inter-firm relationships in the form of a group of firms or of an "industrial district (ID)" may enhance the internationalisation of SMEs, especially in developing countries. A simple theoretical model of an ID is presented. Then, the hypothesis of the internationalisation of the ID driven by a "leader firm" is studied. In our model, co-operation with the developing country's firms may ease the productive undertaking in the developing country. To the aim of preliminary testing this hypothesis in the social and economic context of Latin America, we analysed the experience of groups of SMEs and of "quasi-IDs" in some countries (Argentina, Brazil, Mexico), with the perspective of future co-operation with the Italian IDs, and further international expansion.

J.E.L. Classification: D23, F21

Keywords: Industrial districts, Interntional cooperation.

[+] Already published in : van Dijk M.P. and Rabellotti R. (eds.), Enterprise Clusters and Networks in Developing Countries, EADI Book Series 20, London: Frank Cass, 1997.

1   Introduction: Theoretical Hypotheses and the "Stages" of Internationalisation[*]

The idea of the existence of different "stages" in the process of firms' internationalisation has been acknowledged in the literature for some time (Rullani and Vaccà, 1983). These stages range from the simple access to the international market through the exports of goods and services, to export consortia and joint ventures, to the foreign involvement in production in the form of foreign direct investment (FDI).[1] A *continuum* of "intermediate" forms ranges between these extremes, including equity and non-equity agreements.[2]

From this approach it follows that trade theory and the theory of FDI may be considered within the same theoretical context (Ramazzotti e Schiattarella, 1989). This is further confirmed by the new approach that emphasises firm-level sources of comparative advantage and international competitiveness. Thus, in addition to the more conventional explanations based on industry- and country-level factor endowments, the inter-firm gaps in technological capabilities, and the duration and effectiveness of the learning process may determine a competitive edge internationally (Pietrobelli, 1998, 1992).

Moreover, these intermediate forms of internationalisation cannot be regarded as *second best* entrepreneurial choices, but actual *first best* options depending on the specific firms' and markets' characteristics. Under this perspective, the choice of

---

[*] This study was financed by the Italian National Research Council - CNR-PFI Project 3.5.2. Preliminary versions were presented at CNR seminars in Milan and at Tor Vergata University, Rome, and at the Economic Commission for Latin America (ECLAC), Buenos Aires, Argentina, at the Universidad Federal de Santa Catarina (UFSC), Florianopolis, Brazil, and at an EADI workshop on industrialization in LDCs in Vienna. We wish to acknowledge the useful comments of Professor G. Becattini, and of B.Chauduri, M.P.van Dijk, R.Rabellotti, and H.Schmitz. Responsibility for errors and omissions is only ours. This paper is the outcome of a joint effort of the authors. However, Bagella drafted sections 1, 4.1, 4.2 and 6, and Pietrobelli sections 2, 3, 4.3, 4.3, 4.4, 4.5, and 5.

[1] Becattini identifies two main categories: "commercial" and "productive" (or "developed") internationalisation (Becattini, 1993). Writing of "stages" of internationalisation does not necessarily imply a pre-defined and always identical sequence. Thus, FDI does not always need to be preceded by exports, although exporting to a country often allows valuable learning.

[2] Among the main "intermediate" forms of internationalisation are: joint ventures, trade and production licensing, management contracts, "turn-key" and "ready-made" contracts, production-sharing contracts, international sub-contracting (Oman, 1984a).

the preferred "stage" of internationalisation takes a "strategic" dimension.[3] However, the "strategic" choice of international expansion of a Small and Medium-sized Enterprise (SME) is crucially different from that of a large corporation. This reflects the different capabilities to influence and cope with a complex external environment characterised by asymmetric information, different risk propensities, and different opportunities to exploit economies of scale and scope. Sometimes these capabilities are available in-house, but they often need to be purchased from outside. It is well-known that a large corporation is often capable of internalising these capabilities: in contrast, a SME will have to rely on real and financial services purchased from the market, and these services will be more varied and complex the more "developed" is the "stage" of internationalisation. For these reasons, and for the high transaction costs involved in the process, *ceteris paribus* SMEs are expected confine their activities to the simpler stages of internationalisation

The aim of this paper is twofold. First, we describe the forms that the foreign involvement of Italian enterprises has taken in some developing countries on the basis of some recent and new empirical evidence. Second, we explore, at a theoretical level, the possibility that organisations such as Industrial Districts (IDs) may foster the internationalisation of SMEs. Some experiences of the foreign involvement of Italian firms in Latin America, and the policies designed to promote this process, are analysed in sections 2 and 3. In section 4 the central thesis is explored, and some case-studies of Latin-American IDs are assessed from the perspective of international co-operation with the Italian IDs in section 5. Section 6 summarises and concludes.

2 New Evidence on the International Expansion of Italian Firms in Latin America

Two recent studies analyse the forms of productive involvement chosen by a sample of Italian SMEs in Latin America, and their sources of competitive strength and weakness (Carisano, 1994, Pietrobelli, 1994).[4] The universe from which the evidence was drawn was made of 1000 firms belonging to the 23 export consortia dealing with Latin America that are associated to the National Federation of Export Consortia (Federexport). These firms were reached by a postal questionnaire, and 126 firms responded. Out of them, only the SMEs

---

[3] By "strategy" we mean the purposeful action of an agent aiming at the acquisition of power over other agents, even to the cost of giving up present profits in exchange for future (expected) profits (Acocella, 1989).

[4] These studies were carried out as part of the CNR-PFI project 3.5.2., together with other studies, of which we report some results. These include: Angori, 1994, Bagarani, 1994, Becchetti, 1994, Bercovich, 1995, Carisano, 1994, Feistein, 1994, LoCicero, 1995, Pietrobelli, 1994b, and 1992, Quintar *et al.*1995, Rabellotti, 1995.

having some relationship with Latin America in 1989 were selected, to generate a sample of 30 enterprises that is considered well representative of the universe.[5] The main results of these studies are the following:

(i) the sample firms show a good attitude towards the international market, with an export propensity of over 40 per cent of their overall sales. However, the empirical evidence shows only a relatively "easy" stage of foreign involvement, confined to exporting. FDI are virtually non-existent, and only ten per cent of the sample firms set up some kind of agreement with local producers, mostly of a commercial nature.[6] Over 50 per cent of total exports go to the nearer and more accessible markets of the European Community (EC), 23.7 per cent to other industrial countries, and 11.4 per cent to Latin America is by far the most important market among the Least Developed Countries (LDCs). Exports are concentrated in intermediate and investment goods, mainly in machinery and metalworking, rubber and plastic products, consistently with what one would expect on the basis of country endowments (and the ensuing international specialisation).[7]

(ii) The main obstacles to exports are related to the complex custom and administrative procedures, and to the scarce information on foreign markets.[8] The more export success depends on "non-price" factors, such as product and firm's reliability, trade-marks, a good product and process technology, the more valuable is information on the market and on the characteristics of demand. However, price-based competitiveness is especially relevant for exports to Latin America and East-Asia, while exports to the US and Japan rely on technology and product quality to a greater extent. Thus, specialised real services could be more beneficial for the latter markets. Additional obstacles are related to the fragmented sale and

---

[5] For the sampling technique and other specific aspects of the questionnaire, see Carisano, 1994, and Pietrobelli, 1994b. In 1989 the average sample firm employed 69 workers, had sales for L.It.14 bn. (about US$8,7mill.) and exports for L.It.6 bn. (about US$ 3,7mill.). The sample mainly included Nothern Italy firms.

[6] Only two examples of technology transfer agreements have been recorded. These results confirm what already discovered in other surveys on the international agreements of Italian firms (e.g. Cespri-Bocconi, 1988).

[7] Evidence from a sample of SMEs from Tuscany (Italy) confirms the conclusion that Italian SMEs mainly expand internationally by exporting rather than investing abroad (Manuelli, 1994).

[8] The information available on Latin American markets appears to be, perhaps surprisingly, as scarce as information on South-East Asia, that is much geographically and "culturally" farther from the Italian business community. Services providing information on the markets and on the procedures to get access to them have not been available in sufficient quantity/quality.

distribution network.[9] Efficient production is often not sufficient to ensure stable export competitiveness, in the absence of adequate distribution networks. The small firm-size and the lack of economies of scale and scope represent a clear obstacle in this sense. The sample firms often emphasised the inadequacy of Italian public policies to specifically support financially and with real services distribution and sale in overseas markets.

In contrast, the presence of Italian large companies in Latin America is much more extended and takes various forms. Becchetti, 1994, in an analysis focused on the experiences of IRI and ENI (the two largest State-owned conglomerates), shows that these firms have been much more active in Latin America than the SMEs, both in the form of FDI and of inter-firm agreements and exports. Contrary to the evidence for SMEs, the main obstacles to large firms' international expansion have had a financial nature, related to the foreign debt crisis and to the macroeconomic instability in the region. In fact, these large corporations had the capabilities in-house to operate in the South-American "imperfect" markets, characterised by limited and asymmetric information.

Furthermore, there is evidence that belonging to a "group" led by a large corporation has been a critical condition to set up international agreements of various kinds. This is shown by Vitali, 1994, on the basis of evidence on the agreements between Italian and Latin American firms during 1987-90 in the clothing and food industries: out of 26 agreements, 9 were signed by enterprises that are part of the Benetton group, 5 of the Stefanel group, and all the others by firms of other industrial groups (i.e. Ellesse, IRI, Zegna, Tachella, Armani).

3   Support Policies to SMEs' Foreign Involvement: The Case of the Italian Development Co-operation with Argentina

In recent years, Italian foreign aid policies have had two related sets of objectives: the promotion of international collaboration in production, especially through international joint ventures, and the use of development co-operation as a strategic tool of foreign economic policy (Cortellese and Pietrobelli, 1993).

However, the explicit target of supporting the joint ventures between Italian and LDCs' firms has not been reached. Article No.7 of the law regulating development co-operation (L.49/1987), provides specific support for the setting up of international joint ventures, but it has been applied only in very few circumstances, and the financial incentives offered have not been sufficient to boost the active involvement of the Italian partners.

Within this context, the innovative mechanism of the "Treaty of Privileged Relationship" between Italy and several other LDCs was introduced (Angori,

---

[9] The sample firms rely primarily on local importers (50 per cent), and secondarily on sale agents (33 per cent) for their exports.

1994). The first of these treaties was signed by the Italian government with Argentina in 1987 (*Tratado de Relación Asociativa Particular entre Argentina e Italia*), followed by others with Brazil and Venezuela (Pietrobelli, 1990). However, it is acknowledged that the results have generally been very limited and far below expectations.[10] A central weakness, that has been detected by an empirical assessment of the results and the procedures of the Treaty with Argentina, is the excessive emphasis on financial aspects, with a general neglect of the need for real production-related services (Pietrobelli and Cortellese, 1994).

A survey based on a sample of 400 Argentine enterprises usefully highlights the different expectations and obstacles of Italian and local partners (Feinstein, 1994). Major obstacles have been the complex bureaucratic procedures and the lack of established acquaintance among the partners. Argentine enterprises expected to gain easier access to new product and process technologies and modern equipment, offering the Italian partners low labour costs, raw materials, and a quick access to the regional market and to the *Mercosur*. However, the small size of the Argentine partners, their limited technical and marketing capabilities, and their little access to credit, have all contributed to the successful establishment of only very few joint ventures. Financial support proved insufficient to ensure their success.

The experience of the Italy-Argentina Treaty prompts several interesting considerations, especially on the methodology employed. Thus, when assessing an SME's interest to set up a joint venture in a LDC, one has to take into special consideration the special environment of origin, as well as its capability to introduce technological changes and its sources of competitive advantage.

Summarising, given the evidence of Italian SMEs' internationalisation only confined to exporting, and of their difficulties to undertake a more complex international expansion, an alternative route needs to be taken. Thus, in view of these considerations, SMEs' international expansion may benefit from concepts and analyses that, especially in Italy, have contributed to a better understanding of their organisation and operation. To our present aim, the concept of Industrial District (ID) and the evidence from some concrete historical examples may be useful and promising.

4   Obstacles to SMEs International Expansion: Elements for a Theory of the Internationalisation of Industrial Districts

4.1. In addition to the difficulties that Italian SMEs faced to expand their reach of activities internationally, the foreign productive involvement of clusters and

---

[10] In addition, the treaties with Brazil and Venezuela, after promising declarations of all partners, have never been actually implemented.

groups of SMEs[11] is constrained by many difficulties. These include the co-ordination of individual actions and the structure of incentives to collaborate in all the activities related to product and process design, raw material and equipment procurement, technology selection, adoption and adaptation, the management of production, marketing and distribution. Collaboration in exporting poses less problems, and it is often efficiently carried out through organisations like export consortia.

We discussed above the structural difficulties that SMEs face to proceed to the more complex stages of internationalisation, often due to problems of insufficient and asymmetric information, diseconomies of scale and of scope, high transaction costs.. Given the existence of these obstacles, the internationalisation of SMEs together with other SMEs sharing a tradition of fruitful collaboration on the home market may provide an easier alternative. The Italian IDs provide a clear and successful example in point, with the consolidated interaction of SMEs sharing a common productive specialisation, location, and a high social and cultural homogeneity of workers and entrepreneurs.[12]

4.2. Some of these conditions may be represented in a simple analytical model that helps to single out those factors that affect IDs' competitiveness, summarised by its average productivity. Such factors, in the case of a single-product ID, are the following:

$$P = f(K, L, RSERV, XEFF) \tag{1}$$

$$\frac{P}{L} = f\left((\frac{K}{L}, \frac{RSERV}{L}, \frac{XEFF}{L})\right) \tag{2}$$

$$RSERV = f\left((\frac{P}{L}, NF, \frac{X}{P}, \frac{M}{P}, Ypc)\right) \tag{3}$$

$$XEFF = f(HK, COOP, PAR) \tag{4}$$

Symbols stand for: P = production, K = physical capital; L = labour; RSERV = real services for the SMEs belonging to the ID; XEFF = "X-efficiency"; P/L = average labour productivity in the ID; HK = human capital; COOP = inter-firm cooperation; PAR = principal-agent relationships; Ypc = per-capita income; NF =

---

[11] "Group" of SMEs is a broader and looser concept than ID: the latter is a group of SMEs with also special characteristics, including a common location and productive specialisation. Cluster emphasises physical proximity, not necessarily identical productive specialisation.

[12] Essential references on the industrial districts are Becattini, 1979 and 1987, and Pyke, Becattini and Sengenberger, 1991.

number of firms in the industry; X = exports of the ID; M = imports of the ID; All variables refer to the aggregate of the ID.

This model refers to the production P of a single-product ID as a function of labour and capital, of some real services needed in various phases of production, and of an index of X-efficiency. One hypothesis is that real services (e.g. providing information on goods and factors markets) are available within the ID, and that they are an important input of production. We assume that production is positively related to the quantity (and/or quality) of such services, that also lower transaction costs. Similarly, the expected sign of K and L is also positive, as well as of the index of X-efficiency. This concept (Leibenstein, 1966) may be useful to detect the presence of an ID. In fact, when the business environment is positively affected by individual habits, routines and procedures, as it happens in an ID, each enterprise's production process is enhanced. Methods, routines, procedures, implicit and explicit codes, schedules, plans, are central determinants of efficiency, and in an ID these dimensions importantly contribute to raise global productivity.

Equation (2) expresses ID average productivity as a function of a number of variables. Among them, "belonging" to the ID operates through numerous positive externalities (primarily of a technological kind), and is the one that most positively affects the productivity of each enterprise, and thereby of the whole ID. If this applies, then $P_d/L_d > P_i/L_i$ (where d and i stand for district and industry respectively), i.e.: the ID average productivity must be higher than the industry national average. This constraint implies that the high geographical concentration of many firms active in the same industry or with substantial backward and forward linkages, enhances collective efficiency through the working of many external economies. In addition, cooperation may also contribute to raise collective efficiency, and this is explicitly considered in equation (4)

Equation (3) is a supply function of real services, that is positively influenced by some variables, including the ID average productivity. One can expect that a higher ID productivity may itself spur the offer of increasingly more appropriate services, that are in turn capable of raising productivity. In other words, a positive and dynamic cumulative interaction would be sparked. Other relevant variables are: the number of firms active in the industry within the same ID, the international orientation of the ID, summarised by the export and import ratios (X/P and M/P), per capita income, as a proxy for the development and complexity of the socio-economic environment. The international orientation of the ID firms positively affects the endogenous offer of real services within the ID, due to the increased flow of knowledge that a wider international openness allows, and to the stronger inducement to compete.[13] Moreover, this itself has a positive and direct

---

[13] This is consistent with Paganetto and Scandizzo, 1992.

linkage with the degree of foreign involvement of the ID. We expect that the number of firms in the ID is correlated with the supply of RSERV, as the demand from a higher number of firms will itself induce a more intense response of the same enterprises and of different agents in a co-operative interaction. In other words, the supply of real services depends on the existence of a critical mass of firms, not necessarily of small dimension. Thus, all the partial derivatives of equation (3) are expected to be positive. To these variables, one could add more policy-variables (e.g. industrial policies and other selective support policies) that could exogenously raise the quantity and quality of services, and indirectly also ID productivity.

Equation (4) makes explicit some of the determinants of X-efficiency. In general, it may depend on the quality of human capital that is available in the productive and service sectors within the ID (HK). Moreover, X-efficiency depends on the extent and quality of inter-firm cooperation (COOP), that in addition to the prevailing external economies, may improve collective efficiency. Inter-firm cooperation itself reflects the environmental conditions prevailing, that include, among other things, the quality of social life, the firm-union relationships, the co-operative attitude towards some common purpose that is shared by every participant, and the quality of the organisational settings, of the routines and of the procedures, and it is bound to improve XEFF in the ID. In a hierarchically structured ID, where some kind of "leadership" emerges, X-efficiency also depends on the relationships between the leader-firm and the others. As it is well known, such interaction may be portrayed as a principal-agent relationship.[14] This theory argues that there may be a contrast of interests between the two agents, so that in our case the agent-firms may not be induced to seek productivity gains as actively as the leader firm. The agent-firms are often only sub-contracted, whereas the leader-firm may hold the responsibility of the entire project. In such instance, fulfilling all the requirements of a project of internationalisation may demand an effort that is higher than the routine effort demanded to the sub-contracted firms. For example, product design and realisation should be faster than it is usually required, but the leader-firm could not be in the position to perfectly observe and monitor the agents' activity. Insofar as these potential contrasts become difficult and harsh, the X-efficiency of the entire ID-system would be hindered, and relevant to our aims, the project of internationalisation would be delayed. Therefore, a good principal-agent relationship (PAR),where it applies, may improve XEFF, and thereby the ID average productivity.

Concluding on this, a group of firms may be considered a real ID if the following relationships apply:

(i) $P_d/L_d > P_i/L_i$, that, given K/L, is fulfilled subject to:

(ii) $RSERV_d > RSERV_i$

---

[14] Hart and Holmström, 1988, Nalebuff and Stiglitz, 1983.

(iii) $XEFF_d > XEFF_i$

The second and third conditions imply that real services and X-efficiency in the ID must be of a quantity and/or quality that is higher relative to the industry at the national level. If (ii) and (iii) *ceteris paribus* apply, necessarily also (i) is satisfied.[15]

4.3. Equations 1-4 may represent a starting point to measure some statistical indicators of the existence of an ID. A first attempt in this direction was made by Bagarani, 1994, along the lines first set by Sforzi, 1987, with a model that allows to overlap statistical indicators of the characteristics of the population with the distribution of enterprises in the area, in order to emphasise the existence/absence of some of the necessary elements, although not sufficient, for the existence of an ID. Through a principal components and cluster analysis, this method highlighted areas in the territory that are homogeneous in terms of the structure of population and of specialisation of industrial activities. This method was successfully applied to the regions of Umbria and Emilia Romagna in Italy, and could be applied also in the LDCs with the aim of determining *a priori* the potential for the establishment of an organisational set up of the kind of the ID, that might spur the internationalisation of an Italian ID, or with which it could usefully interact.

The studies of the Latin American experiences of clustering of firms and ID-like settings, presented in the following section 5 represent original and interesting material to test the hypothesis of a foreign involvement of the Italian IDs in the LDCs. Under a co-operative perspective, some Italian SMEs belonging to an ID might get access to some real services that the local cluster may offer.

4.4. Having described a simple analytical tool to encompass all the main features of an ID, and the sources of its competitive advantages, we derive the central hypothesis that this paper aims at discussing and testing with the empirical evidence available: Can the network of collaboration and relations existing among the SMEs belonging to an ID or to a cluster boost more complex stages of internationalisation (i.e. joint ventures, FDI)? In other words, can these external economies foster the process of international expansion? Inter-firm communication and interaction may in fact produce important "clustering" advantages, related to the acquisition of information of product and factor markets, to human capital and training, to the adoption of advanced technologies (and to the learning, adaptation and improvement efforts that are necessary with it), to technology diffusion, to the development of new products and processes, to the access to new markets. May these advantages give a competitive edge also in a process of international expansion?

---

[15] Work in progress by the authors includes an analytical model portraying the hypothesis that the activity of a "leader-firm" may enable the other firms operating in the ID to reduce their risk and transaction costs, that may be especially heavy in an internationalisation project.

A preliminary question we must answer is the definition of what we mean by "internationalisation of the ID". To this aim, we need to separate conceptually the internationalisation of the individual firms of the ID, from the internationalisation of the ID itself (in its unity). Bagarani (1994) argues that the latter case requires some kind of "formalisation" of the ID, like for example a consortium, an association, a trade-mark, or the Law No.317/91, initially requiring some degree of formalisation for the ID to get access to soft loans to finance technological innovation. This is not needed in the event of internationalisation of the individual SMEs, even belonging to the ID. In this paper we do not adopt a rigid definition, but we will examine the case of internationalisation of clusters of SMEs not necessarily united by a formal constraint, but all sharing a strong interest to collaborate in the international market. The "strength" of the interest to collaborate for the individual SME may be evaluated on the basis of a cost-benefit assessment, as costs and benefits can be measured. Yet, their measurement in distant markets where information is scarce and costly is difficult. An additional problem may be represented by the higher unit costs of information that a SME has to face *ceteris paribus* relative to a large company, and the ensuing lower propensity to direct foreign productive involvement in the presence of costlier information needs.

This obstacle may be overcome if we consider the case of a "Hierarchical" ID based on the existence of a "leader firm", that is also already operating (or ready to begin operating) in international markets. The leader firm may be defined as that firm that, on the basis of past experience, has internalised information and knowledge of the international markets and of their functioning, and therefore has a special mastery of the information on foreign markets to be able to evaluate correctly risks and positive and negative externalities. In this case, the leader firm would be able to bear the initial cost of the internationalisation project, without sharing it with other firms from the beginning. This firm could prepare a pre-feasibility study of a project of FDI or joint venture (JV), and propose it to other SMEs located in the "input" and "output subsectors" of its production, as well as to the service suppliers that are located "horizontally" to its production activity, and to other SMEs engaged in production of the same goods (Diagram 1). Such proposal is expected to be more credible and effective if it comes from a leader-firm belonging to the ID and sharing with the ID firms common values, norms and attitudes.

If, for example, we take the case of a leader firm in the machinery industry, it could set up a fruitful interaction with other input- and output-firms, and also with service suppliers, in order to carry out a FDI or JV project in Latin America. In this case, if local partners operate in the output sub-sector, the leader firm might facilitate the involvement of other Italian firms active in the same ID, thereby supplying not only technology and machinery, but also all the necessary skills and expertise to obtain a competitive product. Initially the leader firm would appraise costs and benefits of the project (and the risks involved). Later, also the other firms involved would participate in the appraisal.

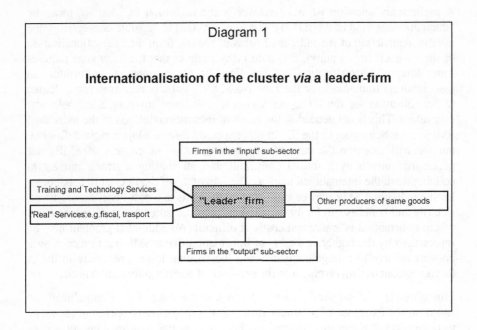

In other words, one could imagine a firm pulling and carrying other firms with it in the process of internationalisation. The final target is a FDI in an area in a foreign country. Moreover, if an ID, or a quasi-ID were operating therein, it may happen that the local SMEs in the ID would resist to the foreign firms willing to get access to the external economies generated within the ID. In order to avoid a competition that could be damaging for everyone, there is a need to realise various forms of <u>co-operation among local and Italian enterprises,</u> with the aim of finding areas of common interest to set up locally all the flows of information, factors and goods that are necessary for the existence of a larger and more efficient ID.[16] Summarising, a developed form of internationalisation of clusters of enterprises appears as a possibility insofar as the necessary conditions for the existence of an ID are reproduced locally.

4.5. The strategic choice of the stage of internationalisation may still be explained by the local availability of at least one source of comparative advantage (e.g. skilled and/or cheap labour, raw materials, access to third markets and to regional markets or custom unions - e.g. *Mercosur* and NAFTA in the American hemisphere). In addition, the availability of some favourable institutional conditions may foster the international expansion of groups of SMEs. Under this respect, Lo Cicero, 1995, has explored the peculiar function that a financial

---

[16] The advantages from cooperation have been analysed by the so-called models of "coordination failure". See Cooper and John, 1988.

intermediary like a merchant bank or a local bank having a sound knowledge of the socio-economic environment of the ID may perform. This intermediary, due to its solid experience and its intangible asset of reputation, could supply not only financial services, but also real services in support of the international expansion of the ID. This financial intermediary, thanks to the mastery he has on the stock of information on the economic and political context in which the business takes place, may supply services that are related to three possible functions, that are briefly outlined below.

(i) Following one popular line of interpretation, IDs would have been born as organisations to replace markets that did not allow the flow of information, finance and productive factors that is necessary for any entrepreneurial activity.[17] The gamut of inter-personal relationships that pre-existed the ID, and that derive from the common localisation and productive specialisation, made possible such flows. From the viewpoint of internationalisation, the spatial expansion of the ID activities could make the persistence of these flows harder: hence, the intermediary might facilitate these flows also when the important advantage of geographical proximity is inevitably reduced. It has been argued that the international expansion of an ID may dilute the co-operative and community-like relationships among the ID firms, that are central for the success of the ID, and that this may be highly risky for the future development of the ID (Becattini, 1993). The effectiveness of the activity of this intermediary is strengthened if he operates in accordance with a leader-firm acting as a true engine of the international expansion of the ID. In this event, the support provided by the intermediary may be seen as a strength of the project portrayed in Diagram 1, and improve the credibility of the project before other SMEs get involved. This would reduce the risks of the principal-agent relationship.

(ii) The intermediary might perform the role of a seconding manager in the design of the strategic international expansion of the ID, and in the monitoring of the implementation of the project in the absence of a leader-firm. In other words, this could be seen as a sort of leasing of the high strategic management skills, necessary for a developed foreign involvement, when it is not available locally. This would imply not only assisting in the project design (what normally happens with merchant banking), but also nurturing its actual implementation, at least initially.

(iii) Thirdly, the intermediary, provided that he has sufficient knowledge of the local environment, might link up with another intermediary in the LDC or with an international agent, and provide the guarantee in the contractual and post-contractual relationships of an international business. In this sense, his role would

---

[17] The prevailing conditions also inhibited the growth of a larger company capable of internalising markets.

be similar to that of an arbitrator of post-contractual behaviour between the foreign firms and those belonging to the ID, as well as within the ID.[18]

5   Industrial Districts in Latin America and Possible Collaboration with the Italian IDs

Having defined this theoretical framework, we would like to assess the actual opportunities open to Italian enterprises belonging to some IDs to get access to the advantages of co-operation with similar organisations abroad (i.e. what we call potential ID, having some of its essential characteristics). To this aim, we investigated the feasibility of *equity* or *non-equity* agreements with groups of local firms. Following the hypothesis that the international expansion of an Italian ID would be easier if it could find a similar network and organisation abroad. Therefore, some groups of firms in selected Latin-American countries have been analysed, as they were expected to have some of the features of an ID *alla italiana*.

These studies focused on the three countries that have reached the highest levels of industrial development in the region: Argentina, Brazil and Mexico. The experiences that have been object of analysis, in spite of their differences, all refer to SMEs, mostly in the manufacturing sector, that have been remarkably dynamic in the recent past. We overview them in sequence.

5.1. The case of <u>Rafaela in Argentina</u> is especially interesting and promising, from the viewpoint of the international expansion of Italian SMEs. Rafaela, located in the centre-east of the Santa Fé province, appears an interesting cluster of firms with a variety of manufacturing activities (agro-industry, chemical, industrial machinery, auto components, agricultural machines), and also a metalworking ID (Quintar *et al.*, 1995).

An interesting dimension, that in spite of many differences, makes this area comparable to other Italian experiences, is represented by the high social homogeneity, based on the common Italian heritage of a large part of the population, that emigrated from Piemonte in the 1870s. This area has recorded a dynamism and an export propensity much higher than the national average: in 1992 the firms located in the quasi-ID exported US$ 20 mill., i.e. 20% of total sales, with a 300% increase relative to 1988. This appears remarkable in view of the average export propensity of Argentine enterprises, that was only 7% in the '80s . The increasing openness to the international market of the firms in Rafaela is also revealed by the substantial rise of imports, mainly of foreign machinery.

---

[18] These proposals for a possible role for credit intermediaries, like for example a merchant bank, all stem from the hypothesis, that is common to the new theories of the firm, that a firm is a network of contracts, more or less explicit and formalised, to manage complex production processes profitably (Lo Cicero, 1995).

The metalworking district (110 establishments in 1990) includes on the one hand metal and machinery producers, and on the other hand vehicle and car components. An in-depth analysis of this experience has shown the existence of some specific elements that generated an industrial climate conducive to the creation of dynamic comparative advantages based on a permanent process of technical progress, growing inter-firm linkages, and external economies (Quintar *et al.*, 1995). However, some of the necessary conditions for the existence of an ID *alla italiana* are still missing. The size of the local industrial network is still minimal, and this hinders further productive specialisation and a deepening of labour specialisation. Moreover, inter-firm relationships follow the traditional idiosyncratic modes of Argentine industry, limiting the development of quasi-market linkages.[19] Nevertheless, a good synergy between the private and the public sector has favoured the creation of institutions favouring external economies. Among these, it is worthwhile reminding the Association of Metalworking Industrialists and the *Delegación nor-oeste de la dirección de asesoramiento y servicios tecnológicos* (DAT, Direction of Support and Technological Services for SMEs), that is a provincial support body for SMEs, founded in 1983 and supplying laboratory services geared to quality control, managerial training, technological innovation.

However, in spite of the larger export and import propensities of the enterprises in Rafaela, other forms of international expansion are still very limited. Partial exceptions are represented by the agreements signed by some enterprises in Rafaela with enterprises from the US, Germany, Canada, Denmark, Italy, Brazil and India, that regulate the exchange of intermediate products and components for the automotive industry, and the provision of specialised technical assistance. Moreover, the *Cámara de Comercio Exterior* (Foreign Trade Chamber) and the *Municipalidad* of Rafaela have created a *Fundación para el Desarrollo Regional* (Foundation for Regional Development) that carries out training programs and fosters the exchange of technological information and inter-firm co-operation.[20] In October 1992, in order to strengthen the relationships with the Italian economy, it was signed an agreement with the Modena Chamber of Commerce, within the framework of the *Tratado de Relación Asociativa Particular* aiming at promoting economic, industrial and technological co-operation among enterprises in Modena and Rafaela. This agreement included: industrial co-operation and technology transfer, exchange of information on sales markets, training and exchange of

---

[19] Sub-contracting is seldom used (41% of the local firms never sub-contract anything), and the observed tendency to the increase of vertical integration, has been partly due to the prevailing macroeconomic conditions of uncertainty: in these conditions, the internalisation of a good share of the production process and of the market-linkages was a rational and inevitable response.

[20] To this aim, the Foundation signed two cooperation agreements with Spanish institutions: the *Asociación de Investigación Tecnológica TEKNIKER* at Eibar, and the *Centro Tecnológico de Materiales INASMET* in San Sebastián.

professionals and specialised engineers, diffusion of information on sub-contracting and joint ventures.

From the perspective of the Italian SMEs, such experience of interaction among Argentine enterprises of a quasi-ID, and their interest for international co-operation, may offer some favourable conditions for a more developed international involvement of the Italian IDs. In other words, the supply of real services, and the opportunities for external economies of scale, of scope and of organisation that already exist in that area, given the active and effective interaction between local firms, might ease an international expansion of groups of Italian SMEs towards Argentina.

5.2. The case of a quasi-ID analysed in Brazil differs from the previous experience for two main reasons: the greater productive specialisation in the furniture sector, and the simultaneous presence of SMEs and of medium-large enterprises in the same location. In Sao Bento do Sul, Santa Catarina State, in south-eastern Brazil, are located 120 furniture plants employing about 6000 workers, almost one half of the urban population (Bercovich, 1995). This pole especially developed since the early 1970s, and at very high rates: in 1992 Sao Bento do Sul produced 5% of Brazilian furniture, and exported US$ 60 mill., that is equivalent to 50% of the country's total. The study of this experience has revealed that medium-size vertically-integrated enterprises (i.e. with about 200 workers) coexist with many SMEs that, due to the low entry-barriers, to the considerable external economies made possible by the presence of medium-size enterprises, and to a growing demand, were born at high rates during the past few years. Remarkable external economies are related to: good markets for raw materials and for second-hand equipment, efficient services for foreign trade, a high mobility of specialised manpower, a technology institute set up by the entrepreneurs themselves in 1978 (*Fundacao de Tecnologia, Ensimo e Pesquisa*, FETEP), an extended network of micro-enterprises supplying specialised services in some stages of production. However, the export expansion of the Sao Bento do Sul cluster is still mainly due to the exports of the larger firms. A few agreements with foreign firms have been signed, mainly for the purchase of machinery, related technical assistance, and for some occasional sub-contracting. The tendency to set up more complex and multi-dimensional agreements with groups of SMEs appears still very limited.

5.3. Thirdly, Rabellotti, 1995, recently made an effort to read with systemic glasses the experience of two areas densely populated by SMEs in Mexico. Respectively 1200 and 1700 shoe manufacturers (about 60% of the country's total) are localised in the regions of Guadalajara and Leon. These firms, after the trade liberalisation of 1988, opened up to international relations, and increased their exports. Among the factors that explain their good performance are: good inter-firm co-operation, mostly of an informal nature and among very small firms, and a good institutional assistance.[21]

The analysis of this Mexican experience has shown the special interest of the SMEs in the area for better and more intense relationships with Italian shoe manufacturers, considered as an example to imitate. What could be the interest of Italian SMEs in establishing commercial, technological, and productive linkages with the shoe manufacturers from Guadalajara and Leon? The recently implemented NAFTA (North American Free Trade Agreement, linking Mexico, United States and Canada in a custom union) offers new opportunities for firms operating with Mexican partners. The co-operation with Mexican shoe manufacturers may provide Italian SMEs with an interesting chance to break into some *niches* of the North-American market, otherwise impossible due to the competition from other producers from Brazil, Mexico, and East-Asia. Moreover, a strategy of international decentralisation of production is already being followed by competing firms from South Korea and Taiwan, that have moved their plants to cheap labour locations like Thailand, Indonesia and the Philippines. Under this respect, a closer co-operation with Mexican firms and IDs might offer Italian SMEs the opportunity to exploit the advantage deriving from their advanced know-how, and face the emerging trend of a shift of shoe productions towards LDCs. To this aim, the agreement between the Association of Brenta Craftsmen (*Associazione Artigiani del Brenta*) and the Employers'Association of Guadalajara and Leon looks very promising. The target pursued with the agreement is not confined to the transfer of the entire plant or of some phases of the production process, but also extends to the transfer of some elements of the Italian mode of industrial organisation and production.

6   Summary and Conclusions

The hypothesis that SMEs face substantial difficulties in their international expansion, in particular if beyond the simpler and less risky exports, has been confirmed by many empirical analyses. Among the obstacles to a more developed stage of SMEs internationalisation (e.g. inter-firm agreements or FDI) towards LDCs are: the market failures related to risk and uncertainty, the economies of scale and scope to operate at an international scale, both for manufacturing and distribution of all the product varieties demanded by export markets. In addition, the alternative option of internalising transactions within the borders of the firm is not open to them.

However, in spite of these difficulties, a more developed foreign involvement of the Italian SMEs may be fostered by various forms of inter-firm agreements, in particular if they derive from a long-experienced tradition of co-operation based

---

[21] The *Istituto Tecnológico del Calzado*, created in 1984 in Guadalajara, is a good example of effective institutional support to technology training and R&D.

on some common elements such as a common social and human base, a geographic proximity, and the same productive specialisation. These are some of the basic characteristics of the Italian IDs, that have importantly contributed to their success. These assets of inter-firm co-operation and collaboration may represent a key determinant of the further development of the Italian SMEs' international expansion towards emerging economies.

In some Latin-American countries, where already exist forms of industrial organisation that have been defined quasi-districts, some of the conditions to generate external economies and favour the international expansion of Italian IDs towards those areas are present. The presence of quasi-IDs observed in Latin America may attract the Italian IDs, given the good level of organisation observed and the high propensity to collaborate. Support to these forms of international expansion may come from numerous institutional agents, like for example a specialised financial intermediary or a leader-firm. Further research will be needed to address some of the specific issues outlined in this paper, and to test empirically the validity of the hypotheses proposed.

References

Acocella N., 1989, Efficienza e strategia nel processo di multinazionalizzazione: verso una teoria più generale, in Acocella N. E Schiattarella R. (eds.) Teorie della internazionalizzazione e realtà italiana, Napoli: Liguori.

Angori E., 1994, La funzione svolta dagli accordi bilaterali: il caso Italia-Argentina. Aspetti istituzionali, *Studi di Economia e Diritto*, 2/94.

Bagarani M., 1994, Metodologia per rilevare l'esistenza di un distretto industriale: indicatori significativi per l'internazionalizzazione,Working paper CNR-PFI.

Bagella M. (ed.), 1992, Politiche ed interventi per l'internazionalizzazione di imprese medio-piccole italiane in America Latina. 2 Volumes, mimeographed, Dipartimento di Economia ed Istituzioni, Università di Roma Tor Vergata.

Becattini G. (ed.), 1987, *Mercato e forze locali: il distretto industriale*, Bologna: Il Mulino.

Becattini G., 1979, Dal settore industriale al distretto industriale. Alcune considerazioni sull'unità d'indagine dell'economia industriale, Economia e Politica Industriale, 1.

Becattini G., 1993, Presentazione a 'Distretti industriali e mercato unico europeo' di M.Mistri, Milano: Franco Angeli - Ist.Tagliacarne.

Becchetti L., 1994, La grande impresa pubblica in America Latina: l'esperienza IRI, l'offerta endogena di servizi reali, la dimensione degli investimenti, il project financing, *Economia, Società e Istituzioni*, Vol.VI N.1.

Bercovich N., 1995, Analisi dell'internazionalizzazione del settore del mobile di Sao Bento do Sul (Santa Catarina, Brasil) alla luce dell'esperienza dei distretti industriali italiani, *Economia e Diritto del Terziario*, 1.

Carisano R., 1994, La piccola e media impresa in America Latina. L'assetto attuale dei rapporti e problemi di inserimento: un'indagine sul campo, *Economia, Società e Istituzioni*, Vol. VI N.1.

CESPRI-BOCCONI, 1988, La cooperazione internazionale delle imprese italiane: analisi generale e prospettive degli accordi delle PMI in Europa, report for the Task Force on SMEs for the EEC, Bruxelles.

Cooper R. and John A., 1988, Coordinating Coordination Failures in Keynesian Models, *Quarterly Journal of Economics,* 103, August

Cortellese C. and Pietrobelli C., 1993, La strategia per la ricostruzione economico-sociale nei PVS: quale ruolo per la cooperazione internazionale?, Studi di Economia e Diritto, Vol.XXXXIII, No. 3.

Dei Ottati G., 1992, Fiducia, transazioni intrecciate e credito nel distretto industriale, *Note Economiche*, XXII, n.1-2.

Feistein H.A., 1994, L'indagine campionaria sui progetti di cooperazione presentati alla CGI argentina nell'ambito dell'Accordo italo-argentino., *Studi di Economia e Diritto*, Vol.XXXXIV, No. 3.

Hart O. and Holmström B., 1988, The Theory of Contracts, in BEWLEY T. (ed.) Advances in Economic Theory, Econometric Society Monographs N.,12, Cambridge, U.K.: Cambridge University Press.

Leibenstein H., 1966, Allocative Efficiency Vs. X-Efficiency, *American Economic Review*, 56.

Lo Cicero M., 1995, Internazionalizzazione dei distretti industriali: un ruolo possibile per il merchant banking, *Economia e Diritto del Terziario*, 1.

Manuelli A., 1994, *Internazionalizzazione e trasferimento tecnologico in aree a minor sviluppo. Le problematiche nei sistemi locali di piccole imprese in Toscana*, Firenze: IRPET.

Mistri M., 1993, *Distretti Industriali E Mercato Unico Europeo*, Milano: Franco Angeli and Istituto Tagliacarne.

Nalebuff B.J., and Stiglitz J.E., 1983, Prizes and Incentives: towards a General Theory of Compensation and Competition, *Bell Journal of Economics*, 14.

Oman C., 1984a, New Forms of International Investment in Developing Countries, Paris: OECD.

Paganetto L. and Scandizzo P.L., 1992, Quality, International Trade and Endogenous Growth, *Rivista di Politica Economica*, 11, Nov.

Pietrobelli C., 1998, Industry, Competitiveness and Technological Capabilities in Chile. A New Tiger from Latin America?, London and New York: Macmillan and St.Martin's.

Pietrobelli C., 1994, Internazionalizzazione delle PMI italiane in America Latina e progresso tecnologico: una nota da un'indagine empirica, Economia, Società e Istituzioni, Vol. VI N.1.

Pietrobelli C., 1992, Il ruolo del progresso tecnologico nei processi di internazionalizzazione delle imprese, Studi di Economia e Diritto, Vol.XXXXII, No. 4/92.

Pietrobelli C., 1991, Tecnologia e Sviluppo. L'inserimento internazionale di un'economia emergente, Roma: Edizioni Lavoro.

Pietrobelli C., 1990, Italia-Brasile: Logica Di Un Accordo, Andes, 9.

Pietrobelli C., Cortellese C., 1994, Joint Ventures E Relazioni Economiche internazionali: l'esperienza del Trattato tra Italia e Argentina, Studi di Economia e Diritto, Vol.XXXXIV, No. 3.

Pietrobelli C. and Rabellotti R., 1992, Relaciones extramercado entre firmas y sus efectos en el desarrollo industrial de los países de menor desarrollo. El caso de un Parque Industrial en Santiago de Chile, Revista Latinoamericana de Estudios Urbanos y Regionales - EURE, XVIII, No.54, and Economia, Società ed Istituzioni, IV (1).

Pyke R., Becattini G. and Sengenberger W. (eds.), 1991, Industrial Districts and Inter-firm Cooperation in Italy, ILO, Geneva.

Quintar A., Ascua R., Gatto F. and Ferraro C., 1995, Rafaela (Argentina): un quasi-distretto italiano alla argentina, Economia e Diritto del Terziario, 1/95.

Rabellotti R., 1995, Distretti industriali in Messico: il caso del settore calzaturiero a Guadalajara e Leon, Economia e Diritto del Terziario, 1/95.

Ramazzotti P. and Schiattarella R., 1989, Investimenti diretti ed esportazioni tra mercato ed impresa, in Acocella N. E Schiattarella R. (eds.) Teorie della internazionalizzazione e realtà italiana, Napoli: Liguori.

Rullani E. and Vacca' S., 1983, Oltre il modello classico di impresa multinazionale, Finanza, Marketing, Produzione, 1-2.

Sforzi F., 1987, L'identificazione spaziale in Becattini (ed.), reprinted as: The Geography of Industrial Districts in Italy, in Goodman E. and Bamford J. (eds.), 1989, Small Firms and Industrial Districts in Italy, London and New York: Routledge.

Vitali G. 1994, Paper presented to the Conference CNR-PFI, Università Tor Vergata, Roma, 24.3.1994.

Appendix

Appendix. Firms belonging to GA areas and their relative specialisation in the Mediocredito sample

N. of GA area	Province	Council	Relative specialisation of the GA area	N. of firms included in the sample by activity (firms whose activity is not part of the relative specialisation of the GA area are underlined)
546	BA/TA	Locorotondo, Martinafranca	textile, footwear, clothing, metal products, mechanical equipment	Second transformation and treatment of metals (4) Apparel and clothing accessories, automated production Tools and final metal products
543	BA	Putignano	textile, footwear, clothing, metal products, mechanical equipment, furniture	(2) Second transformation and treatment of metals Paper and cardboard transformation
539	BA	Barletta	footwear	(2) Footwear, automated manufacturing Tricots, socks and other stockings
503	CH	Fara Filiorum Petri	textile, clothing, metal products, mechanical equipment, furniture	Tools and final metal products
495	TE	Teramo, Corropoli,Torri cella Sicura, Sant'Omero, Bellante	textile, clothing, metal products, mechanical equipment, furniture	Office machinery and automatic data processing (2) Apparel and clothing accessories, automated production Furniture and wood furnishing industry Flax, ramitè and true hemp yarn industry Wool industry Other knitted outer garments Boiler and tanks construction Chemical products for agriculture and industry Plastic products
493	TE	Notaresco, Alba Adriatica,Giuli anova, Mosciano Sant'angelo, Tortoreto, Roseto Degli Abruzzi	textile, clothing, metal products, mechanical equipment, furniture	Tricots, socks and other stockings (2) Leather products (2) Production and base transformation of non ferrous metals (2) Furniture and wood furnishing industry Other textiles (3) Apparel and clothing accessories, automated production Production and base transformation of non ferrous metals Stone and non-metallic mineral manufacture Electrical instruments for means of transport and industry, cells and accumulators Electric wires and cables Vegetable and animal fat industry Rubber

N. of GA area	Province	Council	Relative specialisation of the GA area	N. of firms included in the sample by activity (firms whose activity is not part of the relative specialisation of the GA area are underlined)
491	TE	Pineto Atri	textile, clothing, metal products, mechanical equipment, furniture	Plastic products (3) Furniture and wood furnishing industry Parts and fittings of passenger cars and trailers production
458	AV	Solofra	leather, housing	(2)Leather
456	AV	Montemiletto, Torre Le Nocelle	leather, housing	Tools and final metal products Metal structure construction
436	BN	Molinara	housing, transport equipment	Tools and final metal products
419	FR	Castelliri, Broccostella, Castelliri	clothing, textile, mechanical equipment	Electrical instruments for means of transport and industry, cells and accumulators Paper and cardboard transformation Other textiles
395	VT-RE	Gallese, Castel Sant'Elia, Fabrica Di Roma, Gallese, Nepi	mineral extraction, electrical equipment, appliance, chemicals-pharmaceuticals, mechanical equipment	(3)Pottery production Printing industry Cheese industry
388	PG	Todi	clothing, textile, leather, petroleum pr. refin., rubber-plastics	Concrete, asbestos, lime and gypsum building materials' production Radio receivers, television receivers, control systems production
369	SI	Torrita Di Siena, Sinalunga, Torrita Di Siena,	metal products, mechanical equipment, rubber-plastics, non-metallic minerals, furniture, wood	Tricots, socks and other stockings Plastic products Tools and final metal products
366	SI	Colle Val D'elsa Barberino Val D'elsa Poggibonsi Castellina In Chianti Casole D' Elsa	Metal Products, Mechanical Equipment, Rubber-Plastics, Non-Metallic Minerals, Furniture, Wood	(2)Glass Industry Pottery Production Road Vehicles, Construction and Assembling Production and Base Transformation of Non Ferrous Metals Tools and Final Metal Products Other Mechanical Prepared Animal Feeds Furniture and Wood Furnishing Industry Steel Tubes Manufacture
358	AR	Pieve Santo Stefano	Jewellery, Clothing,	
356	AR	Bibbiena	Wood, Jewellery, Clothing, Paper, Metal Products, Mechanical Equipment, Mechanical Equipment, Printing	Concrete, Asbestos, Lime and Gypsum Building Materials' Production Tricots, Socks and Other Stockings

N. of GA area	Province	Council	Relative specialisation of the GA area	N. of firms included in the sample by activity (firms whose activity is not part of the relative specialisation of the GA area are underlined)
355	AR	Arezzo Castiglion Fibocchi Capolona Civitella In Val Di Chiana Castiglion Fiorentino	Jewellery, Clothing, Clothing	Tricots, Socks and Other Stockings Tools and Final Metal Products (3)Apparel and Clothing Accessories, Automated Production (10)Jewellery, Silver, Gift Shop, Precious Stone Cutting Electrical Instruments for Means of Transport And Industry, Cells and Accumulators Motors, Generators, Transformers, Switch and Other Electric Materials Production Metal Working Machinery (2)Construction of Electrical Machinery, Telecommunication and Electromedical Machinery (2)Plastic Products (5)Leather Paper and Cardboard Transformation (7)Footwear, Automated Manufacturing
353	PI, FI	San Miniato Fucecchio Santa Maria A Monte Castelfranco Di Sotto Santa Croce Sull'arno	Chemicals, Machinery, Non-Metallic Minerals, Wood, Leather, Paper, Metal Products, Mechanical Equipment, Textile	(5)Leather (7)Footwear, Automated Manufacturing Paper and Cardboard Transformation (2)Plastic Products
352	AP	Grottammare	Chemicals, Mechanical Equipment, Rubber-Plastics, Printing	Apparel and Clothing Accessories, Automated Production
343	FI	Vaiano	Leather, Metal Products, Mechanical Equipment, Paper, Textile	Other Knitted Outer Garments (2) Wool Industry
342	FI	Vaiano Montemurlo Cantagallo Poggio a Caiano Carmignano Prato Agliana	Leather, Metal Products, Mechanical Equipment, Paper, Textile	Concrete, Asbestos, Lime and Gypsum Building Materials' Production Metal Structure Construction Bread, Biscuits And Bakery Products Industry (11)Wool Industry Flax, Ramitè and True Hemp Yarn Industry (4)Tricots, Socks And Other Stockings
339	FI	Empoli,Cerreto Guidi, Montelupo Fiorentino, Montespertoli, Vinci	Leather, Metal Products, Mechanical Equipment, Paper, Textile	(2)Glass Industry (2)Apparel and Clothing Accessories, Automated Production Paper and Cardboard Transformation Footwear, Automated Manufacturing Apparel and Clothing Accessories, Automated Production Bread, Biscuits and Bakery Products Industry Cocoa Power, Chocolate, Ice-Cream Industry Base Chemicals Production

N. of GA area	Province	Council	Relative specialisation of the GA area	N. of firms included in the sample by activity (firms whose activity is not part of the relative specialisation of the GA area are underlined)
338		Gambassi Terme, Certaldo		Other Wood Manufacture (Excluding Furniture) Paper and Cardboard Transformation
336	PI-PT	Pistoia, Quarrata, Pisa	Chemicals, Machinery, Non-Metallic Minerals, Wood, Leather, Paper, Metal Products, Mechanical Equipment, Textile	(2)Other Textile Articles Furniture and Wood Furnishing Industry Printing Industry (3)Furniture And Wood Furnishing Industry Food nd Chemical Industry Machinery Radio Receivers, Television Receivers, Control Systems Production
335	PT	Buggiano Larciano Monsummano Terme Ponte Buggianese Chiesina Uzzanese Montecatini Terme Montelupo Fiorentino Pieve a Nievole Uzzano	Leather, Metal Products, Mechanical Equipment, Paper, Textile	(4) Footwear, Automated Manufacturing Printing Industry Apparel And Clothing Accessories, Automated Production Cork, Straw, Reed And Wicker, Brush And Paintbrush Products Wool Industry Leather Products Noodle Products Vegetable And Fruit Transformation And Conservation Dyeing, Tanning And Colouring Materials Metal Working Machinery
333	LU	Pietrasanta	paper, rubber-plastics, leather, metal products, mechanical equipment	Foundries Second transformation and treatment of metals
332	LU	Lucca, Altopascio, Capannori	paper, rubber-plastics, leather, metal products, mechanical equipment	Pneumatics, vulcanisation and repair (2)Pulp, paper and cardboard production Footwear, automated manufacturing Second transformation and treatment of metals Bread, biscuits and bakery products industry Paper and cardboard transformation Electric wires and cables
330	LU	Barga Bagni Di Lucca Borgo A Mozzano	paper, rubber-plastics, leather, metal products, mechanical equipment	(2)Glass industry (2)Pulp, paper and cardboard production Concrete, asbestos, lime and gypsum building materials' production
328	AP	Fermo	chemicals, mechanical equipment, rubber-plastics, electrical equipment, appliance	Footwear, automated manufacturing
324	AP	Porto Sant'elpidio Sant'elpidio A Mare	chemicals, mechanical equipment, rubber-plastics, electrical equipment, appliance	(2)Footwear, automated manufacturing

N. of GA area	Province	Council	Relative specialisation of the GA area	N. of firms included in the sample by activity (firms whose activity is not part of the relative specialisation of the GA area are underlined)
323	AP	Rotella	chemicals, mechanical equipment, rubber-plastics, electrical equipment, appliance	Miscellaneous edible products and preparations
322	AP	Monte San Pietrangeli	chemicals, mechanical equipment, rubber-plastics, electrical equipment, appliance	Footwear, automated manufacturing
321	AP	Montegranaro, Ascoli Piceno	chemicals, mechanical equipment, rubber-plastics, electrical equipment, appliance	(2)Footwear, automated manufacturing (3)Footwear, automated manufacturing Metal structure construction Bread, biscuits and bakery products industry
320	AP	Ponzano Di Fermo, Magliano Di Tenna	chemicals, mechanical equipment, rubber-plastics, electrical equipment, appliance	Second transformation and treatment of metals Footwear, automated manufacturing
319	AP	Montefiore Dell'aso	chemicals, mechanical equipment, rubber-plastics, electrical equipment, appliance	Footwear, automated manufacturing
318	AP	Fermo, Monte Urano	chemicals, mechanical equipment, rubber-plastics, electrical equipment, appliance	(2)Footwear, automated manufacturing Leather
314	MC	Urbisaglia	mineral extraction, leather, rubber-plastics	Apparel and clothing accessories, automated production
313	MC	Appignano, Treia	mineral extraction, leather, rubber-plastics	(3)Furniture and wood furnishing industry Apparel and clothing accessories, automated production Leather
312	MC	Tolentino	mineral extraction, leather, rubber-plastics	Leather products
311	MC	San Ginesio	mineral extraction, leather, rubber-plastics	Footwear, automated manufacturing
310	AN	Loreto	rubber-plastics, mechanical equipment	Tools and final metal products
309	MC	Morrovalle	mineral extraction, leather, rubber-plastics	Rubber Footwear, automated manufacturing
307	MC	Civitanova Marche Montecosaro, Potenza Picena	mineral extraction, leather, rubber-plastics	Plastic products Chemical products for agriculture and industry Second transformation and treatment of metals Tools and final metal products (11)Footwear, automated manufacturing
306	MC	Cingoli	mineral extraction, leather, rubber-plastics	Zootechnics agriculture machinery
304	AN	Serra De' Conti, Montecarotto	rubber-plastics, mechanical equipment	(4)Footwear, automated manufacturing

N. of GA area	Province	Council	Relative specialisation of the GA area	N. of firms included in the sample by activity (firms whose activity is not part of the relative specialisation of the GA area are underlined)
303	AN	Senigallia, Corinaldo	rubber-plastics, mechanical equipment	Furniture and wood furnishing industry Radio receivers, television receivers, control systems production
301	AN	Ostra, Ostra Vetere	rubber-plastics, mechanical equipment	Printing industry Stone and non-metallic mineral manufacture Zootechnics agriculture machinery Plastic products
300	AN	Camerano, Castelfidardo Filottrano Osimo	rubber-plastics, mechanical equipment	Second transformation and treatment of metals (2)Tools and final metal products (2)Metal working machinery Food and chemical industry machinery Motors, generators, transformers, switch and other electric materials production Electrical instruments for means of transport and industry, cells and accumulators Construction of electrical machinery, telecommunication and electromedical machinery Radio receivers, television receivers, control systems production Installation: electrical machinery, apparatus and appliance (2)Apparel and clothing accessories, automated production Other textile articles (2)Furniture and wood furnishing industry Printing industry Plastic products (2)Musical instruments
299	AN	Jesi, San Paolo Di Jesi	rubber-plastics, mechanical equipment	Zootechnics agriculture machinery Car body and trailers construction Rubber Food and chemical industry machinery Radio receivers, television receivers, control systems production
296	PS	Montecalvo In Foglia Fermignano, Urbino	wood, furniture, mechanical equipment	Furniture and wood furnishing industry Production and base transformation of non ferrous metals Tools and final metal products
295	PS	Peglio, Urbania	wood, furniture, mechanical equipment	(2)Apparel and clothing accessories, automated production Taylormade clothing and underwear
294	PS	Macerata Feltria	wood, furniture, mechanical equipment	Taylormade clothing and underwear

N. of GA area	Province	Council	Relative specialisation of the GA area	N. of firms included in the sample by activity (firms whose activity is not part of the relative specialisation of the GA area are underlined)
291	PS	Montelabbate, Pesaro	wood, furniture, mechanical equipment	(6)Furniture and wood furnishing industry Tools and final metal products (3)Machinery for wood, paper, leather and shoes industry, sanitary, laundry and ironing equipment Printing industry 140
287	PS	Mondolfo, Barchi, Monte Porzio	wood, furniture, mechanical equipment	Second transformation and treatment of metals Taylormade clothing and underwear Metal structure construction Precision instruments
286	PS	Sant'ippolito	wood, furniture, mechanical equipment	Furniture and wood furnishing industry
285	PS	Fano Saltara	wood, furniture, mechanical equipment	Metal structure construction Apparel and clothing accessories, automated production Furniture and wood furnishing industry
284	PS	Piobbico	wood, furniture, mechanical equipment	Metal structure construction
283	FO	Civitella Di Romagna	petroleum pr. refin., metal products, mechanical equipment, rubber-plastics, wood, clothing	Precision instruments
280	FO	San Clemente	petroleum pr. refin., metal products, mechanical equipment, rubber-plastics, wood, clothing	Pottery production
278	FO	Sarsina	petroleum pr. refin., metal products, mechanical equipment, rubber-plastics, wood, clothing	Tools and final metal products Electrical lighting equipment
277	FO	Bertinoro Castrocaro Terme E Terra Del Forli'	petroleum pr. refin., metal products, mechanical equipment, rubber-plastics, wood, clothing	Metal structure construction (3)Plastic products Carpentry, woodwork and wood floor Foundries (2)Furniture and wood furnishing industry Concrete, asbestos, lime and gypsum building materials' production (2)Transmission tool equipment

N. of GA area	Province	Council	Relative specialisation of the GA area	N. of firms included in the sample by activity (firms whose activity is not part of the relative specialisation of the GA area are underlined)
272	RA	Alfonsine Bagnacavallo Fusignano Lugo, Massa Lombarda	petroleum pr. refin., metal products, mechanical equipment, rubber-plastics, wood, clothing	Power generating machinery and equipment for extractive industries, non metallic manufacturing, civil engineering, building, iron and steel industry Footwear, automated manufacturing (2)Zootechnics agriculture machinery (2)Food and chemical industry machinery Electrical household equipment Vegetable and fruit transformation and conservation Miscellaneous edible products and preparations (3)Footwear, automated manufacturing Apparel and clothing accessories, automated production Printing industry Rubber
271	RA	Faenza	petroleum pr. refin., metal products, mechanical equipment, rubber-plastics, wood, clothing	Vegetable and fruit transformation and conservation (2)Tools and final metal products Base chemicals production
266	FE-BO-MO	Cento, Pieve Di Cento, S.Agata Bolognese, San Giovanni In Persiceto Sant'agostino	metal products, mechanical equipment, mechanical equipment, chemicals, housing, innovazione tecnologica, r&s, transport equipment	(2)Tools and final metal products Precision instruments Road vehicles, construction and assembling Motors, generators, transformers, switch and other electric materials production Power generating machinery and equipment for extractive industries, non metallic manufacturing, civil engineering, building, iron and steel industry Pottery production Metal working machinery Foundries
265	FE-BO	Argenta, Molinella	metal products, mechanical equipment, mechanical equipment, chemicals, printing, transport equipment	Electric wires and cables Footwear, automated manufacturing
261	BO-MO	Bazzano Castelvetro Di Modena Marano Sul Panaro Monteveglio Vignola Vignola Di Modena	metal products, mechanical equipment, mechanical equipment, chemicals, printing, transport equipment	(2)Transmission tool equipment Parts and fittings of passenger cars and trailers production Plastic products Precision instruments Metal structure construction Meat and meat preparation

N. of GA area	Province	Council	Relative specialisation of the GA area	N. of firms included in the sample by activity (firms whose activity is not part of the relative specialisation of the GA area are underlined)
260	RE-MO	Casalgrande, Fiorano Modenese, Formigine, Maranello, Sassuolo	metal products, mechanical equipment, chemicals, transport equipment, pottery	Building brick materials (18)Pottery production Forging, pressing, drawing and shearing of metals (2)Metal structure construction (4)Metal working machinery (4)Power generating machinery and equipment for extractive industries, non metallic manufacturing, civil engineering, building, iron and steel industry Transmission tool equipment Car body and trailers construction (2)Tricots, socks and other stockings Apparel and clothing accessories, automated production Printing industry Rubber Power generating machinery and equipment for extractive industries, non metallic manufacturing, civil engineering, building, iron and steel industry
256	MO	Bomporto, Campogalliano, Castelfranco Emilia, Castelnuovo Rangon,E Modena	metal products, mechanical equipment, chemicals, transport equipment	Iron and steel industry (3)Pottery production Forging, pressing, drawing and shearing of metals Second transformation and treatment of metals (3)Tools and final metal products (3)Zootechnics agriculture machinery Food and chemical industry machinery (3)Power generating machinery and equipment for extractive industries, non metallic manufacturing, civil engineering, building, iron and steel industry Transmission tool equipment (3)Precision instruments Motors, generators, transformers, switch and other electric materials production Electrical household equipment (2)Road vehicles, construction and assembling (4)Meat and meat preparation Tapestry and carpets (3)Apparel and clothing accessories, automated production (2)Printing industry 837 Electrical household equipment

N. of GA area	Province	Council	Relative specialisation of the GA area	N. of firms included in the sample by activity (firms whose activity is not part of the relative specialisation of the GA area are underlined)
255	MO	Cavezzo, Finale Emilia, Mirandola, San Felice Sul Panaro, San Possidonio	metal products, mechanical equipment, chemicals, transport equipment	Pottery production Power generating machinery and equipment for extractive industries, non metallic manufacturing, civil engineering, building, iron and steel industry Motors, generators, transformers, switch and other electric materials production Parts and fittings of passenger cars and trailers production (3)Medical and surgical instruments (2)Tricots, socks and other stockings Other textiles Transmission tool construction
253	MO	Carpi	metal products, mechanical equipment, chemicals, transport equipment	(5)Apparel and clothing accessories, automated production Zootechnics agriculture machinery Power generating machinery and equipment for extractive industries, non metallic manufacturing, civil engineering, building, iron and steel industry (5)Tricots, socks and other stockings (3)Other textiles Machinery for wood, paper, leather and shoes industry, sanitary, laundry and ironing equipment

N. of GA area	Province	Council	Relative specialisation of the GA area	N. of firms included in the sample by activity (firms whose activity is not part of the relative specialisation of the GA area are underlined)
252	RE	Albinea, Bagnolo In Piano, Casina, Cavriago, Gattatico, Montecchio Emilia, Reggio Emilia, Sant'ilario D'enza, Scandiano	clothing, rubber-plastics, electrical equipment, appliance	(3)Pottery production Base chemicals production (2)Second transformation and treatment of metals Metal structure construction Boiler and tanks construction (3)Tools and final metal products Zootechnics agriculture machinery Metal working machinery (2)Food and chemical industry machinery (2)Power generating machinery and equipment for extractive industries, non metallic manufacturing, civil engineering, building, iron and steel industry Transmission tool equipment (7)Precision instruments (4)Electrical instruments for means of transport and industry, cells and accumulators (3)Electrical instruments for means of transport and industry, cells and accumulators Radio receivers, television receivers, control systems production Electrical household equipment Noodle products Bread, biscuits and bakery products industry (2)Apparel and clothing accessories, automated production Wood intermediate products Paper and cardboard transformation (2)Printing industry Rubber (2)Plastic products Transmission tool construction
251	RE	Castelnovo Di Sotto, Gualtieri	clothing, rubber-plastics, electrical equipment, appliance	Tools and final metal products Concrete, asbestos, lime and gypsum building materials' production Car body and trailers construction Second transformation and treatment of metals Electrical household equipment Food and chemical industry machinery
250	RE	Correggio, San Martino In Rio	clothing, rubber-plastics, electrical equipment, appliance	Power generating machinery and equipment for extractive industries, non metallic manufacturing, civil engineering, building, iron and steel industry Motors, generators, transformers, switch and other electric materials production Noodle products (3)Plastic products (2)Zootechnics agriculture machinery

N. of GA area	Province	Council	Relative specialisation of the GA area	N. of firms included in the sample by activity (firms whose activity is not part of the relative specialisation of the GA area are underlined)
248	RE	Castellaranocas tellarano Fr. Roteglia	clothing, rubber-plastics, electrical equipment, appliance	(4)<u>Pottery production Paper and cardboard transformation</u>
246	PR	Calestano, Collecchio, Colorno, Fontevivo, Montechiarugolo, Parma, San Secondo Parmense, Sorbolo, Trecasali	clothing, metal products, mechanical equipment	Glass industry Pottery production (2)Pharmaceuticals Soap and detergent, personal hygiene and perfumery products production <u>Second transformation and treatment of metals</u> (3)<u>Tools and final metal products</u> (4)Food and chemical industry machinery Power generating machinery and equipment for extractive industries, non metallic manufacturing, civil engineering, building, iron and steel industry (3)Precision instruments (2)Meat and meat preparation Cheese industry Vegetable and fruit transformation and conservation Noodle products Cocoa power, chocolate, ice-cream industry Miscellaneous edible products and preparations Pulp, paper and cardboard production <u>Paper and cardboard transformation</u> (2)<u>Printing industry Rubber</u> (2)<u>Plastic products</u> (2)Transmission tool construction
245	PR	Langhirano, Lesignano De'bagni	clothing, metal products, mechanical equipment	<u>Printing industry</u> Meat and meat preparation
244	PR	Fornovo Di Taro	clothing, metal products, mechanical equipment	Food and chemical industry machinery
242	PR	Busseto	clothing, metal products, mechanical equipment	<u>Plastic products</u>
238	PC	Cadeo, Fiorenzuola D'arda, Lugagnano Val D'arda	metal products, mechanical equipment, mineral extraction	<u>Concrete, asbestos, lime and gypsum building materials' production Radio receivers, television receivers, control systems production Prepared animal feeds</u> Zootechnics agriculture machinery Food and chemical industry machinery
237	PC	Nibbiano, Ziano Piacentino	metal products, mechanical equipment, mineral extraction	Boiler and tanks construction <u>Meat and meat preparation</u>
233	PN	Maniago, Montereale Valcellina	rubber-plastics, furniture, machinery	(3)Tools and final metal products Metal working machinery Plastic products Precision instruments Transmission tool equipment Foundries Rubber

N. of GA area	Province	Council	Relative specialisation of the GA area	N. of firms included in the sample by activity (firms whose activity is not part of the relative specialisation of the GA area are underlined)
229	UD	Buia, Buttrio, Cividale Del Friuli, Codroipo, Coseano, Gemona Del Friuli, Manzano, Martignacco, Osoppo, Pasian Di Prato, Pozzuolo Del Friuli, Premariacco, San Daniele Del Friuli, San Giovanni Al Natisone, Tavagnacco, Trivignano Udinese, Udine	chemicals, paper, wood, steel	(2)Iron and steel industry Concrete, asbestos, lime and gypsum building materials' production Stone and non-metallic mineral manufacture Glass industry Base chemicals production (2)Dyeing, tanning and colouring materials Chemical products for agriculture and industry (2)Second transformation and treatment of metals Metal structure construction Tools and final metal products Metal working machinery Power generating machinery and equipment for extractive industries, non metallic manufacturing, civil engineering, building, iron and steel industry Machinery for wood, paper, leather and shoes industry, sanitary, laundry and ironing equipment Motors, generators, transformers, switch and other electric materials production Meat and meat preparation Bread, biscuits and bakery products industry Beer and malt industry Non alcoholic beverage and mineral water industry Other knitted outer garments Footwear, automated manufacturing (6)Furniture and wood furnishing industry Paper and cardboard transformation (2)Printing industry Transmission tool construction
220	RO	Melara	textile, clothing, clothing, furniture	Metal working machinery
218	RO	Adria	textile, clothing, clothing, furniture	Plastic products

N. of GA area	Province	Council	Relative specialisation of the GA area	N. of firms included in the sample by activity (firms whose activity is not part of the relative specialisation of the GA area are underlined)
217	PD-TV	Albignasego, Brugine, Cadoneghe, Campodarsego, Carrara San Giorgio, Casier, Cervarese Santa Croce, Limena, Padova, Piove Di Sacco, Ponte San Nicolo', Rubano, Saonara, Selvazzano Dentro, Stra, Torreglia, Vigonza, Villanova Di Camposampiero	textile, leather, rubber-plastics, mechanical equipment, non-metallic minerals, gold	(2)Iron and steel industry Cement, lime and gypsum production (2)Pottery production (2)Dyeing, tanning and colouring materials (3)Second transformation and treatment of metals (2)Metal structure construction Boiler and tanks construction (8)Tools and final metal products (3)Zootechnics agriculture machinery Metal working machinery Food and chemical industry machinery (2)Power generating machinery and equipment for extractive industries, non metallic manufacturing, civil engineering, building, iron and steel industry Machinery for wood, paper, leather and shoes industry, sanitary, laundry and ironing equipment (2)Precision instruments Motors, generators, transformers, switch and other electric materials production (2)Electrical instruments for means of transport and industry, cells and accumulators Radio receivers, television receivers, control systems production Electrical household equipment (2)Installation: electrical machinery, apparatus and appliance Parts and fittings of passenger cars and trailers production Printing industry Cocoa power, chocolate, ice-cream industry Distilled alcoholic beverage, ethyl alcohol and mandy industry Tricots, socks and other stockings Other textiles (3)Footwear, automated manufacturing Apparel and clothing accessories, automated production (4)Paper and cardboard transformation (6)Printing industry Publishing industry Rubber Plastic products Photographers' studios and cinema industry Transmission tool construction

N. of GA area	Province	Council	Relative specialisation of the GA area	N. of firms included in the sample by activity (firms whose activity is not part of the relative specialisation of the GA area are underlined)
215	PD	Bagnoli Di Sopra, Monselice, Pernumia,	textile, leather, rubber-plastics, mechanical equipment, non-metallic minerals, gold	Steel drawing, ironing and rolling Apparel and clothing accessories, automated production Plastic products <u>Soap and detergent, personal hygiene and perfumery products production</u> Metal structure construction <u>Base chemicals production</u>
213	PD	Campo San Martino, Carmignano Di Brenta, Cittadella, Fontaniva, Galliera Veneta, Gazzo, Grantorto Padovano, Piazzola Sul Brenta, San Giorgio Delle Pertiche, San Giorgio In Bosco, Tombolo, Villa Del Conte	textile, leather, rubber-plastics, mechanical equipment, non-metallic minerals, gold	<u>Production and base transformation of non ferrous metals Concrete, asbestos, lime and gypsum building materials' production</u> Tools and final metal products Zootechnics agriculture machinery Food and chemical industry machinery Precision instruments <u>Meat and meat preparation Non alcoholic beverage and mineral water industry</u> Silk and chemical fibre industry Flax, ramitè and true hemp yarn industry Apparel and clothing accessories, automated production (2)Taylormade clothing and underwear <u>Pulp, paper and cardboard production Printing industry</u> Plastic products Others manufacturing
208	MI-TV	Vittorio Veneto	textile, leather, rubber-plastics, mechanical equipment, non-metallic minerals, gold	Precision instruments Plastic products

N. of GA area	Province	Council	Relative specialisation of the GA area	N. of firms included in the sample by activity (firms whose activity is not part of the relative specialisation of the GA area are underlined)
207	TV	Arcade, Carbonera, Casale Sul Sile, Maserada Sul Piave, Paese, Ponzano Veneto, Preganziol, Quinto Di Treviso, Roncade, San Biagio Di Callalta, Silea, Spresiano, Treviso, Villorba,	textile, leather, rubber-plastics, mechanical equipment, non-metallic minerals, gold	(3)Building brick materials Cement, lime and gypsum production (2)Concrete, asbestos, lime and gypsum building materials' production Pottery production (6)Metal structure construction (2)Other mechanical Zootechnics agriculture machinery Metal working machinery (2)Food and chemical industry machinery Machinery for wood, paper, leather and shoes industry, sanitary, laundry and ironing equipment Radio receivers, television receivers, control systems production Electrical household equipment Car body and trailers construction Wool industry Cotton industry (6)Tricots, socks and other stockings (6)Apparel and clothing accessories, automated production Wood intermediate products (2)Carpentry, woodwork and wood floor (2)Furniture and wood furnishing industry Pulp, paper and cardboard production (2)Paper and cardboard transformation Plastic products (2)Transmission tool construction
206	TV	Refrontolo, Valdobbiadene	textile, leather, rubber-plastics, mechanical equipment, non-metallic minerals, gold	Tools and final metal products Wine industry
205	TV	Cimadolmo, Fontanelle, Gorgo Al Monticano, Mansue', Motta Di Livenza, Oderzo, Ormelle, Ponte Di Piave, Salgareda,	textile, leather, rubber-plastics, mechanical equipment, non-metallic minerals, gold	Mole production Glass industry Pottery production Metal structure construction Radio receivers, television receivers, control systems production (2)Electrical household equipment Tricots, socks and other stockings Wood intermediate products Other wood manufacture (excluding furniture) (6)Furniture and wood furnishing industry Printing industry Plastic products

N. of GA area	Province	Council	Relative specialisation of the GA area	N. of firms included in the sample by activity (firms whose activity is not part of the relative specialisation of the GA area are underlined)
204	TV	Asolo, Caerano Di San Marco, Cornuda, Giavera Del Montello, Maser, Montebelluna, Nervesa Della Battaglia, Volpago Del Montello	textile, leather, rubber-plastics, mechanical equipment, non-metallic minerals, gold	Metal structure construction Tools and final metal products Food and chemical industry machinery Precision instruments Meat and meat preparation (7)Footwear, automated manufacturing Handmade footwear (2)Apparel and clothing accessories, automated production Plastic products
203	TV	Conegliano, Gaiarine, Mareno Di Piave, Orsago, San Vendemiano, Santa Lucia Di Piave, Susegana, Vazzola	textile, leather, rubber-plastics, mechanical equipment, non-metallic minerals, gold	(5)Tools and final metal products Zootechnics agriculture machinery Machinery for wood, paper, leather and shoes industry, sanitary, laundry and ironing equipment Electrical instruments for means of transport and industry, cells and accumulators Radio receivers, television receivers, control systems production Bread, biscuits and bakery products industry Silk and chemical fibre industry Tricots, socks and other stockings Apparel and clothing accessories, automated production Wood, sawing and industrial processing (4)Furniture and wood furnishing industry Paper and cardboard transformation Printing industry (2)Plastic products
202	PD-TV	Camposampiero, Castelfranco Veneto, Castello Di Godego, Piombino Dese, Riese Pio X, Trebaseleghe	textile, leather, rubber-plastics, mechanical equipment, non-metallic minerals, gold	Foundries (2)Second transformation and treatment of metals Tools and final metal products Food and chemical industry machinery (2)Power generating machinery and equipment for extractive industries, non metallic manufacturing, civil engineering, building, iron and steel industry Precision instruments Electrical lighting equipment Parts and fittings of passenger cars and trailers production Cocoa power, chocolate, ice-cream industry (2)Printing industry
200	BL	Calalzo Di Cadore, Domegge Di Cadore	Optical industry	
199	BL	Pieve D'alpago	Optical industry	Electrical household equipment

N. of GA area	Province	Council	Relative specialisation of the GA area	N. of firms included in the sample by activity (firms whose activity is not part of the relative specialisation of the GA area are underlined)
194	VI	Altavilla Vicentina, Arcugnano, Bolzano Vicentino, Bressanvido, Caldogno, Camisano Vicentino, Costabissara, Creazzo, Dueville, Grisignano Di Zocco, Grumolo Delle Abbadesse, Quinto Vicentino, Sovizzo, Torri Di Quartesolo, Vicenza,	textile, leather, rubber-plastics, mechanical equipment, non-metallic minerals, gold	(2)Iron and steel industry Stone and non-metallic mineral manufacture Pharmaceuticals Foundries Metal structure construction Tools and final metal products (2)Metal working machinery (2)Food and chemical industry machinery (2)Machinery for wood, paper, leather and shoes industry, sanitary, laundry and ironing equipment Precision instruments (2)Motors, generators, transformers, switch and other electric materials production (2)Electrical instruments for means of transport and industry, cells and accumulators Radio receivers, television receivers, control systems production Cotton industry Tricots, socks and other stockings (6)Apparel and clothing accessories, automated production (2)Paper and cardboard transformation (3)Printing industry Rubber (3)Plastic products (5)Jewellery, silver, gift shop, precious stone cutting

N. of GA area	Province	Council	Relative specialisation of the GA area	N. of firms included in the sample by activity (firms whose activity is not part of the relative specialisation of the GA area are underlined)
192	VI	Arsiero, Breganze, Caltrano, Carre', Fara Vicentino, Lugo Di Vicenza, Sandrigo, Sarcedo, Thiene, Velo D'astico, Villaverla, Zane',	textile, leather, rubber-plastics, mechanical equipment, non-metallic minerals, gold	Concrete, asbestos, lime and gypsum building materials' production Dyeing, tanning and colouring materials (3)Forging, pressing, drawing and shearing of metals (2)Second transformation and treatment of metals Metal structure construction Zootechnics agriculture machinery Textile machinery Power generating machinery and equipment for extractive industries, non metallic manufacturing, civil engineering, building, iron and steel industry (3)Machinery for wood, paper, leather and shoes industry, sanitary, laundry and ironing equipment Precision instruments Motors, generators, transformers, switch and other electric materials production (2)Electrical instruments for means of transport and industry, cells and accumulators Construction of electrical machinery, telecommunication and electromedical machinery Shipbuilding industry Cheese industry (6)Wool industry Silk and chemical fibre industry (2)Tricots, socks and other stockings (2)Other knitted outer garments (6)Apparel and clothing accessories, automated production (2)Other textile articles (2)Furniture and wood furnishing industry (2)Paper and cardboard transformation Jewellery, silver, gift shop, precious stone cutting

N. of GA area	Province	Council	Relative specialisation of the GA area	N. of firms included in the sample by activity (firms whose activity is not part of the relative specialisation of the GA area are underlined)
191	VI	Malo, Marano Vicentino, San Vito Di Leguzzano, Santorso, Schio, Torrebelvicino, Valli Del Pasubio,	textile, leather, rubber-plastics, mechanical equipment, non-metallic minerals, gold, textile, metals	<u>Pottery production Pharmaceuticals</u> Foundries Second transformation and treatment of metals (2)Metal structure construction Tools and final metal products (2)Other mechanical (3)Metal working machinery Textile machinery (3)Food and chemical industry machinery (2)Power generating machinery and equipment for extractive industries, non metallic manufacturing, civil engineering, building, iron and steel industry (2)Machinery for wood, paper, leather and shoes industry, sanitary, laundry and ironing equipment Precision instruments Precision instruments Wool industry Cotton industry (2)Tricots, socks and other stockings (4)Apparel and clothing accessories, automated production <u>Wood, sawing and industrial processing</u> Plastic products
190	VI	Marostica, Molvena, Nove	textile, leather, rubber-plastics, mechanical equipment, non-metallic minerals, gold	(3)Apparel and clothing accessories, automated production Metal working machinery (2)Plastic products Electrical lighting equipment <u>Pottery production</u>
189	VI	Barbarano Vicentino, Campiglia Dei Berici, Castegnero, Cologna Veneta, Lonigo, Orgiano, Sarego, Sossano,	textile, leather, rubber-plastics, mechanical equipment, non-metallic minerals, gold	Second transformation and treatment of metals <u>Stone and non-metallic mineral manufacture Concrete, asbestos, lime and gypsum building materials' production Artificial and synthetic fibre production Base chemicals production</u> (2)Metal working machinery <u>Glass industry</u> Tricots, socks and other stockings Office machinery and automatic data processing

N. of GA area	Province	Council	Relative specialisation of the GA area	N. of firms included in the sample by activity (firms whose activity is not part of the relative specialisation of the GA area are underlined)
188	VI-MO	Bassano Del Grappa, Cartigliano, Cassola, Paderno Del Grappa, Romano D' Ezzelino, Rosa', Rossano Veneto, San Zenone Degli Ezzelini, Tezze Sul Brenta, Valstagna	textile, leather, rubber-plastics, mechanical equipment, non-metallic minerals, gold, metal products, mechanical equipment, transport equipment	Base chemicals production Second transformation and treatment of metals Metal structure construction (2)Tools and final metal products (2)Metal working machinery Power generating machinery and equipment for extractive industries, non metallic manufacturing, civil engineering, building, iron and steel industry Motors, generators, transformers, switch and other electric materials production Radio receivers, television receivers, control systems production (2)Electrical household equipment (3)Leather Footwear, automated manufacturing (7)Apparel and clothing accessories, automated production Carpentry, woodwork and wood floor Pulp, paper and cardboard production Paper and cardboard transformation Printing industry (3)Jewellery, silver, gift shop, precious stone cutting Others manufacturing Transmission tool construction
186	VI	Altissimo, Arzignano, Brendola, Chiampo, Montebello Vicentino, Montecchio Maggiore, Montorso Vicentino, Zermeghedo	textile, leather, rubber-plastics, mechanical equipment, non-metallic minerals, gold	Stone and non-metallic mineral manufacture Metal working machinery Food and chemical industry machinery Precision instruments (3)Electric wires and cables Motors, generators, transformers, switch and other electric materials production Radio receivers, television receivers, control systems production Road vehicles, construction and assembling Prepared animal feeds Tricots, socks and other stockings (12)Leather Leather products Apparel and clothing accessories, automated production Pulp, paper and cardboard production Printing industry Plastic products

N. of GA area	Province	Council	Relative specialisation of the GA area	N. of firms included in the sample by activity (firms whose activity is not part of the relative specialisation of the GA area are underlined)
184	VR	Castelnuovo Del Garda, Costermano, Dolce', Peschiera Del Garda	mechanical equipment, paper, clothing, transport equipment	Apparel and clothing accessories, automated production Power generating machinery and equipment for extractive industries, non metallic manufacturing, civil engineering, building, iron and steel industry (2)Stone and non-metallic mineral manufacture Tools and final metal products
183	VR	San Giovanni Ilarione	mechanical equipment, paper, clothing, transport equipment	Footwear, automated manufacturing
182	VR	Arcole, Belfiore, Caldiero, Colognola Ai Colli, San Bonifacio, Soave, Tregnago,	mechanical equipment, paper, clothing, transport equipment	Prepared animal feeds Zootechnics agriculture machinery (2)Apparel and clothing accessories, automated production Precision instruments Boiler and tanks construction Foundries Printing industry Wool industry Paper and cardboard transformation
178	VR	Casaleone	mechanical equipment, paper, clothing, transport equipment	Furniture and wood furnishing industry
176	VR	Bovolone, Oppeano	mechanical equipment, paper, clothing, transport equipment	Furniture and wood furnishing industry Bread, biscuits and bakery products industry
172	TN	Calliano, Rovereto	rubber-plastics, textile, mechanical equipment, chemicals	Plastic products Parts and fittings of passenger cars and trailers production Tools and final metal products Printing industry Chemical products for agriculture and industry Pneumatics, vulcanisation and repair (2)Food and chemical industry machinery
158	TN	Borgo Valsugana	rubber-plastics, textile, mechanical equipment, chemicals	Iron and steel industry
140	MN	Viadana	clothing, mineral extraction, mechanical equipment, wood	Base chemicals production Building brick materials Footwear, automated manufacturing Medical and surgical instruments
139	MN	Suzzara, Pegognana,	clothing, mineral extraction, mechanical equipment, wood	Motors, generators, transformers, switch and other electric materials production Other wood manufacture (excluding furniture) Electrical household equipment Meat and meat preparation
137	MN	San Giovanni Del Dosso, Serravalle A Po, Poggio Rusco	clothing, mineral extraction, mechanical equipment, wood	Meat and meat preparation (2)Concrete, asbestos, lime and gypsum building materials' production

N. of GA area	Province	Council	Relative specialisation of the GA area	N. of firms included in the sample by activity (firms whose activity is not part of the relative specialisation of the GA area are underlined)
136	MN	Marcaria, Castellucchio, Rivarolo Mantovano,	clothing, mineral extraction, mechanical equipment, wood	(2)Meat and meat preparation Apparel and clothing accessories, automated production Tools and final metal products Tricots, socks and other stockings
134	BG-MN	Castiglione Delle Stiviere, Cavriana	clothing, mineral extraction, mechanical equipment, wood	Transmission tool construction Carpentry, woodwork and wood floor (2)Tricots, socks and other stockings Cheese industry Transmission tool equipment
133	MN	Canneto Sull'oglio, Castel Goffredo, Asola, Ceresara, Gazoldo Degli Ippoliti, Remedello,	clothing, mineral extraction, mechanical equipment, wood	Toys and sporting goods (3)Tricots, socks and other stockings Forging, pressing, drawing and shearing of metals Transmission tool construction Boiler and tanks construction
132	CR	Soresina	steel industry, mechanical equipment, clothing	Printing industry Power generating machinery and equipment for extractive industries, non metallic manufacturing, civil engineering, building, iron and steel industry
131	OR-CR	Malagnino, Sospiro, Pozzaglio Ed Uniti, Castelverde, Pizzighettone	steel industry, mechanical equipment, clothing	Apparel and clothing accessories, automated production (2)Plastic products Machinery for wood, paper, leather and shoes industry, sanitary, laundry and ironing equipment Silk and chemical fibre industry
130	VA-CR	Cremona, Madignano, Bagnolo Cremasco, Crema, Ripalta Cremasca, Spino D'adda, Romanengo	steel industry, mechanical equipment, clothing	(2)Iron and steel industry (2)Zootechnics agriculture machinery Food and chemical industry machinery Motors, generators, transformers, switch and other electric materials production Parts and fittings of passenger cars and trailers production Vegetable and animal fat industry Meat and meat preparation Leather products Paper and cardboard transformation Printing industry (2)Plastic products Transmission tool construction
129	CR	Fiesco, Ripalta Arpina	steel industry, mechanical equipment, clothing	Metal working machinery Base chemicals production
128	CR	Casalmaggiore, Gussola, Sabbioneta	steel industry, mechanical equipment, clothing	Paper and cardboard transformation Wood, sawing and industrial processing

N. of GA area	Province	Council	Relative specialisation of the GA area	N. of firms included in the sample by activity (firms whose activity is not part of the relative specialisation of the GA area are underlined)
126	PV-MI	Vigevano, Abbiategrasso, Corbetta, Boffalora Sopra Ticino, Marcallo Con Casone, Ossona, Mesero	leather, mineral extraction, clothing, non-metallic minerals	Second transformation and treatment of metals Metal structure construction Tools and final metal products Other mechanical Metal working machinery Textile machinery (2)Food and chemical industry machinery (6)Machinery for wood, paper, leather and shoes industry, sanitary, laundry and ironing equipment Precision instruments Motors, generators, transformers, switch and other electric materials production Parts and fittings of passenger cars and trailers production Other knitted outer garments Footwear, automated manufacturing Taylormade clothing and underwear
122	PV	Mortara, Palestro, Robbio, Cilavegna,	leather, mineral extraction, clothing, non-metallic minerals	Plastic products Printing industry Paper and cardboard transformation Wood intermediate products Textile machinery
121	PV	Sannazzaro De'burgondi, Pieve Del Cairo	leather, mineral extraction, clothing, non-metallic minerals	Metal working machinery Tricots, socks and other stockings Wool industry
120	BS	Vestone, Barghe, Odolo, Agnosine	mineral extraction, transport equipment, steel industry, mechanical equipment	Plastic products Iron and steel industry Electrical instruments for means of transport and industry, cells and accumulators Iron and steel industry (2)Foundries Tools and final metal products
118	BS	Nuvolera, Villanuova Sul Clisi, Prevalle, Roe' Volciano, Salo'	mineral extraction, transport equipment, steel industry, mechanical equipment	Stone and non-metallic mineral manufacture (2)Plastic products Paper and cardboard transformation Wool industry Textile machinery
116	BS	Seniga	mineral extraction, transport equipment, steel industry, mechanical equipment	Foundries

N. of GA area	Province	Council	Relative specialisation of the GA area	N. of firms included in the sample by activity (firms whose activity is not part of the relative specialisation of the GA area are underlined)
114	BS	Palazzolo Sull'oglio, Pontoglio, Adro, Capriolo, Erbusco, Castelli Calepio, Grumello Del Monte, Palosco, Bolgare,	mineral extraction, transport equipment, steel industry, mechanical equipment	(2)Foundries Metal structure construction Textile machinery Food and chemical industry machinery Power generating machinery and equipment for extractive industries, non metallic manufacturing, civil engineering, building, iron and steel industry Radio receivers, television receivers, control systems production Wool industry (4)Cotton industry Other knitted outer garments Other textiles (2)Leather products Apparel and clothing accessories, automated production Costruzione di imballaggi in wood Other wood manufacture (excluding furniture) (2) Rubber
113	BS	Maclodio	Mineral Extraction, Transport Equipment, Steel Industry, Mechanical Equipment	Wool Industry
111	BS-BG	Leno, Orzinuovi, Verolanuova, Montichiari, Bassano Bresciano, Manerbio, Verolanuova	Mineral Extraction, Transport Equipment, Steel Industry, Mechanical Equipment	Production And Base Transformation of Non Ferrous Metals Zootechnics Agriculture Machinery Electrical Household Equipment Installation: Electrical Machinery, Apparatus And Appliance (2) Vegetable And Animal Fat Industry Cotton Industry Leather Products Apparel And Clothing Accessories, Automated Production (2) Plastic Products
110	BS	Villa Carcina, Lumezzane, Gardone Val Trompia, Sarezzo,	Mineral Extraction, Transport Equipment, Steel Industry, Mechanical Equipment	Metal Working Machinery Foundries (2)Tools And Final Metal Products (2)Second Transformation And Treatment of Metals Precision Instruments
108	BG-BS	Provaglio D'iseo, Paratico, Villongo, Sarnico	Mineral Extraction, Transport Equipment, Steel Industry, Mechanical Equipment	Electrical Instruments For Means of Transport And Industry, Cells And Accumulators Cotton Industry Footwear, Automated Manufacturing Others Manufacturing Rubber Wool Industry Shipbuilding Industry
106	BS	Sellero	Mineral Extraction, Transport Equipment, Steel Industry, Mechanical Equipment	Second Transformation And Treatment of Metals

N. of GA area	Province	Council	Relative specialisation of the GA area	N. of firms included in the sample by activity (firms whose activity is not part of the relative specialisation of the GA area are underlined)
105	BS	Bedizzole, Lonato, Desenzano Del Garda, Calcinato	Mineral Extraction, Transport Equipment, Steel Industry, Mechanical Equipment	Base Chemicals Production Iron And Steel Industry Forging, Pressing, Drawing And Shearing of Metals Electrical Instruments For Means of Transport And Industry, Cells And Accumulators Glass Industry Second Transformation And Treatment of Metals Food And Chemical Industry Machinery
104	BS	Breno, Berzo Inferiore	Mineral Extraction, Transport Equipment, Steel Industry, Mechanical Equipment	Forging, Pressing, Drawing And Shearing of Metals Iron And Steel Industry
103		Rudiano, Rovato, Chiari, Coccaglio, Cologne		Steel Drawing, Ironing And Rolling Production And Base Transformation of Non Ferrous Metals Tools And Final Metal Products (3)Metal Working Machinery Food And Chemical Industry Machinery Precision Instruments Cotton Industry Tricots, Socks And Other Stockings Carpentry, Woodwork And Wood Floor Paper And Cardboard Transformation Plastic Products

N. of GA area	Province	Council	Relative specialisation of the GA area	N. of firms included in the sample by activity (firms whose activity is not part of the relative specialisation of the GA area are underlined)
102	BS	Brescia, Castel Mella, Castenedolo, Cellatica, Rezzato, Nave, Ospitaletto, Mazzano, Flero, Paderno Franciacorta, Passirano, Rodengo-Saiano, Dello, Bovezzo	Mineral Extraction, Transport Equipment, Steel Industry, Mechanical Equipment	(6)Iron And Steel Industry Steel Tubes Manufacture Production And Base Transformation of Non Ferrous Metals Stone And Non-Metallic Mineral Manufacture Chemical Products For Agriculture And Industry (3)Foundries (6)Second Transformation And Treatment of Metals (4)Tools And Final Metal Products Zootechnics Agriculture Machinery (7)Metal Working Machinery (5)Textile Machinery Food And Chemical Industry Machinery Precision Instruments Electric Wires And Cables (2)Electrical Instruments For Means of Transport And Industry, Cells And Accumulators Construction of Electrical Machinery, Telecommunication And Electromedical Machinery Radio Receivers, Television Receivers, Control Systems Production Parts And Fittings of Passenger Cars And Trailers Production Cheese Industry Bread, Biscuits And Bakery Products Industry Miscellaneous Edible Products And Preparations Leather (3)Apparel And Clothing Accessories, Automated Production Taylormade Clothing And Underwear (4)Printing Industry (2)Publishing Industry (3)Plastic Products Transmission Tool Construction
99	Bg-Mi	Fara Gera D'adda, Casirate D'adda, Arcene, Melzo, Cassano D'adda, Calvenzano, Caravaggio, Trezzano Rosa, Treviglio, Lurano, Trezzo Sull'Adda	Textile, Mechanical Equipment, Non-Metallic Minerals, Wood, Rubber-Plastics	Pottery Production Pharmaceuticals (3)Second Transformation And Treatment of Metals (3)Tools And Final Metal Products Other Mechanical Zootechnics Agriculture Machinery Metal Working Machinery Motors, Generators, Transformers, Switch And Other Electric Materials Production Other Knitted Outer Garments Printing Industry Publishing Industry Plastic Products Jewellery, Silver, Gift Shop, Precious Stone Cutting

N. of GA area	Province	Council	Relative specialisation of the GA area	N. of firms included in the sample by activity (firms whose activity is not part of the relative specialisation of the GA area are underlined)
98	BG	Cividate Al Piano, Urgnano, Antegnate, Cologno Al Serio, Calcinate, Covo, Martinengo, Isso	Textile, Mechanical Equipment, Non-Metallic Minerals, Wood, Rubber-Plastics	Second Transformation And Treatment of Metals Tools And Final Metal Products Textile Machinery Electrical Instruments For Means of Transport And Industry, Cells And Accumulators Construction of Electrical Machinery, Telecommunication And Electromedical Machinery Meat And Meat Preparation (4)Other Knitted Outer Garments Other Textiles Leather Apparel And Clothing Accessories, Automated Production Paper And Cardboard Transformation Printing Industry
96	BG	Villa D'ogna, Parre,	Textile, Mechanical Equipment, Non-Metallic Minerals, Wood, Rubber-Plastics	Plastic Products Electrical Instruments For Means of Transport And Industry, Cells And Accumulators Wool Industry Artificial And Synthetic Fibre Production

N. of GA area	Province	Council	Relative specialisation of the GA area	N. of firms included in the sample by activity (firms whose activity is not part of the relative specialisation of the GA area are underlined)
95		Valbrembo, Bergamo, Ponteranica, Verdellino, Albano Sant'alessandro, Carobbio Degli Angeli, Lallio, Chignolo D'isola, Seriate, Villa D'adda, Ciserano, Almenno San Salvatore, Pedrengo, Mozzo, Azzano San Paolo, Ponteranica, Boltiere, Grassobbio, Sorisole, Gorle, Brembate Di Sopra, Dalmine, Curno, Filago, Bottanuco, Orio Al Serio, Levate, Stezzano, Verdellino, Chignolo D'isola, Mapello, Torre Boldone, Treviolo, Osio Sopra, Comun Nuovo, Medolago, Gorle, Alme', San Paolo D'argon, Lallio, Scanzorosciate, Presezzo, Villa D'alme', Suisio, Carvico, Sant'omobono Imagna, Pedrengo, Comun Nuovo, Orio Al Serio, Ponteranica	Textile, Mechanical Equipment, Non-Metallic Minerals, Wood, Rubber-Plastics	(2)Iron And Steel Industry Steel Tubes Manufacture Steel Drawing, Ironing And Rolling Cement, Lime And Gypsum Production (2)Concrete, Asbestos, Lime And Gypsum Building Materials' Production Stone And Non-Metallic Mineral Manufacture Pottery Production Base Chemicals Production Pharmaceuticals Soap And Detergent, Personal Hygiene And Perfumery Products Production (3)Foundries (9)Second Transformation And Treatment of Metals (7)Metal Structure Construction (3)Tools And Final Metal Products (4)Metal Working Machinery (3)Textile Machinery Food And Chemical Industry Machinery 2)Power Generating Machinery And Equipment For Extractive Industries, Non Metallic Manufacturing, Civil Engineering, Building, Iron And Steel Industry (2)Machinery For Wood, Paper, Leather And Shoes Industry, Sanitary, Laundry And Ironing Equipment (4)Precision Instruments (3)Motors, Generators, Transformers, Switch And Other Electric Materials Production Electrical Instruments For Means of Transport And Industry, Cells And Accumulators (2)Electrical Household Equipment (3)Electrical Lighting Equipment (3)Installation: Electrical Machinery, Apparatus And Appliance Meat And Meat Preparation Prepared Animal Feeds Beer And Malt Industry Wool Industry (3)Cotton Industry Silk And Chemical Fibre Industry (3)Other Knitted Outer Garments (6)Apparel And Clothing Accessories, Automated Production Other Textile Articles Carpentry, Woodwork And Wood Floor Furniture And Wood Furnishing Industry Paper And Cardboard Transformation (3)Printing Industry Publishing Industry Rubber (12)Plastic Products Transmission Tool Construction

N. of GA area	Province	Council	Relative specialisation of the GA area	N. of firms included in the sample by activity (firms whose activity is not part of the relative specialisation of the GA area are underlined)
93	PV	Belgioioso, Villanterio, Spessa	Leather, Mineral Extraction, Clothing, Non-Metallic Minerals	Cereals And Cereals Transformation Wood Intermediate Products Prepared Animal Feeds
91	MI	Guardamiglio, Lodi Vecchio, Codogno, Galgagnano, Borgo S.Giovanni	Paper, Electrical Equipment, Appliance, Steel Industry, Chemicals, Printing	Plastic Products Electrical Household Equipment Parts And Fittings of Passenger Cars And Trailers Production Metal Working Machinery Foundries
90	MI-CO	Carate Brianza, Ceriano Laghetto, Lissone, Desio, Seveso, Mariano Comense, Renate, Macherio, Arosio, Giussano, Cesano Maderno, Meda, Seregno, Muggio', Varedo, Crosio Della Valle, Inverigo, Ceriano Laghetto	Paper, Electrical Equipment, Appliance, Steel Industry, Chemicals, Printing, Textile, Furniture, Wood	Iron And Steel Industry Steel Tubes Manufacture Steel Drawing, Ironing And Rolling Building Brick Materials Base Chemicals Production 259 Artificial And Synthetic Fibre Production Second Transformation And Treatment of Metals (4)Tools And Final Metal Products (5)Metal Working Machinery Food And Chemical Industry Machinery Radio Receivers, Television Receivers, Control Systems Production Installation: Electrical Machinery, Apparatus And Appliance Car Body And Trailers Construction Parts And Fittings of Passenger Cars And Trailers Production Other Knitted Outer Garments Other Textiles Apparel And Clothing Accessories, Automated Production Other Textile Articles Carpentry, Woodwork And Wood Floor (7)Furniture And Wood Furnishing Industry Pulp, Paper And Cardboard Production Paper And Cardboard Transformation Printing Industry (4)Plastic Products Transmission Tool Construction
86	SO	Dubino		Forging, Pressing, Drawing And Shearing of Metals

N. of GA area	Province	Council	Relative specialisation of the GA area	N. of firms included in the sample by activity (firms whose activity is not part of the relative specialisation of the GA area are underlined)
79	BG-CO-MI-BG	Caprino Bergamasco, Calolziocorte, Cisano Bergamasco, Merate, Costa Masnaga, Lecco, Perego, Rogeno, Bulciago, Valmadrera, Vercurago, Nibionno, Cremella, Barzago, Missaglia, Barzano', Valgreghentino, Cisano Bergamasco, Dolzago, Calolziocorte, Sirone, Osnago, Bosisio Parini, Oggiono, Mandello Lario, Cassago Brianza, Bulciago,	Paper, Electrical Equipment, Appliance, Steel Industry, Chemicals, Printing, Textile, Furniture, Wood	(2)Iron And Steel Industry (4)Steel Drawing, Ironing And Rolling Building Brick Materials Forging, Pressing, Drawing And Shearing of Metals (3)Second Transformation And Treatment of Metals (5)Tools And Final Metal Products (3)Metal Working Machinery Precision Instruments Motors, Generators, Transformers, Switch And Other Electric Materials Production Radio Receivers, Television Receivers, Control Systems Production Meat And Meat Preparation Bread, Biscuits And Bakery Products Industry Wool Industry (3)Cotton Industry Silk And Chemical Fibre Industry Tapestry And Carpets Apparel And Clothing Accessories, Automated Production Pulp, Paper And Cardboard Production (2)Printing Industry (3)Plastic Products

N. of GA area	Province	Council	Relative specialisation of the GA area	N. of firms included in the sample by activity (firms whose activity is not part of the relative specialisation of the GA area are underlined)
78	CO-PV	Como, Bregnano, Valbrona, Pusiano, Villa Guardia, Erba, Lipomo, Rovello Porro, Cermenate, Figino Serenza, Casnate Con Bernate, Turate, Appiano Gentile, Fino Mornasco, Cantu', Maslianico, Rovellasca, Olgiate Comasco, Lurate Caccivio, Veniano, Limido Comasco, Vertemate Con Minoprio, Anzano Del Parco, Albavilla, Canzo, Cernobbio, Montano Lucino, Albese Con Cassano, Figino S.	Textile, Clothing, Furniture, Wood, Paper	Iron And Steel Industry Base Chemicals Production Soap And Detergent, Personal Hygiene And Perfumery Products Production (2)Forging, Pressing, Drawing And Shearing of Metals Second Transformation And Treatment of Metals Tools And Final Metal Products (2)Textile Machinery Precision Instruments Motors, Generators, Transformers, Switch And Other Electric Materials Production Electrical Household Equipment Road Vehicles, Construction And Assembling Medical And Surgical Instruments Non Alcoholic Beverage And Mineral Water Industry (3)Wool Industry Cotton Industry (11)Silk And Chemical Fibre Industry Tricots, Socks And Other Stockings (4)Other Knitted Outer Garments Tapestry And Carpets Leather Products(2)Furniture And Wood Furnishing Industry Paper And Cardboard Transformation (5)Printing Industry Rubber Plastic Products Jewellery, Silver, Gift Shop, Precious Stone Cutting

N. of GA area	Province	Council	Relative specialisation of the GA area	N. of firms included in the sample by activity (firms whose activity is not part of the relative specialisation of the GA area are underlined)
75	VA	Induno Olona, Venegono Inferiore, Malnate, Varese, Tradate, Cislago, Castronno, Gazzada Schianno, Morazzone, Venegono Superiore, Arcisate, Casciago, Daverio, Locate Varesino, Bisuschio, Mornago	Metal Products, Mechanical Equipment, Rubber-Plastics, Leather, Electrical Equipment, Appliance, Optical Industry	Second Transformation And Treatment of Metals (4)Metal Working Machinery Power Generating Machinery And Equipment For Extractive Industries, Non Metallic Manufacturing, Civil Engineering, Building, Iron And Steel Industry (2)Electrical Instruments For Means of Transport And Industry, Cells And Accumulators Road Vehicles, Construction And Assembling Parts And Fittings of Passenger Cars And Trailers Production Airship Construction And Repair Printing Industry (2)Cheese Industry Cocoa Power, Chocolate, Ice-Cream Industry (2)Silk And Chemical Fibre Industry Tricots, Socks And Other Stockings Other Textiles Leather Products (3)Other Textile Articles (2)Paper And Cardboard Transformation Printing Industry Publishing Industry Plastic Products (2)Toys And Sporting Goods

N. of GA area	Province	Council	Relative specialisation of the GA area	N. of firms included in the sample by activity (firms whose activity is not part of the relative specialisation of the GA area are underlined)
72	VA	Somma Lombardo, Gallarate, Sumirago, Lonate Pozzolo, Cassano Magnago, Samarate, Cardano Al Campo, Carnago, Besnate, Golasecca, Cavaria Con Premezzo, Solbiate Arno	Metal Products, Mechanical Equipment, Rubber-Plastics, Leather, Electrical Equipment, Appliance, Optical Industry	Iron And Steel Industry (2)Base Chemicals Production (3)Foundries (3)Second Transformation And Treatment of Metals Metal Structure Construction (2)Tools And Final Metal Products Other Mechanical Metal Working Machinery Textile Machinery Food And Chemical Industry Machinery Power Generating Machinery And Equipment For Extractive Industries, Non Metallic Manufacturing, Civil Engineering, Building, Iron And Steel Industry Electrical Instruments For Means of Transport And Industry, Cells And Accumulators (2)Airship Construction And Repair Cotton Industry (2)Tricots, Socks And Other Stockings (5)Other Knitted Outer Garments Tapestry And Carpets Other Textiles Leather Products (3)Apparel And Clothing Accessories, Automated Production Other Wood Manufacture (Excluding Furniture) Printing Industry (4)Plastic Products Jewellery, Silver, Gift Shop, Precious Stone Cutting

N. of GA area	Province	Council	Relative specialisation of the GA area	N. of firms included in the sample by activity (firms whose activity is not part of the relative specialisation of the GA area are underlined)
71	VA-MI	Castano Primo, Turbigo, Busto Arsizio, Parabiago, Nerviano, San Giorgio SU Legnano, Solbiate Olona, Gorla Minore, Cerro Maggiore, Rescaldina, Castellanza, Gorla Maggiore, San Vittore Olona, Rescaldina, Olgiate Olona, Fagnano Olona, Marnate, Castellanza, Robecchetto Con Induno, Cuggiono, Parabiago, Canegrate, Arconate, CanegratE	Paper, Electrical Equipment, Appliance, Steel Industry, Chemicals, Printing, Metal Products, Mechanical Equipment, Rubber-Plastics, Leather, Electrical Equipment, Appliance, Optical Industry	Steel Drawing, Ironing And Rolling (5)Base Chemicals Production (2)Chemical Products For Agriculture And Industry Soap And Detergent, Personal Hygiene And Perfumery Products Production Foundries (2)Second Transformation And Treatment of Metals (2)Tools And Final Metal Products Other Mechanical (2)Zootechnics Agriculture Machinery (4)Metal Working Machinery (2)Textile Machinery Food And Chemical Industry Machinery (2)Power Generating Machinery And Equipment For Extractive Industries, Non Metallic Manufacturing, Civil Engineering, Building, Iron And Steel Industry (2)Precision Instruments Electrical Instruments For Means of Transport And Industry, Cells And Accumulators Construction of Electrical Machinery, Telecommunication And Electromedical Machinery (2)Radio Receivers, Television Receivers, Control Systems Production Electrical Household Equipment Road Vehicles, Construction And Assembling Wool Industry (9)Cotton Industry (3)Silk And Chemical Fibre Industry Flax, Ramitè And True Hemp Yarn Industry (4)Tricots, Socks And Other Stockings (4)Other Knitted Outer Garments (2)Footwear, Automated Manufacturing (2)Apparel And Clothing Accessories, Automated Production Other Textile Articles Pulp, Paper And Cardboard Production (4)Paper And Cardboard Transformation (4)Plastic Products Jewellery, Silver, Gift Shop, Precious Stone Cutting Photographers' Studios And Cinema Industry Transmission Tool Construction

N. of GA area	Province	Council	Relative specialisation of the GA area	N. of firms included in the sample by activity (firms whose activity is not part of the relative specialisation of the GA area are underlined)
49	NO-AL	Ovada, Belforte Monferrato, Momo, Tagliolo Monferrato,	Clothing, Textile, Machinery	<u>Furniture And Wood Furnishing Industry</u> (2)Metal Working Machinery Transmission Tool Equipment Motors, Generators, Transformers, Switch And Other Electric Materials Production Soap And Detergent, Personal Hygiene And Perfumery Products Production Power Generating Machinery And Equipment For Extractive Industries, Non Metallic Manufacturing, Civil Engineering, Building, Iron And Steel Industry <u>Tools And Final Metal Products</u>
46	AL	Mombello Monferrato	Clothing, Chemicals, Rubber-Plastics, Leather, Jewellery, Gold	
42	TO-AT	Bruino, Mombercelli	Transport Equipment, Wine, Paper, Electrical Machinery	Precision Instruments Wood Intermediate Products
41	AT	San Marzano Oliveto, Canelli	Wine	<u>Paper And Cardboard Transformation</u> Distilled Alcoholic Beverage, Ethyl Alcohol And Mandy Industry
34	CN	Farigliano, Dogliani	Mineral Extraction, Clothing, Wood, Rubber-Plastics, Metal Products, Mechanical Equipment	Others Manufacturing <u>Printing Industry</u>
32	AT-CN-LU	Bubbio, Cortemilia, Altopascio	Mineral Extraction, Clothing, Wood, Rubber-Plastics, Metal Products, Mechanical Equipment, Wine	(2)Electrical Instruments For Means of Transport And Industry, Cells And Accumulators Paper And Cardboard Transformation
31	CN	Nucetto, Ceva	Mineral Extraction, Clothing, Wood, Rubber-Plastics, Metal Products, Mechanical Equipment	<u>Installation: Electrical Machinery, Apparatus And Appliance</u> Meat And Meat Preparation
30	CN	Carru'	Mineral Extraction, Clothing, Wood, Rubber-Plastics, Metal Products, Mechanical Equipment	Tricots, Socks And Other Stockings
24	NO	Omegna, Casale Corte Cerro, Anzola D'ossola, Casale Corte Cerro,	Clothing, Textile, Machinery	<u>Second Transformation And Treatment of Metals</u> Soap And Detergent, Personal Hygiene And Perfumery Products Production <u>Electrical Instruments For Means of Transport And Industry, Cells And Accumulators</u> Tricots, Socks And Other Stockings <u>Foundries</u> (3)Tools And Final Metal Products
23	NO	Oleggio	Clothing, Textile, Machinery	Apparel And Clothing Accessories, Automated Production

N. of GA area	Province	Council	Relative specialisation of the GA area	N. of firms included in the sample by activity (firms whose activity is not part of the relative specialisation of the GA area are underlined)
18	NO-MO	Borgomanero, Pella, Gattico, Cressa, Pogno, Arona, Briga Novarese, Fontaneto D'agogna	Clothing, Textile, Machinery, Transport Equipment, Chemicals, Metal Products, Mechanical Equipment	Base Chemicals Production Metal Working Machinery Machinery For Wood, Paper, Leather And Shoes Industry, Sanitary, Laundry And Ironing Equipment (3)Precision Instruments 340 Bicycles And Motorcycles Assembled And Parts Thereof Precision Instruments Cotton Industry Footwear, Automated Manufacturing Apparel And Clothing Accessories, Automated Production Plastic Products Transmission Tool Construction
15	VC	Briona, Ghemme, Arborio	Textile, Machinery	Electrical Instruments For Means of Transport And Industry, Cells And Accumulators Apparel And Clothing Accessories, Automated Production Other Knitted Outer Garments
13	VC	Trivero, Lessona, Quaregna, Portula, Pray, Strona, Cossato, Coggiola, Valle Mosso, Caprile	Textile, Machinery	(2)Textile Machinery Car Body And Trailers Construction (14)Wool Industry Silk And Chemical Fibre Industry
11	VC	Pollone, Biella, Vigliano Biellese, Massazza, Sandigliano, Verrone, Candelo, Mongrando, Andorno Micca	Textile, Machinery	(9)Wool Industry (2)Other Knitted Outer Garments Apparel And Clothing Accessories, Automated Production Pneumatics, Vulcanisation And Repair
8	VC-TO	Tollegno Cuorgne' Rivarolo Canavese Ponte Canavese Lusiglie' Busano Valperga Bairo	Transport Equipment, Paper, Textile, Machinery, Electrical Machinery	(2)Forging, Pressing, Drawing And Shearing of Metals (2)Second Transformation And Treatment of Metals Transmission Tool Equipment Precision Instruments Radio Receivers, Television Receivers, Control Systems Production Wool Industry Wood Intermediate Products

Contributions to Economics

Sabine Spangenberg
**The Institutionalised Transformation
of the East German Economy**
1998. ISBN 3-7908-1103-3

Hagen Bobzin
Indivisibilities
1998. ISBN 3-7908-1123-8

Helmut Wagner (Ed.)
**Current Issues in Monetary
Economics**
1998. ISBN 3-7908-1127-0

Peter Michaelis/Frank Stähler (Eds.)
**Recent Policy Issues in Environmental
and Resource Economics**
1998. ISBN 3-7908-1137-8

Jessica de Wolff
**The Political Economy
of Fiscal Decisions**
1998. ISBN 3-7908-1130-0

Georg Bol/
Gholamreza Nakhaeizadeh/
Karl-Heinz Vollmer (Eds.)
**Risk Measurements, Econometrics
and Neural Networks**
1998. ISBN 3-7908-1152-1

Joachim Winter
**Investment and Exit Decisions
at the Plant Level**
1998. ISBN 3-7908-1154-8

Bernd Meyer
Intertemporal Asset Pricing
1999. ISBN 3-7908-1159-9

Uwe Walz
Dynamics of Regional Integration
1999. ISBN 3-7908-1185-8

Michael Carlberg
European Monetary Union
1999. ISBN 3-7908-1191-2

Giovanni Galizzi/
Luciano Venturini (Eds.)
**Vertical Relationships and
Coordination in the Food System**
1999. ISBN 3-7908-1192-0

Gustav A. Horn/
Wolfgang Scheremet/
Rudolf Zwiener
Wages and the Euro
1999. ISBN 3-7908-1199-8

Dirk Willer
**The Development of Equity Capital
Markets in Transition Economies**
1999. ISBN 3-7908-1198-X

Karl Matthias Weber
**Innovation Diffusion and Political
Control of Energy Technologies**
1999. ISBN 3-7908-1205-6

Heike Link et al.
**The Costs of Road Infrastructure
and Congestion in Europe**
1999. ISBN 3-7908-1201-3

Simon Duindam
Military Conscription
1999. ISBN 3-7908-1203-X

Bruno Jeitziner
**Political Economy of the
Swiss National Bank**
1999. ISBN 3-7908-1209-9

Irene Ring et al. (Eds.)
Regional Sustainability
1999. ISBN 3-7908-1233-1

Katharina Müller/Andreas Ryll/
Hans-Jürgen Wagener (Eds.)
**Transformation of Social Security:
Pensions in Central-Eastern Europe**
1999. ISBN 3-7908-1210-2

Stefan Traub
Framing Effects in Taxation
1999. ISBN 3-7908-1240-4

Pablo Coto-Millán
Utility and Production
1999. 3-7908-1153-X

Frank Riedel
**Imperfect Information
and Investor Heterogeneity
in the Bond Market**
2000. ISBN 3-7908-1247-1

Kirsten Ralf
Business Cycles
2000. ISBN 3-7908-1245-5